To Richard Lloyd-Jones

Contents

Introduction   xi

Acknowledgments   xiii

1 Our Other Voices   1

In truth we are not "individuals"; rather we are many individuals in one personality, like the actor who plays many parts. Our several personalities derive from our concepts of what we want our lives to be. When we have contacts with other people, as in speaking or writing, we select one of our individualities, our choice depending on our audience and our estimate of the situation. Then we "speak" in the "voice" of that individuality.

2 Collecting Information   21

The writer begins with information; he finds this in his own experience or in the experience of others. A major source of information is in libraries and other public places where the recorded and interpreted experience of others is stored. This chapter offers techniques for locating sources of information, and for making information our own, once a source is located.

3 Our Language   53

Contacts with others and with their recorded experiences depend on the medium of our language. Language is a very complex phenomenon with origins perhaps as ancient as man himself. Moreover, language is a fluid, sensitive, symbolic, and potentially influential medium, whose functions are often more than we perceive.

4   Words at Work   71

From the beginnings of our records, language has had a magical and sometimes mystical import for many people. Often it is so closely identified with the world of experience that language and experience are confused with one another. For these two reasons and many others, language often takes on many qualities beyond its first function of identifying the elements of our experience.

5   Order and Knowledge   101

In a world that tends always toward the anarchical, many of us look for order and reason. Our language reflects that search and our best beliefs about our universe even though (as we have seen in the previous chapter) it also tends toward anarchy.

6   Motion   127

We live in a universe of flux and change, of time which flows like a river carrying us along with it. Our language therefore is a language of action and motion; it reflects our anxiety over what is happening and who is causing or directing activities.

7   Patterns of Persuasion   141

Everybody seems to be competing for the time and attention of others; everyone seems too busy competing (or just being busy) to pay attention to us and our ideas. When we have something worth saying, we must get our listener's attention and then we must hold it until he has got our message.

8   Definition, Description, Narration   167

In a world of flux and change, there are some constants; no matter what our voice is, what our message is, what our purpose or audience is, the strategies we use for informing others are as old as language itself. Our audience wants to know what we mean, what things look like, what incidents took place. The skills for using these constants must be learned, but they need not restrict or inhibit us.

9   Evaluating, Judging, and Directing   197

Whether we like it or not, we must make choices and decisions in this world: which Little League team we play on, which mate we live with, which airline we fly on, which political system we cling to. Moreover, more people than we may think look to us for our judgments: "What do *you* think?" is a constant question. The answer to the old question, "Are you a man or are you a mouse?" may take more thought than we realize.

10   The Organization of Language   221

If there were no sentence or paragraph (in the abstract sense), man would invent one. We all create sentences and paragraphs of sorts—but if we are to inform and motivate others, we ought to be more systematic about it. It is our ability to make system and sense and reason out of anarchy that usually impresses others. And is there anyone who isn't trying to impress someone?

11   Structure   259

Structure is democracy at work, the Mets or Jets winning a contest, the motion picture we praise to our friends, the conglomeration of wheels and "cubes" and hardware which makes up an automobile. We admire good structures, deplore or reject bad ones. Here are four good *writing* structures—one of them helped to make your world what it is.

12   Something to Write About   273

If you are seeking for something to unlock the power of *your* mind, you may find some help here.

Appendix   289

"On a Piece of Chalk," Thomas Henry Huxley   291
"A Philosophy of Handicap," Randolph Bourne   309
"Once More to the Lake," E. B. White   317
"How to Write Short Stories," Ring Lardner   323

Index   327

A few words of introduction to the expert in language usage

You are an expert, you know. All of your life you have been using that skill called language as a principal means of getting your daily thing done—whether it was wheedling your parents for something you wanted (but probably didn't need), arguing with your siblings (we all did it), working around a teacher (we all did that, too), wheeling and dealing with your peers, rapping with members of the opposite sex (in my day it was called "our line"), applying for a job, taking part in games and contests or arts and crafts—all of this with more language expertise than you thought you had.

Now don't misunderstand this appeal to you. I'm only partially trying to soften you up, by polishing the apple and playing the sycophant, to get you to read this book. In any case, your teacher will have his own techniques of persuasion or coercion, and, probably, you will still read or not as it pleases you. What I am actually leading up to is both the degree and *kind* of your expertise, and why you ought really to read this book despite all the temptations not to.

Up to now your kind of expertise is probably what we here in the Middle West call visceral or "gut" expertise—in plainer words, you have used language primarily to get you through typical family, social, educational, personal, work, and participant kinds of relationships. You have used language for these aims pretty much without thinking, doing what comes naturally, probably more often than not ignoring or not using a great deal of what you had been taught in the classroom.

Now the time is not far off when you will have to make a choice—whether to continue in the visceral fashion or whether to adapt to the formalities of business, industry, government, education, and other social institutions. If you opt for one of the latter, you will probably be motivated toward uses of the language above and beyond mere "gut" levels. If you are so motivated, you will begin to find it necessary to be rational, logical, persuasive, argumentative. Specifically, you will find it necessary to propose, support, report, narrate, direct, correspond, abstract, record, make choices and judgments.

Some of these activities will take place in face to face confrontations. Some will require that you fill in blank spaces on printed forms. Some will require that you write a good deal—both for people you know and for people you don't know. And some of your activities will require that you read things that others have written. In any of these cases, you ought to know what you are doing—and you ought to know what is being done to you.

If you are one of those who are opting for the latter set of choices mentioned above, then the skills and techniques outlined in this book are for you.

Time to stop polishing the apple and get on with the eating of it.

A statement of appreciation and obligation

What I know about the subject of writing has been learned in many ways—from my reading in books, magazines, and newspapers; from my attempts at free-lance writing; from my work as a technical writer; from my work as an editor; from my efforts to teach the subject; from students' papers; and from my teachers in the Cedar Rapids, Iowa, public schools; from Alex MacGibbon at the Sheldon, Iowa, Junior College; and from Professor William Porter, formerly of the University of Iowa School of Journalism. I owe an especial obligation to the uncommonly good common sense and judgment of Richard Lloyd-Jones of the University of Iowa who has more than once set my erratic mental wanderings on the straight and narrow path of sound learning.

In the actual preparation of this text, I owe an obligation to Terry K. Andrews, who, in the process of aiding in the preparation of the index, uncovered a number of errors (only I am responsible for any which are still present), and to Bette Thompson, who typed the manuscript with diligence, speed, and a fine sense for the quality of her work. For some sound advice at a critical moment, I thank Mr. Robert Sutherlin of Iowa City.

WRITING: Growth Through Structure

1

Our

Other

Voices

When we write we are taking part in, and directing, a process that engages our mind and some of our muscles. It is an extremely complex process, so complex that we are in ignorance of many stages of it, or at least parts of many stages. It is a process that has to be learned. Neither the learning nor the process comes easily. Even the man who makes his living as a writer finds writing difficult. "Pleasant agony," one writer, John Mason Brown, called it.

The physical part of writing, though it can be tiring and lead to "writer's cramp," is the easier because it can be willed. We can put in our eight hours a day as a writer just as we can put in our eight hours a day at some other task.

The physical part of writing requires the use of muscle and a mechanical device (a pen, a typewriter) in a sequential operation. The mental part requires the use of our senses and our intellect. All of our intellectual facilities are needed—the imagination, the fancy, the memory, the intelligence, the ability to make associations. We must collect information by observing and discerning, we must perceive and associate, we must organize, we must learn.

That is not the whole of it by any means. When we write:

- We must decide who we are for that specific occasion.
- We must have a body of information.
- We must have an adequate vocabulary for conceiving, storing, and disseminating our information.
- We must have a purpose for writing; we must have a point to make.
- We must have an understanding of the audience we are trying to reach.
- We must have some "rhetorical strategy" in mind. A football team moves the ball down the field by a series of plays, passing, kicking, running, as the situation may warrant, or as the coach or quarterback sees fit—the game pattern. Our "rhetorical strategy" is our pattern—the "plays" ("ploys," if you wish) we use when we want to accomplish some purpose through writing, or speaking also, for that matter.
- We must have a "style."
- We must decide on levels of language usage, on grammatical patterns, on syntactical devices, and on the kinds of figurative speech we will use.
- We must decide on the length of the work, its brevity, its conciseness, its scale and pace.

If we could make each of these decisions sequentially (and probably some others as well), no matter what sequence we chose the writing would come much easier. But we cannot. Practically every one of our choices interlocks with the other choices; they not only interlock, they are dependent on and control each other. Each one of our choices must be weighed in the balance with all others.

If at this point I have made the task of writing seem so difficult that you are ready to close the book and go back to filling in the areas on numbered paintings, bear with me for just a moment.

You talk to people all of the time, you work out problems in mathematics (though mathematics may not be your "bag" either), you dance or swim or golf—and you do these things rather well. They're complex processes, too, and chances are if you practiced writing as often as you practice these other skills you'd be a good writer. Furthermore, you obviously have already done a bit of writing. Quite a bit, probably. You've gotten into the water, and while it was rather unpleasant at first, you've gotten used to it.

If you think I've outlined a difficult season for you, then think of *my* problem. For although you can already make those interlocking decisions which writing demands, although you can handle several mental tasks at a time, I can discuss only one writing condition at a time. This limitation exists despite the fact that all of the other conditions are pounding at the door of my mental closet, demanding to be let out and onto the printed page at once.

That is one of the first limitations on writing. Even though you can hold two or more apposed ideas in your mind at once, you can put down only one idea at a time. The problem of the writer is the problem of the movie maker. You know, the insane white cook has got the Chinese rancher's daughter cornered in her bedroom and is threatening to divide her with the meat cleaver unless—

The scene shifts to the distant desert where our hero is stranded on an island of sand which is rapidly being eroded by a flash flood. He could swim the flood easily enough under normal circumstances, but he has been securely bound to a saguaro by you know who. Furthermore, there are three mean rattlesnakes, two poisonous Gila monsters, and one rabid coyote marooned on the sand with him—and five of the six think he's the one responsible for their dilemma. The other one is merely hungry.

But the movie maker can put three images on a film at once.

My problem is like the movie maker's, except that he is dealing only with imaginary situations—in real life the hero, the insane cook, and one of the rattlesnakes are all good friends and spend their evenings playing pool at the local tavern. My problem is that I have to deal with you, and your classmates, and your teacher as well. And none of you are imaginary. You are all real, live, breathing people, and you can turn me on or off as you wish.

My solution is to take one subject at a time and, where

necessary, relate it to the others. I'll be as fancy in my footwork as I can. I'll try not to be repetitious or to bore you, and I'll let you know when I shift my scene of operations.

As for you, you may follow along page by page, or you may skip around as you please or as your teacher directs. In the latter cases, you'll find the table of contents and the index useful.

Who We Are

A common misconception, held by many would-be writers, and by readers also, is that the real-life author of a written work and its narrator are one and the same person. A second similar misconception is that the narrator is consistently one and the same person.

Robert Louis Stevenson was a native of Scotland. He grew up a frail, sickly boy, all his life tubercular. In 1883 his *Treasure Island* brought him fame and fortune. The narrator of the book is the boy, Jim Hawkins, although at one point the narration has to be turned over to Dr. Livesey in order that the reader may be kept informed as to what is happening while Jim is a prisoner of Long John Silver and the mutineers.

It should be obvious to anyone that Robert Louis Stevenson and young Jim could not be one and the same. At no time had Stevenson undergone the adventures narrated in the book. Likewise, he could not be Dr. Livesey, although it is possible that some of Dr. Livesey's characteristics might be similar to those of Stevenson. But, as Stevenson himself noted, he got the whole idea for the story, not from personal experience, but from an incident in a book by Charles Kingsley.

Let's take as a second example of this same point *The Great Gatsby* by F. Scott Fitzgerald. The first-person narrator of this novel, Nick Carraway, can be identified with his creator in many respects. He came from a "Middle Western City" (Fitzgerald came from St. Paul), and his grandfather was a merchant. But Carraway graduated from Yale whereas Fitzgerald was a drop-out from Princeton. Moreover, as the novel moves along, we find Fitzgerald using some of his own biography for the legendary Jay Gatz. In other words, Fitzgerald is projecting himself into both roles—Carraway's and Gatsby's. If we read either Arthur Mizener's or Andrew Turnbull's biographies of Fitzgerald, we can see the resemblances between narrator and author—but we can also see the differences.

There are several reasons why the real-life author and the

fictional narrator are not the same. For one, truth *is* stranger than fiction. Fiction cannot report on the oddities, the coincidences, the inanities, the pathos and accidents of real life. Real life is often formless, pointless. Fiction must have point and form. Truth is often incredible, but fiction must be credible.

For another, fiction must surpass true life in its power to move people. Hamlet wonders that the player can mourn over Hecuba and speculates what the actor would do if he had Hamlet's real-life troubles. After two thousand years, the fate of Oedipus still moves us; and the death of Hamlet has the power to stir audiences, even in this violence-ridden century.

But you raise the question: What about the deaths of Jesus on the cross, of Lincoln and John F. Kennedy from an assassin's bullet? Don't these real-life cases move more people than half a dozen play-acted tragedies? Yes, they do. Why? I'll come back to that point in a few moments.

Let's take an even more difficult case first: Richard Henry Dana, Jr.'s *Two Years Before the Mast* is based on a two-year voyage the author took from Boston round Cape Horn to the California coast and back. The voyage is presented in a first-person narrative based on Dana's experiences. The question is a legitimate one; Dana says that his account is "an accurate and authentic narrative." Are Dana and the narrator the same—or not?

I'll answer that question in several ways. First, I'll ask you to accept my argument that people change with time. Dana's adventures had taken place in a remote place under relatively primitive circumstances—in a small sailing-boat on the open seas, in harbors and bays free of man's trammeling devices for restraining the sea, and on land where relatively few people lived and where the seat of government was a thousand miles distant. His book was written several years later in the relatively civilized and urbane city that was nineteenth-century Boston. During those years he had re-entered college and begun work toward a law degree. So the Dana who wrote his book was not the college drop-out who had undergone two years of adventure.

Second, I'll argue that each of us constructs his past life on verbal patterns which he bases on his memories of his past and on his concept of himself. My authority here is Henry David Thoreau:

With thinking we may be beside ourselves in a sane sense. By a conscious effort of the mind we can stand aloof from actions and their consequences; and all things, good and bad, go by us like a torrent. We are not wholly involved in Nature. I may be either the driftwood in the stream, or Indra [the Hindu god of the heavens, thunder, and rain] in the sky looking down on it. I may be affected by a theatrical exhibition; on the other hand, I may not be affected by an actual event which appears to concern me much more. I only know myself as a human entity; the scene, so to speak, of thoughts and affections; and am sensible of a certain doubleness by which I can stand as remote from myself as from another. However intense my experience, I am conscious of the presence and criticism of a part of me, which, as it were, is not a part of me, but a spectator, sharing no experience, but taking note of it, and that it is no more I than it is you. When the play, it may be the tragedy of life is over, the spectator goes his way. It was a kind of fiction, a work of the imagination only, so far as he was concerned. This doubleness may easily make us poor neighbors and friends sometimes. ("Solitude," *Walden*)

Thoreau implies that life is a kind of fiction, a work of the imagination in which we, the authors of our own fictions, stand aside and watch ourselves in action. Thoreau, of course, is not alone in this view: Wordsworth talked of life as a sleep and a forgetting; Shakespeare found that our little life is rounded with a sleep, and Hamlet spoke of the after-life as a dream "that must give us pause"; Rosamond Lehman speaks of the "dusty answer we get from life"; and so on. The idea that life is a dream, a fiction, a play in which we (the men and the women) are just the players has intrigued artists, writers, and thinkers in all times and ages.

If life is a kind of fiction, then who supplies the text, the script? We supply our own, of course, and since all of our life is past (the future doesn't exist as yet, and the present is past at the very instant it occurs), the script is written after the fact.

The author of a fiction selects his *scenes* from all the possible scenes in the lives of his characters. He presents some in great detail, close up, so to speak (see the *Life on the Mississippi* paragraphs in Chapter 12 as an example); he summarizes others, standing further away from them, in a like manner of speaking (see the *Two Years Before the Mast* paragraphs in Chapter 12). The result is a pattern of dramatized scenes and summarized (narrated) scenes, proportioned so as to give the work its *pace*. He alternates serious and tragic scenes with scenes of comedy (comic relief). His work builds to climaxes, highlights, and then falls off again.

George Bernard Shaw corroborates the point in a passage in his *Immaturity:*

Whether it be that I was born mad or a little too sane, my kingdom was not of this world: I was at home only in the realm of my imagination, and at ease only with the mighty dead. Therefore I had to become an actor, and create for myself a fantastic personality fit and apt for dealing with men, and adaptable to the various parts I had to play. (xliii) [1]

Does that remind you at all of the pattern of your own life, the way you react to existence—granting that *you* may not have been born *mad!* We may not all write plays with lengthy prefaces in which we explicate our philosophies of existence, we may not all write books in which we dramatize them, but if we are honest with ourselves, we will admit that we do create fictional patterns. Here, for example, is a teacher:

However, there is another way in which life may sometimes seem to be a fiction to us. Sometimes we seem to stand outside ourselves and watch ourselves as we go through our activities. Now this has happened to me many times when I make a conscious effort to stand aside and take a look at myself as I perform. I can do this easily . . . teaching a class—here I observe myself to see if I am using the right methods, am keeping students interested. . . . Oftentimes we consciously review what we did in a certain situation . . . to see how we performed and to see if we cannot improve our efforts in similar situations. In any case . . . we do behave as if we were actors and as if we were playing out various roles; at times . . . life becomes a "fiction"—if we mean observing oneself going through the acts of his life; and here we mean observing oneself as if he were in a "fiction," in a play. (Richard Price)

All of us create oral fictions; writers create written fictions, projections of themselves on paper. We can see that particularly in biographies. Certainly there is a pattern in *Two Years Before the Mast.* Dana has alternated the tragic scene of the flogging with the comic one of the captain who called on other ship captains, bringing his brig with him! The high drama of furling the sails at the onslaught of a storm or pitching the hides off the steep cliff at Dana Point (see Chapter 12) is set off against the tediousness of everyday labor. So artless is his tale that we have to think about it twice before we are aware of the fictionlike structure of the book.

[1] By permission of The Society of Authors, London, for the Bernard Shaw Estate.

During his voyage Dana was an ordinary seaman before the mast, playing a minor part in the two-year venture. In his book he placed himself on the center of the stage, the chief actor in his narrative. Most of us in our life voyage are the equivalent of ordinary seamen, but in our fictional structures we place ourselves at the center.

Dana had a purpose in selecting and arranging his scenes. He wanted to write a book that people would read. Likewise, we have a purpose in selecting and arranging the scenes in our fiction. We want to present to *ourselves* and to others the best possible image of ourselves. We suppress the scenes that do not fit our image of ourselves—we thrust the scenes out of our mind.

Assignments for Discussion

Shakespeare wrote:

> All the world's a stage,
> And all the men and women merely players.
> They have their exits and their entrances;
> And one man in his time plays many parts . . .

The notion was not unique with Shakespeare. Du Bartas, Montaigne, Thomas Heywood, and Middleton have written lines that paraphrase these. How much does Thoreau echo Shakespeare?

What does an actor do when he portrays a part? Does this activity differ, and if so how, from his real-life actions? In what ways are we actors in our daily lives? Have you ever deliberately "acted" in an encounter?

Thoreau uses the term "experience." What is an experience? How do we know we have had one? When does an experience begin and end? In what ways might our ability to use language shape the nature of an experience?

Assignment for Writing

Write about an experience that at the time seemed unreal to you, an experience about which you said at the time or later: "I just can't believe it! It doesn't seem real! Can this really be me? Can this really be happening to me?"

Now to get back to our reactions when a great religious or political figure dies. Is it not possible that if we build fictional structures about our own lives, we do likewise for those about us? The answer has to be yes. These fictional structures then become involved with other structures—the constructions we have built about our country or our religion, or our belief in the rightness of our traditions, or our attitudes about the dignity and rights of man. The result is a complex set of verbal constructs or patterns, structured along the lines of a drama or a novel, in which we are the chief actors.

Our relationships toward the other actors in this fiction are conditioned by other verbal patterns:

No man is an island, entire of itself; every man is a piece of the continent, a part of the main; if a clod be washed away by the sea, Europe is the less, as well as if a promontory were, as well as if a manor of thy friends or of thine own were; any man's death diminishes me, because I am involved in mankind; and therefore never send to know for whom the bell tolls; it tolls for thee. (John Donne)

When Shakespeare says that all the world's a stage, he is actually saying that there is a dramatic relationship between and among all of us; that just as the player, in the play in *Hamlet,* mourns the death of Hecuba, so we in our own dramas mourn the death of another actor. Lincoln has been dead a hundred years and is at best a name in the history books or a face on a coin or a stamp; very few of us knew John F. Kennedy; but they and others are actors in *our* play. Unlike Hamlet, we do not have to ask:

What's Hecuba to him, or he to Hecuba
That he should weep for her?

Assignment for Discussion

Consider the following: the assassinations of John F. Kennedy, Bobby Kennedy, Martin Luther King, Jr., a child struck down in the streets by an automobile, the death of a Vietnamese citizen in a gunfight between our forces and the Viet-Cong, the death of a Biafran child by starvation. Why does one of these affect us more than another? Does the bell tolling for the Biafran or the Vietnamese toll for us also? How and why?

Assignment for Writing

Write about an instance of someone's death: a friend, a relative, a comrade in battle, a national figure in politics, sports, entertainment, or business (and see Chapter 12). Discuss its effect on you.

Now, I want to go on to the second of two points I raised some time back—that a narrator (or an author) is consistently one and the same person.

In Mark Twain's *Adventures of Huckleberry Finn,* we find this:

NOTICE.

Persons attempting to find a motive in this narrative will be prosecuted; persons attempting to find a moral in it will be banished; persons attempting to find a plot in it will be shot.

BY ORDER OF THE AUTHOR
Per G. G., CHIEF OF ORDNANCE

A page later we find this:

EXPLANATORY.

In this book a number of dialects are used, to wit: The Missouri negro dialect; the extremest form of the backwoods South-Western dialect; the ordinary "Pike-County" dialect; and four modified varieties of this last. The shadings have not been done in a haphazard fashion, or by guess-work; but painstakingly, and with the trustworthy guidance and support of personal familiarity with these several forms of speech.

I make this explanation for the reason that without it many readers would suppose that all these characters were trying to talk alike and not succeeding.

THE AUTHOR

The book begins:

You don't know about me, without you have read a book by the name of *The Adventures of Tom Sawyer,* but that ain't no matter. That book was made by Mr. Mark Twain, and he told the truth, mainly. There was things which he stretched, but mainly he told the truth.

All of the quoted material was written by Mark Twain (or rather by Samuel Langhorne Clemens in his *role* of Mark Twain), but if you will look at it with even moderate care, you will sense the differences among the *voices* that are speaking. The *tone* of the first quotation is impersonally legalistic, but we are puzzled by the harshness of the punishment for the mildness of the crime until we realize that we are being put on by "The Author"—who in this case hides behind the anonymity of "G. G., Chief of Ordnance." The temptation to assume that the second "G" stands for "God" is strong; if the assumption is the case, then we have caught "The Author" speaking in a blasphemous voice.

The tone of the second notice is scholarly, and the passage is maintained in a serious vein with no warning at all that we are being had until the final few words. But in this case the author seems more willing to stand on his own—the fiction of the deputy is missing.

The voice in the third quotation is that of an uneducated boy —except that he knows his "place" well enough to address the author as "Mr. Mark Twain."

Have I made my point—or rather has Mark Twain made it for me? The narrator in a fiction is not *consistently* one and the same person. Like the real self behind him, he "plays many parts" and in each one speaks in a different voice.

The term for the characterization that is projected by the author or narrator is *persona*. The *persona* speaks with one or more voices, and the result of the use of the voices is the *tone* of the work.[2]

Assignments for Discussion

When we are angry the tone of our voice is unlike the tone of our voice when we are not angry. Why?

What is likely to be the tone of our voice when: we are having breakfast or some other meal with the family? we are engaged in

[2] This discussion is based on a kinescript prepared by Professor Walker Gibson for the Commission on English of the College Entrance Examination Board, through whose kind permission the material is used.

a discussion or argument with one or the other of our parents? we are trying to persuade a friend to accompany us on some sort of expedition? we are trying to explain some concept in class? we are engaged in some outdoor or athletic activity?

How can we recognize the tone of voice in something written?

Assignment for Writing

Describe an occasion when you have acted a part in a real-life situation. Perhaps you were talking to a salesman who was trying to sell you something, perhaps you were trying to make points with a girl or boy, perhaps you were complaining to the telephone company about some defect in service. In what ways did you change from your normal self? Did you act in a "phony" way, perhaps? Did you deliberately put on an act? In what way did the tone of your voice reflect your change?

Or, imagine that you have been asked to play the romantic lead in a class play. As you rehearse the play, you gradually fall in love with the other lead. In the play, you say to the other lead: "I love you, (John) (Mary)." That night on the way home, you tell (him) (her), "I love you." Describe the difference in each situation, and the tone of voice that would be used.

─────────────────

When we come to write, then, we assume an identity—we play a role, a part. We choose an appropriate language to suit. Although Mark Twain, one of our great humorists often could not resist the opportunity to make people laugh (and as a consequence often changed his tone unexpectedly), you will not have the same freedom. Moreover, certain kinds of writing demand a certain tone of voice—for instance, when you write directions, your language will be imperative in a mild objective way—most of the time.

Your identity will be reflected in a number of ways. There is the attempt to avoid identity at all costs by the use of phrases such as these:

> It is thought (instead of I *think*)
> The latter method was chosen (instead of I *chose*)

There is the dead hand of corporate or governmental anonymity:

> It is ordered . . .
> This has been done . . .

Some writers cling to such habits of writing because to them the personal pronoun is anathema. But in most of these cases the identity of the human agent is important. Thoughts require people to think them. Choices require someone to choose. Avoiding the personal element is simply avoiding responsibility, but the custom is strong. Even acts that are manifestly personal are evaded in such linguistic impersonalities. And the world apologizes, "It is not done." But the conventions of impersonality have more than once encouraged moral evasiveness.

Compromisers substitute "we." "We" is correct when it is used to mean "several of us"; or "we, the committee believe"; or "we, you and I." The custom of mathematics has made it correct to say, "In equation one, we substitute. . . ." Here the speaker implies that his demonstration is a cooperative intellectual effort. Kings use (or used) "we" to indicate the royal pronouncement as opposed to the personal feeling: "Mr. Browning, we are not amused."

However, one quickly becomes weary of the journalistic royalist and his so-called "editorial we," the thinly disguised effort of a single man to sound as though he were speaking for a number of people: "We believe the mayor is wrong." Likewise a bit of a bore is the false heartiness of the nurse who wakens you in the morning with, "We feel better this morning, don't we?" Choosing "we" as middle ground between the overuse or non-use of a personal pronoun is perhaps worse than either extreme. (But notice the trap I got myself into in the first sentence of this paragraph. I dared not use "we," and "I" would have sounded too much like whining. So I fell back on the impersonal "one" to imply "all of us.")

Or, in a colloquial mood we go to the pronoun "you." Here is the voice of Astronaut Charles Conrad speaking about *his* daily activities from several hundred thousand miles out in space:

> You've got your systems to monitor and you've got to eat and keep yourself clean, get some sleep and except for that, you're free to do a little looking out the window and studying the check lists and maps and things that you're going to be using when you get to the lunar orbit.

Addressing an audience in his paper, a writer may use "I," "one," or "you" as in this text. I am sitting in a sunlit Arizona studio using "you" as if I knew you, and "I" as if you knew me. Sometimes I use "we" to mean both of us. Sometimes I use "one" when none of the others seems particularly appropriate. When I want to be a bit blunt, I am more inclined to use "you." When I feel that I am becoming too blunt, I fall back on "we." But at all times I am conscious of the fact that someday there will be a "you," and I try to guide myself accordingly.

In other words, one of the first decisions I made when I came to write this book was the *point of view*—who I would be, what voice I would use, what tone I would choose—or, to summarize, what part I would play for the next several hundred pages.

Here is an example of a shifting point of view. This type of shift usually occurs when a writer or speaker is concentrating on his subject or his audience or himself in turn. There is nothing morally wrong with such shifts—but as a matter of good writing manners, one ought to correct copy such as this so as to reflect a single point of view before the manuscript is turned over to one's public. With a little practice one can learn how to do it right the first time on a short paper; longer papers probably will require editing and revision.

I depend on two types of pitch—a hard-thrown fast ball and a breaking curve ball, either aimed at a specific point each time in the strike zone. Note that for either pitch I keep the toe of my right foot firmly against the pitcher's rubber, and I bring my left leg across just as I bring my hands together before throwing the ball. This is to avoid tipping the batter off on my pitch. There's no point in your tipping the batter off on what's coming. Lots of young pitchers suffer for this and wonder why they can't get a ball past the batter. The release of the ball is important too. Always let the ball go just at the point . . .

In this example the writer began with a first-person point of view. In his second sentence he expanded his point of view to take in his reader; his first-person point of view thus became a dialogue. No technical problem. In his third sentence he switched to a third-person descriptive point of view, and in the fourth sentence he changed to the impersonal "you" that we all use because in English there is really nothing to serve the purpose of an impersonal pronoun except that "you." In the last sentence, after a second shift to the third-person point of view, he switched to direct discourse or the command viewpoint.

Our Audience

From time to time many of us have kept journals or diaries in which we recorded many of our activities and thoughts.

Have you kept a journal or diary? For whom were you writing? (I waive the question if the record was kept as a part of a classroom exercise.) Did you enter items in your book that you wanted no one to see? Were you absolutely honest with yourself?

Some people—Ralph Waldo Emerson, Nathaniel Hawthorne were two—have kept journals as "bank accounts" on which they drew later for material for stories, poems, and essays.

Two poets—the English Gerard Manley Hopkins and the American Emily Dickinson—wrote poems that they wanted no one to see. Fortunately, for us, their poems were made available to a wider audience after their respective deaths.

But aside from instances such as these, most of us write for an audience. We write letters, we write "themes" for our English teachers, we write "papers" for our other teachers. Some of us have written letters to the editor of a magazine or a newspaper, and a few of us have probably tried our hand at submitting something of a more substantial nature.

When we come to write we must decide who and what our audience is. The task is not easy. Those who succeed very well at this sort of decision usually become editors of large-circulation newspapers and magazines, for they know "how to put their finger on the nation's pulse." It is a very valuable commodity and brings many kinds of rewards—money, fame, status, friendships with important people.

Unfortunately, I cannot teach you this skill any more than I can teach you to be a great writer. Others may argue with me, but I think greatness of many kinds is born within certain people. If this were not so, why haven't our splendid academies produced another Shakespeare?

No, genius does not need academies or teachers. It manages very well on its own. Schools and pedants are for all the rest of us—most of us as a matter of fact. So, if you are a genius— leave us now and go on about your own business. We'll make out, somehow.

There are some things I can teach you about estimating the

interests of an audience. Depending on the situation, it is made up of:

- Your friends. (You can fairly well evaluate these.)
- Your parents and other relatives. These are not necessarily your friends. If the mass media are right (at the time of this writing), this may be one of your more difficult audiences. On the other hand you may not write much for them.
- Your teachers. Usually they are divided into audiences of one to an audience. Here is one place where you often work very hard trying to categorize (or "psych," as you say it) your audience. Success can mean "acing" the course.
- Potential employers. Usually one at a time and only when you are trying to get work. Their employment blanks usually solve that problem.
- Actual employers. Here is a very complex situation, especially in a large organization. Large organizations tend to be multi-layered. Your immediate supervisor may be an engineer, his may be an accountant. The president probably was a high-school dropout. In any case he is also the hardest one to write for. Presidents have an embarrassing habit of asking pointed and meaningful questions. The stupid ones appear only in Hollywood films. (Seriously, some of them have advanced degrees from the Harvard School of Business.)
- Your peers on the job. They may work for some other organization. They may be brighter than you, or not as bright. Some of them grew up in ghettos and the barrios of the Southwest. Some belong to the Country Club; some do not. Some are engineers, some salesmen, some accountants.
- Customers of your employer. They may not always be right, but they always think they are. You don't have to leave all of them happy, but you'd better have a high batting average.
- People who are looking for information. Some of them are geniuses who just don't happen to know much about your area of expertise. Some of them probably have to have their letters of inquiry written for them, and they have trouble making "X's."
- Community-minded people. People associated with you in PTA, Boy Scouts, Camp Fire Girls, community funds, church, and the like. These and the people they want you to write letters to—letters soliciting funds, services, more funds, more services.
- People who work for government agencies. The Mayor, the Superintendent of Garbage Collections (probable title is Chief

Sanitation Engineer), the County Supervisor, the Chief of Police, the Collector of Internal Revenue, the people down at the Selective Service. Some of these people, surprisingly to us non-bureaucrats, are quite bright; others will take longer to read what you have sent to them.

Your audience will vary in terms of its education. In 1930 a high-school diploma was not too common, and only the sons and daughters of ministers, school teachers, doctors, lawyers, and the very rich went to college. In 1972 there is a stigma directed toward the high-school drop-out, large numbers of people have two-year degrees or a corresponding amount of college education, and large numbers of people get college degrees. And all kinds of people keep on going to school—I've had people up to 80 years of age in my classrooms.

I've used the term "education" here in a general sense. You must think of your audience in its specialized sense, too—dental technicians, electronic technicians, engineering draftsmen, nurses, physicians, chiropractors, ministers, and so on *ad in-finitum*.

The army has a system here that is emulated by many industrial firms. The army sets up echelons of maintenance. People who work at each echelon level are trained for that level of work—and handbooks are written accordingly. When you write you must have in mind the quantity and quality of the training and background your reader has.

Your audience will vary in terms of its motivation to read. Affluence has not produced a society with more time to read; instead, it has produced far more demands on your reader's time than he has time for. You will have to make a decision as to how you will motivate your audience—and how much motivation will be needed.

Motivation usually depends upon the reader's uses for what we write. They may be vocational—someone will learn how to perform his work more easily, or do a better job, or make more money at his work. They may be avocational—what does he do with his leisure time? They may be addressed to the reader's personal concerns for his health, his comfort, his safety. They may add to his education, to his supply of knowledge. They may relieve his anxieties about the world he lives in. They may help him find a better job, buy the latest automobile, dress himself in the latest fashions. They may entertain him or respond to the old Adam instinct within us for power or wealth. Readers make infinite uses of what we write—it's up to us to decide before-hand what these uses are likely to be.

You must think of your audience in terms of its language capabilities and preferences. You would not expect an Italian audience to read English—you cannot expect an audience accustomed to literary style or to scientific style or to the plain journalistic style of most of our publications to adapt itself easily to some other style. You cannot expect your audience to read "over its head" either—although you can provide your audience with exotic or esoteric bits of erudition beyond its present periphery of cognition.

You must be aware of the social distinctions and choices that are made on the basis of the language usage habits of people. Just as there are people who make social distinctions and choices based on our manners and mannerisms in personal contacts, so there are people who are quite sensitive to the degree of decorum exhibited in our speaking and writing. Propriety in writing de-pends on many properties of language—word choice, correct forms of nouns, verbs, and pronouns, agreement between verb and subject, avoidance of split infinitives and dangling parti-ciples, avoidance of slang and sub-standard words such as "ain't," and the like.

You must think about your audience's preference for the form in which information is presented. In some cases, however, you will have no choice about the form. The mass media and many rhetorical strategies often require appropriate forms.

Your audience, therefore, is likely to be one that can be described in terms of its general interests. Individual members of the audience will have their idiosyncrasies. When you come to write, you will have to decide not only about the general level of the audience, you will also have to decide what to do about their individual differences. You can't please everyone and you shouldn't try to. There is a mean in every case which you should strive for—and let the extreme idiosyncrasies fall by the way.

Assignments for Discussion

In your daily or Sunday paper, select items from the sports pages, the women's pages, the business pages, the book pages, the editorial pages, and the classified advertisements. How does the language differ in each one? Assuming that the newspaper is published for an average family of four, how do you account for the language differences? Which items will be read by the woman of the house? by the man of the house? Why? What items do you read? What items do you pass over? Why?

It seems to some analysts of the printed media that the media often write in such a way as to produce anxieties that are then resolved by later stories in the media—or in the same story. The sports page is an obvious example with its early-in-the-week concern over the winners of Saturday athletic events. Do you agree with this analysis? Can you support your judgment with evidence in the form of stories? What other examples do you find, assuming that you do?

Assignment for Writing

Examine the pages of a favorite magazine to find instances in which an attempt is being made to motivate you to some action (advertisements are obvious, but some advertising doesn't seem to have as its goal any direct action). Write a brief paper on the magazine's techniques for motivating its readers.

Or, in your examination, make a list of items that appeal to you and items that do not. Then write a brief paper on the reasons for your personal reactions.

Questions for Discussion and Writing

1. James Joyce talked about the "reality of experience." What does the word "reality" mean to you? Just what is an "experience"? When does an experience begin and end? How do we know it has taken place? What gives it the quality of "reality"? How would you differentiate, for instance, between something you think of as an experience and the hallucinations of someone under the influence of drugs?
2. Would you agree with Elizabeth Bowen that an "experience means nothing until it repeats itself"? Have you ever had an experience repeat itself? In what ways, if any, did either experience modify your reactions to the other? Would you agree that "experience is the best teacher"?
3. Henry James wrote in "The Art of Fiction":

   The power to guess the unseen from the seen, to trace the implications of things, to judge the whole piece by the pattern, the condition of feeling life in general so completely that you are well on your way to knowing any particular corner of it—this cluster of gifts may be said to constitute experience. . . . Therefore, if I should certainly say to a novice, "Write from experience and experience only," I should feel that this was a rather tantalizing monition if I were not careful immediately to add, "Try to be one of the people on whom nothing is lost."

What does James mean by "pattern"? "impressions"? Is he saying that only a chosen few may belong to the group on "whom nothing is lost"? Is there anything you can do to insure that you are one of the group? Or is it better to let impressions take care of themselves?

4. Mark Twain said:

We should be careful to get out of an experience only the wisdom that is in it—and stop there; lest we be like the cat that sits down on a hot stove-lid. She will never sit down on a hot stove-lid again —and that is well; but also she will never sit on a cold one anymore. (*Following the Equator, Puddinhead Wilson's New Calendar*)

From this statement, does it seem to you that any incident that happens to you is an experience? If so, is the acquisition of wisdom a continuous process? If not, is an experience an incident that furnishes us additional wisdom? How would you correlate Twain's statement with Miss Bowen's?

2

Collecting Information

To write, we must have something to write about. Long ago, writers believed that their subject came to them through divine inspiration:

> O Muse! the cause and the crimes relate;
> What goddess was provok'd, and whence her hate;
> For what offense the Queen of Heav'n began
> To persecute so brave, so just a man;
> Involv'd his anxious life in endless cares,
> Expos'd to wants, and hurried into wars!
> Can heav'nly minds such high resentment show,
> Or exercise their spite in human woe?
>
> (Dryden's trans. of *The Aeneid*)

They believed that they were imitating nature as they wrote:

To hold, as 'twere, the mirror up to nature; to show virtue her own feature, scorn her own image, and the body of the time his form and presence. (William Shakespeare)

With the Romantic Revolution of the early nineteenth century, there was a considerable change in the writer's philosophy. He now saw himself, not as one who held up a mirror to life, but rather as a lamp that illuminated life. The flame that burned within the lamp was his own genius:

> When I have fears that I may cease to be
> Before my pen has glean'd my teeming brain . . .
> (John Keats)

With the advent of the scientific and technological age in which we now live, the writer often reported information that he acquired as a result of observation:

The finely levigated castings, when brought to the surface in a moist condition, flow during rainy weather down any moderate slope; and the smaller particles are washed far down even a gently inclined surface. Castings when dry often crumple into small pellets and these are apt to roll down any sloping surface. (Charles Darwin)

as a result of experimentation:

Into a second dog we injected 1/100th of that quantity, into a third 1/200th. Rabies showed itself in the first dog on the eighteenth day after the injection, on the thirty-fifth day in the second dog, whilst the third one did not take the disease at all. (Louis Pasteur)

as a result of interview:

He was sitting there, waiting for me to start. Obviously, there was to be no time wasted in small talk or exchange of preliminary pleasantries. "*Fortune* magazine," I began, "said you're now only the *second*-richest American and that Howard Hughes is the first. But *Life* said it was a draw. And I've often seen you referred to in other publications as the richest man in the world. Which are you?" [1]

as a result of sampling:

How many such dedicated vintners are there in California? And how large is their production? I began to find out on my first day in

[1] Helen Lorenson, "Jean Paul Getty, His Golden Age," *Esquire,* October, 1969, p. 84.

San Francisco when I attended a "survey tasting" of thirty-five wines in the impressive cellar of the Russian Hill House. . . . For this and later tastings, I used a professional wine-rating chart which allocates scoring points.[2]

as a result of polling:

A majority of American doctors questioned in a poll say that [a] pregnant [woman] should be able to have an abortion if she asks for one. . . . Of the 27,741 who took part, 62.8 per cent said yes, 37.2 per cent said no. . . . In general, younger physicians were more liberal than the older doctors. Geographically, the East at 73 per cent and the Far West at 72 per cent were the regions most favorable . . . (*The Arizona Republic*, November 3, 1969)

For our information we also rely on our memories, our libraries, our museums, our archives, our galleries; we turn to books, maps, bound newspapers and magazines, letters, photographs, diaries, paintings, films, microfilms, videotapes, records, audiotapes, microfiches, computer cards, and computer tapes. The act of referring to these materials in an organized way is called research or information retrieval.

Other sources are teachers, lecturers, explorers, lawyers, scientists, doctors, inventors, engineers, poets, and fiction writers. There is also the day-to-day output of the mass media—newspapers, films, radio, television, magazines.

We acquire knowledge and information by reading, observing, listening, asking questions, making associations. We collect knowledge and information with pen and notebook (or notecards), a tape recorder, a dictaphone, a camera.

Reading

Printed and written materials may be explicit, that is direct and to the expressed point with no connotations:

After a few days, finding the trade beginning to slacken, we hove our anchor up, set our topsails, ran the stars and stripes up to the peak, fired a gun which was returned from the presidio, and left the little town astern, running out of the bay, and bearing down the coast again for Santa Barbara. (Richard Henry Dana, Jr., *Two Years Before the Mast*)

They may be implicit, that is they may suggest several meanings:

[2] Roy Andries de Groot, "Is There Great Wine in California: An Expert's Opinion," *Esquire*, October, 1969, p. 56.

All visible objects, man, are but as pasteboard masks. But in each event—in the living act, the undoubted deed—there, some unknown but still reasoning thing puts forth the mouldings of its features from behind the unreasoning mask. If man will strike, strike through the mask! (Herman Melville, *Moby Dick*)

They may range from simple statements of fact to obscure symbolism, from allegory to satire, from clarity and precision to ambiguity and equivocation. We must deal with printed information as we find it, not according to preconceived notions.

If we are reading a book, we should begin with the table of contents; it is usually a fair outline of the book. We might first read reviews of the book; these will not only help us to understand it but also give us an authority's evaluation. A biographical sketch might furnish us with information about the author's philosophies, his standing, his way of working. The book's index, if there is one, and the preface may also be helpful.

When we are reading a magazine or a newspaper, we should keep in mind the political reputation of the publication if that is pertinent—is the medium liberal, conservative, or middle-of-the-road? We should also be aware that writers have biases and prejudices; we should, if at all possible, get at least two opinions on a given subject. Even scientists and professors, who theoretically are objective, can differ in their opinions and theories, in both their own areas of expertise and in other areas in which they may be tempted to venture opinions.

As an example, here are two quotations appearing on the same page of a daily newspaper; both refer to the same speech by the President:

President Nixon's nationwide speech on Vietnam was an honest, forthright statement that does credit to the President and the good sense of the American electorate.

Words are treacherous weapons, which can be used either to clarify or confuse, and this presidential speech is one of the classic mystifying clarifications of recent years.

It is commendable, incidentally, that a newspaper should present opposite points of view on an arguable subject. In a case such as this, you can read both writers and then make up your own mind. But pity the poor reader who sees only one point of view and has not the good sense to realize there may be others.

We should be particularly careful about statistics and opinions presented as facts. Today's newspaper carries a statement by a politician that employment is up this year; he bases his statement on government figures. On the next page another politician (from the same party) complains that employment figures released by the government are several months old and unreliable.

As for opinions—they do not appear on only the editorial page. Of eight stories on the first page of the same newspaper, one is obviously opinion, one is labeled "news analysis," one is labeled "news comment," and one is obviously speculative. Yet these four stories appear on the page that most of us believe is limited to "news."

Because "words are treacherous weapons," you should keep a reliable dictionary at hand as you read. Look up new words, if they are undefined in the context. If a familiar word is being used in an unusual context or with an apparently unusual meaning, check on it. For example, there are three meanings of the word "devil" in this sentence:

That devil of a printer's devil had better straighten up or he will find himself between the devil and the deep blue sea.

You will find it easier to understand difficult passages if you learn to paraphrase them. Take this example of a paragraph in a contract:

If this instrument includes livestock, then as additional collateral, Debtor assigns, transfers, and conveys to the Secured Party a security in and to all increase and issue thereof, and additions, replacements, and substitutions therefor, and all feed, both hay and grain, owned by Debtor, all water privileges, and all equipment used in feeding and handling said livestock and also all of Debtor's right, title, and interest in all leases covering lands for pasture and grazing purposes.

Paraphrase: The lender may foreclose on anything of value of the borrower's which is directly or indirectly related to the raising of livestock, or on any livestock owned by the borrower.

Assignments for Writing

Paraphrase this paragraph from *Life:*

That probably accounts more than any single thing for the amazing union between the Republican war horse and the Irish urbanologist, a union which was instrumental in producing a whole new plan for the nation's social ills, a plan which, despite carping from the professional Nixon-haters and exiled social engineers who watch jealously from the sidelines, may prove to be the most important new domestic direction the Administration will take. It seeks, in brief, to strengthen the state, city, community and family and to arrest Potomac elephantiasis. Nobody knows, including Nixon and Moynihan, if it will work but it is an intelligent and brave try. It appears that Nixon, aside from suggesting something sensible, has plugged into a great national yearning, much as he did with his decisions to get out of Vietnam and to seek tax reforms.[3]

Before you can paraphrase you will have to translate: Republican war horse, Irish urbanologist, professional Nixon-haters, exiled social engineers, Potomac elephantiasis, plugged into (Moynihan's full name is Daniel Patrick Moynihan).

When you paraphrase, think of your classmates. Don't try to "snow" your reader with gobbledygook, Latinisms, or your version of school teacher's language.

Now paraphrase this semi-scientific paragraph:

The third biggest item in the interplanetary communication catalogue is noise. Noise interferes with all kinds of messages. Cocktail party talk is notoriously vacuous because too many conversations are going on simultaneously. As the number of drinks consumed rises, an increasing amount of heat is given off in relation to the light conveyed. Electronic ears experience somewhat the same problem. The surface of Earth generates heat, and this registers as noise in the ear if the ear is tilted toward the horizon in order to catch particular messages from the sky.[4]

Troublesome items here may be: interplanetary communication catalogue, electronic ear, vacuous, light, messages. Can you think of a better example than the one used of the cocktail party—which doesn't strike me as being particularly analogous here?

An abstract of a book or article is oftentimes useful in helping you to understand what you are reading. Sometimes—as in

[3] Hugh Sidney, "The Volcano in the Cornfield," *Life* Magazine, August 22, 1969, p. 4, © 1969 Time Inc.
[4] John Lear, "Messages from Mars," *Saturday Review*, October 11, 1969, p. 75.

scientific journals or *Masterplots*—they come to hand; more often they do not.

Locating Sources of Information

The quantities of information available to us are so vast as to stagger our reason. As a result there are complex methods for storing and retrieving information. Some of these are as follows:

Books

Many libraries assign Dewey Decimal numbers to books and store them on the basis of the book number. The system was designed as a limited classification system that divides knowledge into units that are numbered 100, 200, 300, and so on. Each main unit is further divisible by tens; 110, 120, 130. The tens are divisible: 111, 112, 113. Other units are then obtained by adding numerals after the decimal. A book on ores of iron would be 553.3. Dewey's attitudes toward knowledge influenced his system; because, for instance, he did not regard novels as "literature," he classified works of prose fiction in an area separate from poetry and drama.

In many libraries the Dewey system is being replaced or augmented by the Congressional Library classification system, because the Congressional Library is attempting to collect and classify all American printed books. The system uses 26 principal divisions, based on the letters of the alphabet. Additional subdivisions are identified by a second letter. These letters are followed by a combination of numbers and letters. For example, literature (including novels) is indexed under *P*; British literature and American literature receive a second letter based on the country of publication and the century. Thus *Arrow of Love* by Frederick Manfred becomes PS 3525 A523A7. These numbers should not be confused with the Library of Congress *accession number* which is in two parts: two digits which before 1969 indicated the year of accession and since 1969 represent merely a control number, and the serial number designating the book's place in the sequence of accession. Manfred's *Arrow of Love*, published in 1961, is 61–10918; some books published in 1969 had the number 77 as the first two digits. Most publishers print the accession number on the same page as the copyright notice.

All accessions of the Library of Congress are listed in the

catalog of the Library, available in many local libraries. Through this catalog and other sources familiar to reference librarians, any existing American book can usually be located. Current books can be located through catalogs and supplements available in most libraries and bookstores.

A bit of advice: Cultivate the good will of your friendly neighborhood reference librarian. If she can't find what you are looking for, it is probably unobtainable.

Newspapers

Although local libraries, newspapers, and state historical libraries try to maintain files of local papers, there are only two that are regarded as "newspapers of record" and therefore filed by many larger libraries. These are the *Times* of London and the New York *Times*. Both are indexed by topics, and libraries that maintain files also have the indexes. Larger libraries will have the *Union List of Serials in the Libraries of the United States and Canada;* this list tells you where files of newspapers are maintained.

N. W. Ayer and Son's *Directory of Newspapers and Periodicals* is a catalog of current newspapers and magazines. I should warn you that no directory of this kind is complete in the fullest sense of the word; there are too many ephemeral publications.

There are also many specialized catalogs and directories of books, newspapers, and other periodicals.

Magazines, Journals, Quarterlies, and Annuals

No one has any idea as to how many publications of this type there are. *Gebbie Press House Magazine Directory* lists some four or five thousand of that particular type of magazine, but both Gebbie and I know the list is not complete by any means. J. R. Porter, in an essay on the history of scientific journals, says that there are about 25,000 scientific journals in the world; he predicts three times that many by the end of the century. Martin Grant, who made a study of such things, once told me there were 5,000 periodicals in the area of religion and theology in Western Germany alone. And so on.

Magazines may be classified as follows:

• Consumer magazines: The kind ordinarily found on newsstands—*Life, Esquire, Saturday Review, Time, Better Homes and Gardens, McCall's.*

• Industrial and commercial magazines: Magazines published for an industry (smelting, grain processing) or a type of commerce (petroleum product sales, photographic equipment sales). If there is an industry or a type of commerce, it probably is represented in one magazine or several. Many of these magazines publish factual information about their subject. However, because of proprietary problems, some information may not be available. Moreover, opinions and conclusions may be biased. Nevertheless, one of these magazines (*Vend*) was responsible for the revelations of chicanery in high places that led to the unseating of a powerful political figure.

• Fraternal and association magazines: Magazines published for service clubs, fraternities, sororities, organizations, and so on.

• House organs and company magazines: These are of two types, one designed for external consumption (*Ford Times*), the other for internal consumption by employees, stockholders, and the like. Some of the external publications have a propagandistic purpose which is often cleverly concealed behind striking color photography and elaborate typography. One that I know of has as its theme the point that we have always had air and water pollution (from blowing dust and animal excrement, for example) so why be overly concerned about pollution from such circumstances as the presence of chemical plants on sites adjacent to our lakes, streams, and large cities.

• Religious publications: Magazines published by and for members of various religious faiths. The annual *Catholic Press Directory* lists all of the publications written for members of that persuasion.

Magazines are so numerous and varied that there is no one guide to them all. *Ulrich's Periodical Directory* and the annual *Writer's Market* list many of general interest. The *Union List of Serials* catalogs storage places for files of past and present periodicals. Libraries and chamber of commerce offices maintain files of periodicals that may be of local interest.

The *Poole Index to Periodical Literature* and the *Reader's Guide to Periodical Literature* index articles of literary and general interest, the former from 1802 to 1906, the latter from 1900 on. There are also indexes and abstracts of specialized subject-matter periodicals. These can be examined in school, college, and public libraries.

Libraries, Museums, and Galleries

All of us are familiar with our local public library, art gallery, or historical museum. We should also know about others that may be of use in our search for information. Many counties also have libraries, museums, and galleries. Usually each state has a state library, an historical museum or archives storage, and so on. Universities and colleges have similar facilities; the libraries of state universities are often quite extensive. In the United States the Library of Congress has the largest collection of printed books; the National Archives stores many materials available only in manuscript or typescript; the Smithsonian collects artifacts; the National Gallery of Art, painting and sculpture.

Perhaps the world's largest collection of materials is in the British Museum in London. Many American libraries maintain the catalog of the Museum for reference.

Public libraries in cities such as Boston and New York have very fine collections of books and manuscripts; the Huntington Library in San Marino, California, the Newberry Library in Chicago, and the Houghton Library at Harvard are three private libraries having very fine specialized collections. In addition there are small but often unique collections in public and private schools, industrial plants, newspapers, and the like.

Not all of the government documents are in Washington. Many universities and colleges have been designated as depositories for U. S. Government papers and documents. So extensive are such collections that elaborate storage and retrieval systems have been set up for them; the Armed Services Technical Information system (ASTIA) is one of these.

In these libraries you can expect to find many sources of information other than books. Many store public records, letters, manuscripts, typescripts, diaries, journals, business papers, and so on; these pertain to authors, business firms, local governments, private individuals, churches, associations, and the like. Sometimes actual documents are stored; often, the material is kept on microfilm, microfiche, computer tape, film, and videotape.

Book research often presents problems. Many books have been printed in more than one edition, and the editions are not alike. The first edition of Richard Henry Dana's *Two Years Before the Mast* differs considerably from the second edition. George Bernard Shaw's *Caesar and Cleopatra* was never issued in an authorized edition; Shaw seems never to have been able to decide on a particular text. To resolve this kind of dilemma scholars try to produce a *definitive edition*. Such editions, however, are sometimes so replete with footnotes as to be expensive, bulky, limited in interest, and even unreadable.

Then there are books about books. All of Shakespeare's plays and poems can be contained in one volume; the books about Shakespeare and his work would fill a small library. In fact, the Folger Shakespeare Library in Washington, D. C., was built to serve as a repository for materials that would illuminate its subject.

A third kind of book is designed to summarize knowledge, in the form of dictionaries and encyclopedias. The range is broad, from special subjects (*Concise Dictionary of American History*) to general subjects (*Encyclopaedia Britannica*). Yearbooks and supplements bring these up to date periodically.

A fourth kind is the directory—your telephone directory or city directory is a familiar variety. Other directories include *Who's Who in America, Directory of American Scholars,* and the like. Directories of books are called *bibliographies* from the Greek word for book (*biblio*) and writing (*graphies*). The basic bibliography for any research is either Constance M. Winchell's *Guide to Reference Works* (and earlier editions on which this work is based) for American books or Arthur J. Walford's *Guide to Reference Material* for English books. One should also note John Minto's *Reference Books*. These volumes are bibliographies of bibliographies. Bibliographies in turn are directories arranged by subject matter (*A Concise Bibliography for Students of English*), by genre (*Granger's Index to Poetry*), by nation and subject (*The Cambridge Bibliography of English Literature*), by period (*Annals of English Literature 1475–1925*), and so on. *A Concise Bibliography for Students of English* lists 5,438 reference items, for instance.

The most familiar directory of library materials is the Library Card Catalog. A good library card catalog will list books under both the author's name (Frederick Manfred, *Arrow of Love*) and the book title (*Arrow of Love* by Frederick Manfred). Listings under an author's name will also include the titles of books about him and books about his books.

You can find information by reference to book titles, the subject, authors, the names of relevant or pertinent subjects, the names of possible repositories or storage places, bibliographies, or categories. For example, if you wanted to find information on the subject of football, you might look up these and similar names: Grantland Rice, sports, Harold "Red" Grange, Knute Rockne, the University of Notre Dame, *Sports Illustrated,* the Green Bay Packers—and football.

In your home town, or in the town where your college is, you will find many repositories for books. In addition to your college library, there will be a town library, perhaps a county library, one or more high school libraries. Many churches have libraries; many ministers and teachers have accumulated large numbers of books. You will find libraries in industrial plants, chambers of commerce, the headquarters of associations, lodges, fraternities. Lawyers and doctors often have highly specialized libraries.

Assignment for Writing

Write on three slips of paper the names of three subjects in which you are interested or about which you are curious, one name to a slip. Place these in a box in class together with similar slips from your classmates. Shuffle these and then draw three. Of the three you receive, choose one, find what information you can on it, and write a brief essay on the subject. Read this essay in class for the edification or amusement of your classmates. The teacher will ask the student who submitted the topic to evaluate your essay.

A word of caution: There are certain obligatory procedures to follow when abstracting information from a source. They are discussed later in this chapter.

Assignment for Discussion

Discuss all the possible sources of information about your college town. Don't overlook such homely sources as telephone directories, billboards, the local chamber of commerce, county histories, old settlers, cemetery associations, and so on.

Observing

Collecting information from stores of knowledge is one thing. Collecting information from sources you can observe directly is another.

Whenever you collect information, some homework is necessary. Are you reporting a football game—what are the records of the two teams, who are the players and the coaches, what schools do they represent, what kind of a game will each play? That's part of it. Historical facts are also useful—when did the two teams first meet, how many games have they played, who has thrown the longest forward pass in a game? A good source of information is the public relations department of the school, or of the school's athletic department. Where such a department exists, it usually has prepared handouts that provide useful information. But if you stick to this alone, you run the risk of being just another reporter.

Be sure you have adequate note-taking materials. A cassette tape recorder is good—for your own observations, or for those of others. It's also good for collecting sounds. A camera is useful. Be sure you are prepared with the appropriate kind of film, lenses, if possible, artificial lighting devices. If you are photographing objects, be prepared to insert some sort of scale in the picture—a six-foot fold-up carpenter's rule is very good.

Think about observations in terms of your senses. Are you observing a plant? What color is it? Is it rough to the touch? Does it have an odor? What is its taste (sample only very small portions, please)? What is its size? Where did you see it? In the sun or shade? In a damp spot or a dry one? What was the approximate temperature? What is the mean temperature in the area? What other plants were near it? What was the soil—sandy or rocky?

In-Class Project

Design a chart that would be useful to you in observing: a tennis match; a table tennis game; a girls' basketball game; a badminton game; a football, hockey, or baseball game; or a golf match.

Assignment for Writing

Use the chart to observe and collect information about an appropriate game or match. Then, on the basis of the information in your chart, write a description of what you saw.

Interviewing

Before you interview someone, do as much of your homework as possible. Don't ask your subject for basic biographical facts if he is listed in *Who's Who*. If he is an earthworm specialist, read at least an encyclopedia article on earthworms before you interview him. It might help if you knew that earthworms are also called "angleworms," "nightcrawlers," "fishworms," and various other esoteric terms. In the process of the pre-interview, try to come up with questions that will have point for your potential readers. A good interviewer will ask open-ended questions rather than questions that lead to "yes" or "no" answers. Instead of "Are earthworms good for the soil?" ask, "What would cause earthworms to become extinct?" or "How is soil pollution harmful to our friend the earthworm?"

Professional writers usually accumulate files of newspaper and magazine clippings on subjects and people of interest to them. You can accomplish something of the same result if you will look up newspaper or magazine articles by or about your subject before you interview him. And, by the way, if he has written a book, don't be gauche and ask him what the book is about. At least read a review of it. Then you can begin: "Herman Crabpuss says that you don't know what you are writing about. What do you think about that?"

Assignments for Writing

Interview one of your parents, a teacher, your boy- or girl-scout leader, or someone else of whom you have a *low* opinion. Try to produce an *interesting* article about him or her.

Among many journalists, scientists have the reputation of being difficult people to interview. Arrange an interview with a nearby scientist, anticipating that he may be difficult. Write a report of your experience.

Sampling (Polling)

One method for gathering information is sampling. Sampling may be random or organized. Organized sampling has been developed by Gallup, Harris, and others to the point where very small samples are predictive of results. The hypothesis behind their technique is that it is possible to select a small sample of people that will have in proportion the same characteristics as an extremely large sample.

When you *interview,* your questions should be open-ended. When you *sample,* they should be polarized. Don't ask: "What do you think of the Republican party?" Ask: "At this time, on the basis of information available to you, would you vote for the Republican candidate for dogcatcher, the Democratic candidate, or are you undecided?" Don't ask: "How are things going?" Ask: "Has your spendable income increased, decreased, or remained the same this year?"

Although you don't have the resources of Harris or Gallup, you can still conduct a fairly respectable sample poll. On your campus, for example, you can decide what proportions of students are: fraternity, independent, sorority, dormitory, commuter. Then you can proportion your total sample according to your decision. Your interviewees can help you by their answers to such questions as: "Did you earn all, part, or none of your college expenses last year?" Such questions can help you categorize your sample.

The problem is actually one of classification. You decide: What are the categories of the large sample in terms of personal characteristics (age, employment, size of family, religious faith, political persuasion, home ownership, place of residence, education, and so on)?

Class Project

In class, decide on the criteria for a representative sample of your student body, based on some proportion such as four or five students per thousand (or hundred if your school is relatively small) of the total enrollment. Then settle on ways of locating this representative sample—which students will you interview? What will you do if the first student proves to be a poor interviewee? Next, settle on a main topic, which might require several questions or just one question, that you want to ask about. If you are trying to determine student attitudes toward student representation on the campus, you might ask several related questions. On the other hand a poll on grades might be limited to: "Should the grading system on this campus be replaced by some other system?" When the questions have been chosen, poll your sample. Report the conclusions to your campus newspaper.

Digesting or Abstracting

When we refer to the literature of a specific area in search of knowledge or information, we often put to use another set of skills closely connected to the skills of observing or interviewing—the skills of abstracting or digesting.

The abstract or digest is a *synopsis* of a journal, magazine, or newspaper article or of a book. Synonyms for *synopsis* are *summary, précis,* or *brief.* It has several purposes and its substance will vary accordingly.

A title is the briefest form of the abstract. Sometimes titles are used to catch the reader's attention:

> "Hub Fans Bid Kid Adieu"
>
> "Stix Nix Hix Pix"

If titles are to be used in catalogs, in advertisements, or in casual references, they ought perhaps to be more informative:

> *Outlines of Shakespeare's Plays*
>
> *Harper's Dictionary of Classical Antiquities*

Still, a title is also a persuasive device, and the immediate persuasive value may be more important than the long-range historical factor.

A somewhat more elaborate form of the abstract is often used under the title of a magazine article:

"The Silent Arsenal" (title): A United Nations Report on the Production, Use, and Effects of Chemical and Bacteriological Warfare.

"The Greatness of Harry Truman" (title): At night, knowing he was in the White House, even *he* slept better.

A form such as the following is used in library card catalogs or that form of bibliography known as the *annotated bibliography:*

32.5   Brussel, Isidore R. Anglo-American first editions. 2 v. N. Y.
       1935–1936
       Part I, East to West (1862–1900), describes first editions of
       English authors whose books were published in the U. S. prior
       to appearing in England. Part II, West to East (1786–1930),
       similarly treats books by Americans first published in England.

Abstracts of this kind are necessary only if the information
is worth leaving to posterity. There ought to be a moral here; I
leave it to you to find it.

A second kind of abstract is used as an introduction to technical and scientific articles. It is necessary because of the time
limitations we all have. What is the article about? Is it of interest to me? Moreover, in articles that are developed inductively
with the conclusions at the end, it is a key or guide that helps
us understand the unfolding of events or concepts in the article.

Here is an abstract of an article, "Writing for the Younger
Generation," by Mabel Louise Robinson:

Out of her varied experience as a writer and as a teacher of fiction
writing at Columbia University, Miss Robinson offers a number of
vigorous conclusions about the demands and the rewards in writing
for young readers. Her own success and the many fine books which
students in her workshops have published give authority to her comments.

Her article gives the writer of juvenile [fiction] a clear view of his
responsibilities and his opportunities as well as good advice on technical problems. In fact, Miss Robinson writes with such zest about
the responses of this young audience that she may persuade writers
of adult fiction to see what they can do for the younger generation.[5]

Another type of abstract is like that which appears in publications such as *Masterplots* or *The Reader's Encyclopedia*:

As a mere boy, after his mother's death, David [Copperfield] is sent
by his cruel stepfather, Mr. Murdstone, to London to make his living;
here he pastes labels on bottles in a warehouse by day and is the single
lodger of the poverty-stricken though optimistic Mr. Micawber and
his family. David finally runs away to his great-aunt Betsy Trotwood,
who becomes his guardian. After a period of school life in Creakle's
school, he settles down to work with Mr. Wickfield, a lawyer, and finds
a warm friend in Wickfield's daughter Agnes. Unaware of Agnes's
deep devotion to him, David marries Dora Spenlow, a rattlebrained

---

[5] This abstract by Helen Hull is reprinted from *The Writer's Book*. Copyright,
1950, by Authors League of America, Inc.

childlike woman, who dies soon after. Neither his literary success nor his marriage has brought him the happiness and peace he yearns for, and David turns to Agnes with the realization he has always loved her. She is involved in extricating her father from the deceits of the unctuous Uriah Heep, who has gained a financial hold over them. With the help of Mr. Micawber, Uriah Heep is foiled; David marries Agnes and together they find happiness.[6]

The abstracter is in a position of power. When *you* write an abstract to precede your own article or report, you act as your own advance agent; you pick the issues you want stressed. More often, the choice is left to someone else. Editors, interested in the persuasive factor, prefer to write their own, or the author simply overlooks the possibility. A journal of abstracts is important to the research because it provides a short guide of published work; the value of the work may not be recognized if the abstract is not a skillful one, however. Annotated bibliographies, such as the one presented above, require special skill in abstracting, as does any brief summary.

The most faithful abstracts preserve the organization of the original. If the organization is chronological, your abstract is chronological. If the organization is syllogistic, your abstract is syllogistic.

By implication, this means that you list the topic sentences and call the result an abstract; you have kept the language and order of the original. But you may have to add transitions and edit some of the sentences. You may also have to add some sentences of your own for emphasis or clarity. This method works fairly well if the original is well done, and if you are cutting about 50 percent.

However, you may need to cut more, or you may want to report some parts of the original more fully (most articles contain rehash; only the new parts deserve the emphasis), or you are abstracting a useful but badly written article (there are more of these than you may think), or your purpose may be different from that of the original author.

There are two basic techniques you can use. You can cut the routine material to the barest mention and copy large sections of the new material. The resulting abstract is a distortion of the original because the emphasis and proportion of the original is discarded. However, such an abstract is very useful to people who want new ideas quickly.

Or you can throw out the original article altogether. You can make an outline according to your own sense of relevance. Then you can fill it out as much as your assigned space allows. You try to keep the basic terms, but in essence you have written a new article. It is shorter and, you hope, more inclusive than the original, but it is still an honest representation.

The length of the abstract is often arbitrarily decided by the whims of an editor, the number of pieces of 8-point type that can be impressed on a 3 x 5 card, or similar considerations.

Consider the style in which similar abstracts are prepared before beginning yours. What elements of a paper are included in those abstracts? Are conclusions and recommendations, for example, left out, or are they, perhaps, the only items left in?

Keep these things in mind:

• What is the point (or points) that the author makes or tries to make? (The author may not have done the job he tried to do.)
• What are the subpoints or subtopics?
• What organization are you going to give the abstract?
• What is your purpose in abstracting?

Assignments for Discussion

Reader's Digest often abstracts articles from other periodicals (although some *Digest* articles are written for the *Digest*). For instance, the September, 1969, issue contains an article, "Drugs and the Athlete," that was "digested" (abstracted) from three articles appearing in consecutive issues of *Sports Illustrated*. Try to find this set of articles or a similar set. Examine the articles and discuss the *Digest's* treatment of the original.

Paperback books often use abstracts on covers as a means of persuading us to buy. These range from one-liners ("They stole love from a world aflame") to paragraphs. Discuss some of these abstracts in terms of their comprehensiveness, honesty, and effectiveness.

Assignment for Writing

Read an article in a magazine such as *Saturday Review* that does not provide its own abstracts. Then write an abstract for a bibliography, limiting it to 100 words; write a 300- to 500-word abstract for presentation to your class. It would be helpful if two or three of your classmates read the same article and wrote their own abstracts. These could then be compared by the class.

A form of the abstract is *minutes of meetings.* These often appear to be reports of actions similar to those of the reporter or researcher. A useful comparison can be made at this point between apparently unlike situations: a young girl's diary and the official minutes of a meeting. The girl empties her mind as she writes; whatever order there is is subconscious. Meetings, as a rule, occur like the thoughts in the girl's mind, but the recorder gives them the appearance of order. Research, unlike the other two, depends upon intellectual order. The process has a logically necessary sequence; the order comes from outside the researcher's mind.

A court reporter provides a record in perfect sequence, but the order of events has been arranged at least partially by the attorneys. The reporter's record, unlike minutes of ordinary meetings, is necessarily complete; a man's life may hang on a point of information or procedure. Both the court report and the minutes of meetings become legal documents, but minutes of meetings are usually easier to read—and are almost always briefer. Moreover, the court reporter's report often serves as a reference for those charged with making a decision; minutes reflect decisions already made.

Finally, the ordinary meeting usually covers several items of business, not all related by any means. Even the "business conference" or "workshop" is often filled with digressions and false excursions. The meeting has a stated purpose, but the participants may carry it far afield; the unity of the technical process just isn't there. The meeting may appear to be orderly, but the order is more of association than logic.

Ordinarily, the secretary has leeway in reporting what has gone on. What order exists in a set of minutes is imposed by him, even though there is often an *agenda* that has been followed. The unwary think that the secretary merely reports in a short form what really happened; by means of selection, the secretary has actually reported the events that were significant in his view. A good secretary may regroup the events of a meeting in order to get the most emphatic and readable report. When he reads the minutes at a subsequent meeting, the participants in the earlier meeting recognize that he has reported them correctly, and yet they may be a little startled by their reported "wisdom" and incisiveness. The secretary's job is important, but it is quite different from that of the researcher or court reporter.

The secretary is primarily an abstracter or at least an editor. Rarely are the verbatim minutes of a meeting published. To be sure, a good secretary makes fairly complete notes of a meeting, making sure that motions are put down in the mover's words, that the names of movers and seconders are obtained, that amendments are accurately reported, and that all votes are recorded. Written committee reports are obtained; these may be abstracted into the minutes or copies may be sent out to all concerned. But even in such detailed reporting, topical jokes, casual asides, and similar remarks are not reported; and if there is a request for an "executive session" or an "off the record" session, the secretary lays his reporting equipment aside. If errors of fact are committed in the meeting, the secretary is permitted to correct these.

Perhaps 6,000 to 12,000 words are uttered in an hour meeting—the secretary's chore is to cut this down to a page and a half of single spaced typing. The written version is five to ten percent of the original. In the process he must be fair and accurate, but his readers will demand that he cut—and cut again. Therein lies the source of the secretary's power.

A final bit of advice. Report comprehensively. Check motions, amendments with their makers. Verify important incidents with the chairman. Get all titles right, and spell all names correctly. Settle on a style for minutes of all meetings and adhere to it unless requested to change. Have the chairman approve your final draft.

If minutes are important, they should be bound into a book in such a way that they cannot be removed without mutilating the book, and in such a way that additions cannot be made except by authorization of the group which appoints or elects the secretary.

Here is a set of minutes taken from an official minutes book of an honorary fraternity:

Minutes of the Meeting of November 5, 1972

The meeting was called to order at 4:05 P.M. by President Frederick Rolfe upon his ruling that a quorum was present.

The minutes of the meeting of October 4, 1969, were read and approved with one correction. The secretary was instructed to change the minutes to read "Motion to adjourn was made by *Richard* Smith."

The treasurer reported the November 1st balance as $1,036.00 with no outstanding bills.

Irving Herman moved that $500.00 of the balance be transferred to an interest-bearing account in a local bank "so as to bring the highest possible return on the investment." Brown seconded. After a warm and at times heated discussion, a motion to table was approved.

John Butler, chairman of the committee on new members, presented a list of candidates for membership. Several members, noting the increase in the number of names on the list as compared to previous elections, raised the question of higher standards for membership. President Rolfe appointed George Penrod and the secretary as an ad hoc committee to confer with the National Headquarters on the matter. They were instructed to report back at the December meeting.

The list of eligible candidates was then approved.

Motion to adjourn was made by Richard Smith.

Signed

Levy Martin, Secretary

Some notes on these minutes:

The passive voice is frequently used in minutes because meetings consist of actions moved and approved and discussions; the passive voice emphasizes these characteristics. Moreover, too frequent use of the active voice would put too much emphasis on the names and titles of certain people such as the president.

In the second paragraph the name *Richard* is italicized to indicate the desired correction.

In the third paragraph a direct quotation is used and indicated by quotation marks. Such quotations are desirable in cases of possible controversy. In the same paragraph the names of those engaging in the discussion are not important. However, as a matter of good practice, the secretary would record dialogue as carefully as possible, noting who said what. This record would remain in his note file where it would be accessible during his tenure. The minutes ordinarily should record only the names of those making and seconding motions, those presenting committee reports, those appointed to perform some task, and so on. However, if a participant asks that "the record show" his participation in some discussion, or his stand on some issue, the secretary will indicate this fact in the published minutes.

Assignment for Writing

Serve as a reporter for a class discussion. Reduce the minutes to 500–750 words. Present them to the class for approval.

Another form of the abstract is the *review*—of articles, books, films, plays, art exhibits, and so on. To the reviewer is entrusted the handling of other people's work—and he should be prepared to give it special care. No one ever starts from scratch; we all depend upon the wisdom of previous workers. Sometimes the bases for the work are so ancient and so widely accepted that special treatment is unnecessary for that part alone. The problem is commenting on ideas that clearly belong to particular individuals. Thus, in reviewing a dramatization, it is not necessary to review the play if it is a well-known one. All you will have to do is review the presentation, referring to the play only to make a point.

Another name for the review is *criticism,* though there is a difference. Reviews are generally written for publication and are evaluations of work that is unfamiliar to the reader. Criticisms or critiques are evaluations of work that the reader has examined. Obviously a review can overnight become a criticism. Incidentally, the term criticism is used here in its positive sense.

In its most complete form a review or criticism is an evaluation or comparison in the classic pattern. "X's work is an important contribution to the state of the art." To this may be added disclaimers—"but it falls short of giving proper theoretical proof." What follows should contain two evaluations—one based on standards of what is a contribution to the state of the art, the other based on standards of what is proper theoretical proof:

A book of essays and notes is usually "about" something, in the sense that a blueprint is "about" what it describes. Works of art, however, are not "about" some "objective" structure "out there." They speak to the experience of the person who is reading, listening to, seeing them. Being consubstantial with that experience, they cannot be said to be about it.[7]

It is not necessary to state the standards overtly as in the above case—often implicit statement is enough. What standards are implicit in the following paragraph?

Unfortunately, this pedestrian and highly conventional book on Giap by an Australian military officer contributes very little to our understanding of the man or the situation. Robert J. O'Neill has failed to turn up any new biographical information on the North Vietnamese general and contents himself with such pedantic military academy questions as to whether or not Giap ought to be considered a "great strategist." [8]

This review statement is based on standards for what is a "pedestrian" book, what is a "highly conventional" book, and so on. The standards also refer to the needs of the potential reader. This part of the review does not discuss the quality of the writing, something that often concerns a reviewer: "Smith has written a better explanation of the laser beam than has Brown." The latter statement, while not overtly critical of the style, does suggest that we may have to struggle our way through Brown. Such comments are useful, for reviews are often prepared to encourage or discourage busy readers.

The organization of the review presents some problems. The reviewer of a book may present a synopsis, a statement of the author's qualifications, a comparison with other similar books, a note as to what has been attempted, what has succeeded, what has failed, and something about the style. Comments may also be made on the presence or absence of footnotes, a bibliography, an index, a table of contents, the type and binding, illustrations and graphs, and the quality of any of these that are included. The commentator may place his most significant judgments and criteria in either ascending or descending order. In popular reviews some conventions prevail. These begin with the qualifications of the author; sometimes they are more relevant than others. Next is a description of the work, usually large in a review because the reader hasn't read the book. The reader's interests must be kept in mind. Finally, there is the judgment,

[7] Thomas Fitzimmons, review of *For the House Hold . . .* , *Saturday Review,* October 11, 1969, p. 37.

[8] Daniel M. Grady, review of *General Giap: Politician and Strategist, Saturday Review,* October 11, 1969, p. 35.

although a good reviewer will blend judgment and summary. The reviewer may find it necessary to support his judgments.

Always be careful to make a complete identification of the work you are reviewing. Be sure you have the exact title and the author's name as it appears on the title page, or in the official program if you are reviewing a play or film. If the author has sometimes been known by another name, you should mention that. List the publisher by the exact name shown in the book; if several addresses are given, list either the first or the most prominent. Give the year of publication. If you are reviewing a revised or later edition, note the first date of publication as well as the present edition. Add the number of pages, the kind of binding, and a note as to presence or absence of illustrations. For films, plays, and the like, list analogous information. Be sure to include the cast, the parts they play, and the names of people whose work contributed to the performance in a significant way—the designer of the lighting and the director of the orchestra, for example, but not the head usher nor the firm that printed the program.

Assignment for Discussion

In class, discuss a book that many have read or a film or play that many have seen. Concentrate on the criteria for evaluation; the subject, the author or director, the cast, the production or style, a comparison with other works. Decide whether the book, play, or film was "good" or not. Defend or attack the decisions that are made, but be prepared to document your point of view.

Assignment for Writing

Write a review of a book you have read or a play or film you have seen. Find reviews or criticisms written by others; newspapers, *Time, Life, Saturday Review, The New Yorker* are good places to look. Your college library should have anthologies or other books in which reviews and criticisms have been collected. Find some of these and analyze them for techniques, style, and the like. Compare your review or criticism with those you have found, and defend your variations from them.

On the Use of Materials in Books, Magazines, and Newspapers

Books, magazines, and newspapers are printed under the protection of the copyright laws of the nation in which they are published. In the United States such materials are originally copyrighted for a period of 28 years. The copyright may be renewed for a second period of 28 years by the owners of the original copyright. You must always assume that the copyright has been renewed.

The materials in books, magazines, and newspapers thus become the legal property of the copyright holder for a period up to 56 years. The date of the original copyright is the date of publication. In books, which are not dated as magazines and newspapers are, the date of copyright is shown on one of the prefatory pages.

The materials in a letter, manuscript, or typescript are the property of their author. Possession of such material may change hands (as in the mailing of a letter), but the literary rights to what is written or typed on the paper belong to the original author.

In order to reprint copyrighted material, permission must be secured from the copyright owner, his agent, or his successor. Such strictures ordinarily are not applied to student papers submitted only to a teacher. They do apply, however, the instant any further distribution or reproduction of the paper is planned.

In any case, the student should acknowledge his sources for any material taken from any publication, whether or not that publication is copyrighted. Even though the original copyrights have expired and the material is in the "public domain," he should indicate his obligations. To fail to do so results in the act of *plagiarism*. Plagiarism is the unauthorized or unacknowledged use of the ideas of others, either in their original form or in a paraphrase. The act of plagiarism is a serious violation of the principles of good citizenship; in many colleges and universities, conviction of the act is sufficient grounds for automatic expulsion.

Either to avoid charges of plagiarism or to acknowledge our obligations, we follow certain style standards when quoting or paraphrasing. These may vary from place to place; the following are typical procedures.

Direct quotations are set off in quotation marks, following the normal margins if they are five lines or less:

The *MLA Style Sheet* notes that "all quotations should correspond exactly with the originals. . . ."

If the direct quotations run to more than five typewritten lines, it is customary to treat them as an independent body of material. A new left-hand margin may be established, usually five spaces within the normal left-hand margin. For college or university use, these quotations are single-spaced; a double-space is used to separate paragraphs. Paragraphing in the quotation then requires an additional indentation; a standard practice is to begin each paragraph five spaces to the right of the left margin of the quotation. Right-hand margins of quotations are also often indented five spaces from the usual right-hand margin.

We can indicate our obligation to our source in several ways:

Theodore Peterson in his *Magazines in the Twentieth Century* says that "the modern magazine . . . has been the least subject to serious study." *

The three periods in the quotation indicate that a portion of the original copy has been omitted—probably because the omitted portion is irrelevant to the present discussion. The asterisk at the end of the quotation is a signal that some note of explanation has been placed at the bottom of the page—the explanatory note is identified by a matching asterisk placed at the head of the note.

Theodore Peterson says that "the modern magazine [by which he means any magazine published since 1900] . . . has been the least subject to serious study." [1]

The brackets indicate an editorial interpolation; they are used rather than parentheses to avoid confusion with parenthetical remarks in the original.

The superscript figure (1) at the end of the quotation signals a reference to a footnote. In other words, it is a signal telling the reader that the source of the quotation or some further commentary or explanation will be found in a note appended to the regular copy.

In a printed text, footnotes may appear at the bottom of a page, at the end of a chapter, or at the end of the book. When typing footnotes, however, the best procedure is as follows:

Draw a line from margin to margin across the typed page, one space below the nethermost line of the quotation. Repeat the

footnote number at the left-hand margin and one space below
the ruled line. Insert a period and two horizontal spaces after
the number, then type your explanation in single-spaced lines.
Draw another line from margin to margin one space below the
last line of your explanation. Double-space and resume your
typing.

Number footnotes in series. In a book-length manuscript, the
series may continue through the book or may begin anew from
the number (1) in each chapter. In shorter papers, continue the
series throughout the paper. In any case, DO NOT RENEW
the series on succeeding pages of your paper or manuscript. Set
the number about one-half a horizontal space above the line,
thus:

Footnote ^{1} all quotations. ^{2}

A third way to indicate our obligation is often used by
scientists and engineers:

Peterson (1) says that "the modern magazine . . ."

In this case the numeral (1) indicates item number one in the
appended bibliography. In the bibliography, books are listed
alphabetically by the last name of their author or of the primary
author if more than one author is listed. Starting from the top
of the list, the books are then numbered in series, and the series
number is the one used in footnoting. Notice that this method
permits only reference to a title; if you want to explain or
elaborate in a footnote, you must use brackets as explained
earlier.

In your footnote, or bibliography, list book titles in this way:

Richard Henry Dana, Jr., "Preface," *Two Years Before the Mast,*
ed. John Haskell Kemble, illustrated edition, two volumes (Los
Angeles, California: The Ward Ritchie Press, 1964), I, p. xxi.

1. Author or authors in order and form listed on the title
page. Some persons prefer or require that the author's name be
listed last name first, followed by first name and initials, thus:
Dana, Richard Henry Jr.

2. Where pertinent, title of the chapter or portion of the book
cited ("Preface," "Appendix A"), enclosed in quotation marks,
followed by a comma inside the final quotation marks.

3. Title of the work, underlined, followed by a comma unless

the next detail is enclosed in parentheses. Copy the title in its complete form as it appears on the title page. The purpose of underlining is the same as italicizing. Most authorities underline or italicize book titles or magazine names to set them apart from titles of shorter pieces such as magazine articles or short stories. On the other hand some journalists either capitalize the title of a book or magazine or else put it in quotation marks.

4. Editor's or translator's name in the same order as in item 1, preceded by "ed." or "trans." (These abbreviations are not enclosed in quotation marks in your copy.) The name is followed by a comma unless the next item is enclosed in parentheses. This name is not placed in parentheses.

5. Edition used, if known and provided it is not the first, in Arabic numerals, followed by a comma unless the next detail is enclosed in parentheses.

6. The series, if pertinent, not underlined and not in quotation marks, and followed by a comma unless the next detail is enclosed in parentheses.

7. The number of volumes, if pertinent, which have the same title as this one (for example, the *Encyclopaedia Britannica* is published in 24 volumes—therefore, for the *Britannica* item 7 would be 24).

8. Place(s) and date(s) of publication within parentheses; the place is followed by a comma. If the date is not known, the abbreviation "n.d." is used, but not in quotation marks. If the publisher's name is supplied, it is inserted between the place and the date; a colon precedes it and a comma follows it.

9. The volume number, if two or more volumes of the book exist, in capital Roman numerals. Do not use the term "Volume" or "Vol." The volume number is followed by a comma.

10. Page number(s) of reference, if pertinent, in Arabic numerals (unless the quotation is taken from a page numbered in small Roman numerals). The page number is preceded by a comma and followed by a period unless an additional reference is required. The numerals are preceded by "p." (page) or "pp." (pages), but these abbreviations are not placed within quotation marks, thus: p. xxi, pp. 23–25. As indicated the inclusive numbers are listed if a series of pages is referenced; otherwise several random pages are listed thus: pp. 1, 3, 7, 9.

If your footnote refers to a magazine or periodical, follow this style:

Arnold Gingrich, "Business and Youth," *Esquire*, LXII, 4 (October, 1969), 73.

1. Author's name, as above, followed by a comma.
2. Title in full, enclosed in quotation marks, followed by a comma inside the second quotation mark.
3. Name of the periodical or magazine, abbreviated in accordance with good usage, underlined, followed by a comma.
4. Volume number (without "Volume" or "Vol." preceding) in capital Roman numerals, followed by a comma, unless the next detail is enclosed in parentheses. For daily, weekly, or monthly publications the complete date (*i.e.*, October 24, 1969) may be used as an alternate—with commas, not parentheses. Both date and volume number are helpful. Bound volumes of periodicals are sometimes indicated by only one of these indicia.
5. Issue number (or month name) if the pagination of the issue begins with page number one (some periodicals are numbered serially by the volume so that the first page of an issue is not necessarily page one).
6. The year (preceded by the month if necessary) enclosed in parentheses, followed by a comma.
7. Page number(s) in Arabic numerals, without "p." or "pp." preceding, followed by a period unless an additional reference to a footnote is needed.

The above are standard ground rules that are generally used. But matters of style are subject to the whims of teachers, editors, association officers, librarians, graduate college deans, and so on. The rule is: When in Ignorantia do as the Ignorant do. Many publications and organizations have their own style books and these must be followed. In case of doubt, follow the example of a good text or of a reputable dictionary.

One final note—if the paper is to have external publication, don't forget to ask for permission to use quotations. Write to the publisher; he usually is in a position to grant permission. If you are quoting manuscripts, letters, or typescripts, otherwise unpublished, you will have to locate the author or his literary heirs.

Indexing

In dealing with subjects, always index the *noun* or *verb*, never index by qualities unless you have a good reason for so doing:

dictionaries, English   running, long distance
desks, office   fishing, trout
chairs, upholstered   racing, horse

When indexing names, always index last name first:

Sutherland, Mason
Gingrich, Arnold

When indexing titles, list title as written by author or publisher:

National Geographic
David Copperfield

Cross-index synonyms or variant spellings:

Précis (see *Summary*)
Smythe (see also *Smith, Smyth*)

Cross-index pseudonyms or variant names:

Mark Twain (see *Samuel Langhorne Clemens*)
Saturday Review of Literature, The (see *Saturday Review*)

When indexing book titles, names of business firms, titles of organizations, associations, institutions, and the like, always use the complete official title, and index by the first word of the title, unless the first word is an article (a, an, the); in that case, index by the word that follows the article:

State Historical Society of Iowa, The, Iowa City, Iowa

Universal Baseball Association, Inc., The, J. Henry Waugh, Prop.

Sometimes it is helpful to your reader if you cross-index lengthy titles such as these. In such cases index by the term most likely to be familiarly used.

3

Our

Language

Man is a toolmaker. The tools he has devised have enabled him to extend his otherwise limited physical, sensory, and mental capabilities. With his extensions of himself, he has walked on the moon, gazed at stars beyond his range of vision, entered into the world of microorganisms, stored and preserved food against the possibility of famine, made himself comfortable under the most adverse environmental conditions, and all but eliminated the perils of disease.

The extension of himself that has made all of this possible is his language. Without language he could devise at best only the most elementary tools. Moreover, language not only makes toolmaking possible but also gives it meaning and point beyond mere survival. Language is the instrument by which man patterns his life and gives those patterns structure and purpose. An educated man, therefore, ought to know something about this most important tool, for it is the key to his education.

Language as Symbol

Language exists in a number of forms. The mind, for instance, is capable of creating symbols to refer to the actions and objects inferred by the senses as being present within and without man; it not only creates these symbols but stores them and makes associations between and among them. The mind also creates and uses symbols for qualities of the inferred objects and actions, and it creates and uses other symbols to demonstrate relationships between and among objects and actions.

The symbols that the mind creates can be externalized in a number of ways. The sculptor converts his symbols into shaped objects; the painter brushes paint onto a canvas to create two-dimensional representations of his symbols; the composer annotates a sheet of music. All of us convert mental symbols into language; our psychological apparatus motivates our physiological apparatus, air is expelled upward from our lungs and used to create sounds in our throat, oral passage, and nasal passage. The sounds thus created are patterned to form the words and exclamations that make up our oral language. Actually, of course, no words are formed. The shaped and conditioned flow of air from the oral and nasal passages sets up vibrations in the environmental air; these vibrations are picked up by the sensory apparatus of another; the psychological apparatus of that other one translates these vibrations into symbols similar to those in the mind of the transmitter.

Because the life of these vibrations is extremely short, man has devised ways of perpetuating or recording the symbols that the vibrations represent. He first devised symbols for his language by making marks on surfaces; on clay tablets, on leather skins, on the walls of caves, on papyrus. Just as sounds, by convention, represent actions, objects, qualities, concepts, so these marks and combinations of marks came, by convention, to represent both the sound patterns we call words *and* the actual phenomena to which the words referred. Thus the written or printed language can indicate speech, "I love you, Mary Jane," or ideas not necessarily spoken, "love, Mary Jane, girl."

More recently man has devised means for extending the spatial and historical range of sounds through radio, the telegraph, television, motion pictures, recording machines, and the like. In so doing he has opened up a new way of representing language; through the medium of motion pictures or television, we may hear and see language simultaneously—a word is shown on the screen at the same time a voice speaks it.

Each of these kinds of language—language in the abstract, language as it is spoken, language as it is written or printed, language as it is stored or transmitted in the form of sound—represents a convention, an agreement among all of us. Each symbol or set of symbols in the abstract language is a *referent* to the real or the imagined world, or to some set of arbitrary standards. Each sound or set of sounds meaningfully uttered by the voice (and perhaps recorded or transmitted by mechanical, electrical, or electronic devices) refers both to the symbols and the things the symbols stand for. The convention, the agreement that we make is that the symbols or sounds (or set of symbols or sounds) refer to specific objects, actions, qualities, incidents, or concepts.

In other words, when we utter the sounds represented by the symbol "desk," or when we write or print the word *desk,* we all agree that these sounds, or this word, refer to an object in the real world that we all agree is a desk. Such agreements may have no philosophical basis whatever, but they are necessary if we are to get on with our daily work.

You must keep in mind, however, that neither the sound nor the written word is the object—the word is not the thing. But you must be prepared to deal with people who operate all or part of the time on the assumption that the word *is* the thing. Even you will often make this assumption if you are not careful.

Origins of Language

All of this highly abstract stuff probably raises questions in your mind. What was the origin of language? Why does a certain sound represent a certain object? Why do certain marks on paper represent certain sounds or certain objects? If language is conventional, is it fixed—or can it change?

About the only statement we can make with certainty with reference to the origins of language is that it began as an oral language. As a matter of fact, language has been an oral matter for most people down to comparatively modern times. Two of the most influential men in western civilization—Jesus and Socrates—apparently communicated with their disciples only through speech, and it is not possible to point to any body of written work and say that it was written by these men. Paul, the

disciple of Christ, employed scribes to write his epistles. The
Greek epics and plays were heard by large numbers of people who
probably never saw the words written. Until the beginning of
printing, only priests and manuscript copyists were permitted to
read the Bible—the majority of people could not have read the
book if they had been permitted to. Even today, though the spoken
language seems to come "naturally" with a certain maturity,
reading must be learned with the help of someone.

Widespread acquaintanceship with language in written or
printed form derives from the invention of the printing press in
the fifteenth century. Printers at once began printing and disseminating everything they could set in type, and they found a
ready market for their printed sheets among large numbers of
people. Up to that time only the very wealthy or the monasteries
could own a book or a library—now the printed word spread
rapidly among all but the lowest classes of people.

The language that the printers used in England in the fifteenth
century had been common in the country for only the past
thousand years—and even then it had undergone some changes.
When the Romans pulled out of the British Isles in the fifth
century, they left behind groups of people who spoke the Celtic
and Pictic tongues. They also left behind evidences of their
occupation in such words as *valla* (wall) and *castra* (camp);
modern Rochester, Worcester, and Winchester are based on the
latter Roman word.

Soon the Islands were being invaded by Angles, Saxons, and
Jutes from what is now Jutland and Friesland. The language
they brought with them was one of what is called the Indo-
European family of languages; Greek, Latin, German, Italian,
Spanish, and French are in the same family. On the continent
they had had contacts with Roman soldiers and citizens, and so
they brought with them the Roman words for wine, cheese,
highway, camp-follower, and the like.

Transliterated, their language looks like this:

Fæder ūre,
þū þe eart on heofonum,
sī þīn nama gehālgod.
Tōbecume þīn rīce.
Gewurþe ðīn willa on eorðan swā swā on heofonum.
Ūrne gedæghwāmlīcan hlāf syle ūs tō dæg.

And forgyf ūs ūre gyltas, swā swā wē forgyfað ūrum gyltendum.
And ne gelǣd þū ūs on costnunge,
ac ālȳs ūs of yfele. Sōþlīce.

Characteristics of this language are: the use of the digraph
or ligature æ for the sound now represented by the letter *a* in
hat; the thorn, þ, used for the *th* sound in words like *thin;* the
edh (pronounced *eth*), used for the *th* sound in words like *then;*
the pronunciation of the long vowels further back in the throat
so that *we* rhymed with *say, pin* (thine) rhymed with *seen, hlaf*
(loaf) rhymed approximately with the *o* in *odd,* and so forth;
conjugational and declensional endings on nouns, adjectives,
and verbs. In this language every letter in a word stood for a
sound that was uttered; thus *cniht* (our word *knight*) was pronounced *k-nicht,* the *ch* sound being somewhere between our *k*
sound and the German *ch* as in *ich liebe dich.* The pronunciation of the *g* varied according to its position in a word; pronounce the modern words, *goose, geese, ring, good,* and *finger,*
and you will have an idea of what was happening.

How Language Grows and Changes

Until the invention of printing a number of circumstances
produced changes in the language—changes that occurred because the language was primarily oral. There were no dictionaries as such and so scribes either copied previous manuscripts
or interpreted the sounds they heard and transliterated them to
the best of their abilities. In the course of a thousand years
declensional and conjugational endings largely disappeared;
helpan became *help,* but *drifan* became *drive,* the final *e* apparently representing a stage in the pronunciation of the word.
Cniht came to rhyme with *rite,* although the spelling, somewhat
modified, was retained. The *edh* and the *thorn* disappeared, to
be replaced by the letters *th;* the pronunciations did not change
however. All of the long vowels moved forward in the mouth; *I*
no longer rhymed with *see* but came to rhyme with *eye,* and so
on. The sound of *u* in *hus, mus* (rhyming with *goose*) became a
dipthong, and the words were pronounced *house, mouse.* The
plural of *hus* had been *husas* so the plural of *house* became
houses. The plural of *mus* had been *mysena,* so the plural of
mouse became eventually *mice.*

At the same time that orthographic and phonetic changes

were taking place, hundreds of Anglo-Saxon words were disappearing and being replaced by borrowings from the Scandinavian, from medieval French, from Latin, and from Greek. For example, we borrowed the medieval French word *werre* which later became our word *war;* similar borrowings resulted in the words *ward, warden.* More recently the French began pronouncing these words with a *g* as in *c'est la guerre,* and we borrowed the modernized forms: *guard, guardian.*

In the Renaissance, Englishmen began to realize that they had a language of their own. Learned men still spoke Latin and Greek, and some persons used French, but the great mass of people were speaking the language we now call English. Scholars began to be concerned about the wordstock, about the spelling of words, and about the grammar. Attempts were made to fix the wordstock, to eliminate barbarisms in the language. Other attempts were made to establish the English orthography even though the pronunciation of words was changing (and continues to change). Finally, an attempt was made to make the English language conform to the grammar of Latin.

Today sensible students recognize that we cannot identify an English grammar, although we can point with some certainty to a number of standard forms. Despite the pressure of the mass of printed materials, the sounds of words change; *pale* is now a two-syllable word as you can determine for yourself by saying *pale, paler.* There are other instances. Orthography remains relatively fixed despite the efforts of *The Chicago Tribune* to simplify it, and the printed words serve only as a sort of shorthand for the sounds they represent. Consider, for instance: *tough, bough, bought, slough, cough, hiccough, dough.* We each manage to learn our language at our mother's knee; she has the easy job. The task of learning the orthography of our language is nightmarish, indeed; the task of teaching it is almost sheer futility. The 26 letters are not at all adequate; what is needed is an alphabet of somewhat more than that number.

Spoken and Written Language

The spoken language relies on sounds, pitch, stress, and intonation. Consider, for instance, the following:

green house   greenhouse   white house   the White House   sometimes
some times

I am going downtown. Where? (Meaning, I didn't understand you)
Downtown. Where? (What part of downtown)

All of the people are standing in the rain. (Emphasizes the quantity)

All of the *people* are standing in the rain.(The animals know better)

All of the people are *standing* in the rain. (None are sitting)

All of the people are standing in the *rain.* (None are inside)

Notice in these examples how the writer indicates what the speaker is saying.

Until fairly recent times the only means for recording the *spoken* word was through the process of memorization. Forced to memorize, people became so adept that they could memorize such lengthy works as *The Iliad* or *The Odyssey.* (One of the first uses of writing was as a form of shorthand to assist the memory.) To assist in memorizing, *mnemonic* devices such as song, rhymes, meter, metrical schemes, and the like were devised; plays on words helped a lot also. All of these devices aided in retaining the listener's interest as well. The oral tradition fosters ritual tribal organization and togetherness, since it cannot exist unless there are at least two persons present (ignoring the fact of talking to oneself!).

The written tradition retains many of the features of the oral tradition, but others disappear. It is no longer necessary to memorize lengthy works or even short pieces; they can be found in any reliable library. Puns fall into disrespect. The stock of literature available to us multiplies immensely. Reading becomes a private activity; the auditorium is replaced by the silent library. In a book, we can come to grips with any mind, past or present.

In the written tradition sentences and paragraphs are important as markers. In the oral tradition the sentences remain, but the necessity for the paragraph all but disappears. The markers or signals are of a different sort—forms that aid the listener in following the speech and that help hold his attention. Some of these devices are carried over to the printed page. But despite the admonition of teachers of writing to "write as we speak," the advice is probably good only for quite literate people. The speech of most of us is so taken up with false starts, tentative efforts, colloquialisms, incomplete phrasings and sentences, and the like that it will not serve as a model for good writing.

Faithful transcriptions of speech do not always ring true; in fact, one of the difficult tasks facing the writer is managing the *impression* of actual speech.

In the oral tradition we are not concerned with the spelling of words—the pronunciation is what matters. In the written tradition (since the pronunciation of words is not very often accurately represented by our 26 letters), spelling becomes important. No matter that a citizen of Boston pronounces *aunt* one way, and the citizen of Chicago another—both of them write it *aunt*. If the middlewesterner spells it *ant*—according to his pronunciation—his readers, whether from Boston or anywhere, will be puzzled by the apparent cordial relationship between the writer and his "ant Alice."

In the written tradition the system of intonations, stresses, pitches, and partial and full stops must be presented in some way. Punctuation serves much of the time; a stressed word can be indicated by the use of CAPITALS or *italics;* changes in *meaning* can be indicated by joining words together—red dog, "red-dog," black bird, blackbird, Cross Road, crossroad, one way, one-way.

In the oral tradition it is possible through a succession of questions, answers, discussions, debates, and the like to arrive at some kind of understanding. The written tradition is a one-way communications street; therefore, the writer must be careful and insure that his communication is complete. The oral tradition is warm and human; words in type are cold and impersonal. In either case, messages can be misinterpreted, but the speaker has the opportunity to correct the misinterpretation at the time.

Marshall McLuhan and others argue that the advent of radio, films, and television is producing an "electronic revolution" and causing an end to the "Gutenberg galaxy." The emphasis on the oral and the visual is reinstituting the oral tradition. Instant and total communication makes us all members of one tribe. A man begins his first step on the moon, 286,000 miles away; he speaks; and all over the globe, millions of people simultaneously share in the experience. Reading the printed word involves only the visual sense, McLuhan argues; but watching a man on the screen involves the visual and aural sense. From this it is a short remove to total involvement; the discotheque challenges all of our senses at once.

But, right as McLuhan may be, the printing presses daily

grind out more and more copies of the written word. Even the television medium itself is a huge consumer of the printed page. Somebody is going to have to know about the art of writing. So far, that somebody has been, for the most part, the educated man.

Where Our Words Come From

Words are of several sorts:

Names given to individuals and specific places: John, Mary, Kansas City, Mississippi River, Earth.

Names for objects and concepts: animal, dog, truth, hell.

Names of qualities and categories: red, color, tall, height.

Names for general and specific actions: activity, movement, walk, hobble.

Names arbitrarily assigned: radio, inch, pound, unicorn.

Compounds of nouns: airplane, arrowhead, boyfriend.

Compounds of adjectives and nouns: lightweight, redhead, bluebird.

Words created by adding affixes: cheeseburger, spiralize, likewise.

Blends or telescoped words: motel (motor plus hotel), smog (smoke plus fog).

Acronyms, words made from initials: radar, sonar, Nazi, Gestapo.

Nonsense words: brillig, slithy, toves.

Play and game words: pom-pom-pullaway, annie-annie-over.

Onomatopoetic or echoic words: meow, hiss, kapoomcha (the sound made by a mimeograph as a sheet of paper passes through—*Esquire*).

Expletives: oh, ah, ouch, wow.

Iterative words: namby-pamby, wishy-washy, willy-nilly (originally will he, nil he, meaning whether he wills it or opposes it).

Words imitating sounds we make: pssst, uh-uh, m-m-m-m.

Clippings and abbreviations: hypo, photo, phone, TB, TV.

Words demonstrating relationships among words: of, to, for, by.

Words standing for other words: it, she, he, they.

A specific word may shift its function; *smog* was created as a noun, but it became a verb: "the valley is smogging over"; an adjective: "the sky is smoggy." An English teacher once told her class: "*There* is never used as the subject of a sentence." She had to be reminded by her students that she had just used *there* as the subject of a sentence. A character in a Shakespeare play says, "*But* me no *buts*," thereby making a verb and a noun out of a conjunction.

The language of the Anglo-Saxons had perhaps 50,000 to 60,000 words, of which many remain in our language. Many disappeared, either because their referents disappeared ("the long-beaked ships," for instance) or because they were replaced by words borrowed from Latin and French. One consequence of this replacement is the notion that words based on our Anglo-Saxon origins form the language of common people, and words based on the borrowings form the language of educated people. Advocates of this notion argue for the pair concept: *light* and *illumination, heart ailment* and *cardiac disease,* and so on. Such a belief is either due to ignorance or snobbery, as these examples will show. The first, "Wardour Street English," is strongly Anglo-Saxon:

> The day after, by the rede of the shepherd-folk, they turned up into the hills again, for they had no wish to raise the country against them; and to say sooth, Sir Godrick was somewhat pensive that he found enmity so far off his own land. So they rode the hills for five days, falling in with new folk, and going slowly because of the rough ways. Thereafter they needed victual, and had been fain of better lodging might they get it. (William Morris, *The Sundering Flood*)

The second is strongly Latinate:

> On the insensible pavement Don Lelio reclined, almost unconscious, his form enclosed in a ligature, marmoreal in blanched quietude. His terete members but an hour ago so apt and flexuous, were distorted by incessant twitchings and cold as snow. Already his lips were livid; they disclosed the purity of teeth clenched and continually strident. In the pallid throat palpitated a vein with diminishing rhythm. Coerulean stains appeared below the flickering lashes of the half-closed eyes. (Frederick Rolfe, *Don Renato*)

Obviously, most of us, common or uncommon, educated or uneducated, do not use language in either extreme.

The additions to the original Anglo-Saxon wordstock come from many sources:

Borrowings. Greek: tantalize, narcissistic (mythology); socratic, platonic (proper names); Oedipus complex (drama); hypothesis, geopolitics (the sciences).

Latin: Latin borrowings make up a very large amount of our borrowings. They are often based on word-formations, using roots taken from Latin verbs and Latin prefixes and suffixes: *in, ad, com, cum, ate, ion.* To illustrate, here are some words based on the Latin verb *pello,* to drive: compel, compulsion, impel, impulse, repel, repulse, pulse, pulsate, pulsation, repulsive, compulsive, appeal, appealing. Other words are borrowed directly: magisterial, legion, aqueduct, circus, caduceus, caesarian.

Old and medieval French: These two earlier forms of modern French derive directly from Latin (as do Spanish, Italian, and Portugese). Many of our words of Latin origin were borrowed from the OF and MF during the centuries of interaction between the two groups of people separated only by the English Channel. *Channel* is itself such a word, and its appearance in the form *canal* indicates a double borrowing, before and after the *k* sound in canal became palatalized to *ch*. Sometimes the sound changes that have taken place between two borrowings are of so complex a nature that only an expert can recognize what has happened. We borrowed Latin *focus* (fireplace), giving it an entirely different meaning, of course. We also borrowed the French *curfew;* the *-few* is derived from French *feu* (fire). *Feu* in turn derives from *focus* by a series of sound changes which took place.

Modern French: cinema, chauffeur, artillery, garage, limousine, cigarette, champagne, matinee.

We have also borrowed from many other languages; the word borrowings indicate the nature of our debt to other nationalities: tobacco, canoe, vodka, assassin, safari, boor, wampum, cannibal, rumba, palaver, lasso, lariat, canyon, tundra, steppes, gaucho.

Coinages. Some of these originate in our industry and commerce: kodak, kodel, rayon, nylon; some have their sources in Greek: telephone, telegraph, mimeograph, anesthesia; some in slang or argot: fuzz, (illustrating another means of coinage by adapting an old word to a new meaning), cool, square, jive; some in combinations: mugwump (a mugwump is a bird who sits on a fence with his mug on one side and his wump on the other), football, basketball; some from sports: redshirt, spitball, blitz; some in analogies: boatel (boat plus motel), stardom (based on *kingdom*), hipster.

Proper names to common words. Sandwich, morocco, tabasco, lynch, quisling.

Degeneration of meaning. Lovely, great, awful, toilet, gossip.
Regeneration of meaning. Snob, stingy, smock.
Taking on a more restricted sense. Doctor (of medicine),
park (to *park* a car), gas (in domestic use or in the automobile).
Wars. Roadblock, expendable, blockbuster, blitzkrieg, flack.
Science. Allergy, proteins, metabolism, relativity, chain reaction.
Films, television, radio, newspapers, and magazines. Slick,
newscast (by analogy to *broadcast* which in turn is analogous to
the act of sowing grain), movies, situation comedies, fade-out,
mike, the "Press," mass media.
Changes in meanings. Life (January 23, 1970, p. 28) printed
this list of words which had acquired new meanings during the
decade of the 1960's:

acid	pot	grass	turn on
bag	rock	head	silo
bread	demonstration	Wallace	Apollo
bust	stoned	rap	blitz
soul	transplant	tune in	busing
freak	Sen. McCarthy	moratorium	camp
hawk	pill	pig	drop out
mace	AFL	Pueblo	hangup
pad	black	salt	joint
topless	brother	split	militant
Minuteman	Camelot	straight	Dr. Spock
panther	dove	trip	weatherman

One could go on and on in this vein for the language grows
and continues to grow.

Language as a Social Marker

Not all of these words are social equals. Language not only
serves to communicate, it also serves as a social marker. Language can be classified as literary, formal, standard, sub-
standard, colloquial, slangish, jargonistic, dialectal, obscene, or
pornographic. Many features of our culture have a different name
at each level. For instance: Juliet-of-the-night, whore, prosti-
tute, lady of the evening, kept woman, fancy woman, mistress,
bar girl, pig. In our standard language and at other levels, we
tend to use *euphemisms* in place of less acceptable words—
eternal sleep for death, funeral director for undertaker, powder
room for the room where the watercloset is.

Politicians and salesmen often use euphemisms as a means of de-emphasizing some of the unpleasant aspects of the program they are trying to sell. Perhaps it is just as well—we all need escape devices of some kind to get us away from some of life's more unpleasant moments. But at least we ought to know what is being done to us.

A news story presents an example:

The Pentagon is abolishing the term "cost overrun" from the language.

In an unpublicized memo of Nov. 26, David Packard, the deputy secretary of defense, proposes that "cost growth" be substituted in every instance in which the services now use the familiar phrase, "cost overrun."

The memo was addressed to the three secretaries of the services and six other high officials involved with procurement.

According to Packard, the term "cost overrun" creates "confusion in the minds of many" and "casts improper reflections on the true status of events."

His memo recalls that a "task force" was set to work on the problem. "The committee started with a general and imprecise term, 'cost overrun,' and discarded it as unworkable, and replaced it with the term 'cost growth,' including a structured set of definitions related to it, which are workable." (Washington *Post* Service, December 7, 1969)

A number of obvious inferences could be drawn from this story; most of them I leave to your consideration and judgment. One inference is the obvious belief on the part of Pentagon officials that the word is the thing; and that we can change the thing by giving it a different name.

Sometimes these euphemisms represent oversimplifications with a popular appeal that the author hopes will have a persuasive effect, as in the case of this statement by a military officer, made with reference to the President's decision to de-escalate the war in Vietnam:

We're leading 34–7 in the third quarter, and now they are going to call the game. And, what's more, they are going to declare the other guy the winner.

But at the time this statement was made, more serious minds in the Pentagon and in the government were saying something else, which indicated that this euphemistic statement was not the official opinion.

Semantic Growth

Language grows semantically; that is, words take on additional meanings. A *dog,* for instance, is a very common animal, long domesticated for his qualities as a pet, as a watch dog, as a shepherd's helper, as an animal of great attractiveness in his seemingly infinite variety of shapes, sizes, kinds, and colors. A dog carries on his activities in the streets before our eyes; he masticates, defecates, procrastinates, urinates, congregates, fornicates, and argumentates as his inclinations and his company permit. A dog, therefore, has many obvious qualities, and all of these contribute to the several dozen meanings for the word *dog:* the animal itself; the male of the canine species; a low contemptuous fellow; an andiron or firedog; a person, as in lucky dog or gay dog; a sundog; any of several mechanical devices for grappling or holding, as the holding dogs and stepping dogs on a typewriter. There are the derived verbs: a detective dogs a criminal, for example. There are the phrases: dog-tired (where dog means very), a dog's life, dog eat dog, dog in the manger, every dog has his day, let sleeping dogs lie, put on the dog, teach an old dog new tricks, and:

> I am his highness' dog at Kew.
> Pray tell me sir, whose dog are you?
> (Alexander Pope)

Or an old word takes on new forms as in bank, bench; mass, mess; flour, flower—but with a variety of new meanings. In other cases, old words of different forms come together in one form but with different meanings as in *band,* a fastening device (OHG *binta*), and a musical organization (Goth. *bandwa*).

We call such usages metaphors, "a figure of speech in which one thing is likened to another." All language is metaphorical; a little thought will help you see that it rests on abstracted qualities and on the assumption that these abstracted qualities are *ideal* qualities. That is, the power of tenaciousness that is implied in a dog's behavior under certain circumstances is the same power of tenaciousness that a man exhibits under another circumstance. Our metaphorical attributions are made with varying degrees of certainty on our part; we say that Joe is a dog or we say that he is like a dog. When we say that Joe is a workhorse, we are being quite logical; we are saying that Joe : work : : horse : work.

So language grows, out of our recognition of things and the qualities of things, out of our certainty that things and qualities are either alike or unlike, and out of our ability to assign verbal symbols to such things and qualities.

Assignments for Discussion and Writing

1. What activities do you take part in that do not involve language in any way?
2. Describe ways in which you have used language to pattern your life. Concentrate on occasions when: you were deliberately acting a part; you were performing a "phony" act; you were "really being yourself."
3. Have you ever been involved in an accident or some similar crisis in which you felt that "words failed you"? Describe how this was the case and how you knew or understood what was going on.
4. In a standard reference work, such as an encyclopedia, an unabridged dictionary, or the "College Edition" of *Webster's New World Dictionary of the American Language*, read some of the discussions you find on the language. What do the terms "pitch," "intonation," "stress" refer to? What is "Grimm's Law"? "Verner's Law"? How did the letters *k, j, w* come into our language? What does "etymology" mean? Apply Grimm's Law and Verner's Law to the etymology of the word "foot" and the analagous terms listed in *Webster's Third New International Dictionary, Unabridged*.
5. In a standard reference work, read a discussion of our speaking apparatus. Then pronounce the following words and analyze what happens as you utter the required sounds: goose, geese, bush, push, foot, cat, gat, bottle, sing, fend, vend, wend. Try to work out Grimm's Law and Verner's Law in terms of the sounds you make.
6. Based on your own experience, discuss how and why old words take on new meanings. What happens to a word in its old sense when a new sense comes into use? Are these circumstances good or bad for our language?
7. Examine one current magazine, one daily newspaper, and the schedule of programs televised by one TV station in one evening. As you read, watch, and listen, make a list of words and phrases that seem new, unusual, or strange to you.

Identify each word in your list as to its media source and also as to its usage: in a commercial or advertisement, in a news story, editorial or feature story; in a sports story, science story, or entertainment story; in a story about politics, war, industry, older people, young people. Compare your list with those made by friends and settle on words that might some day appear in a dictionary. Evaluate the usage level of each word or phrase; is it literary, formal, standard, substandard, slang, obscene? Write an essay of 500 to 600 words in which you generalize about your word list.

8. Organize a discussion on the subject of levels of usage or acceptance. What distinctions can you make between levels? How do you determine where a particular word belongs? Why is one level of usage praised and another rejected? If the word is not the thing, why do we use euphemisms or prohibit the use of some words? How do nonacceptable words maintain their existence? In what way is language usage related to social acceptability? Why?

9. Examine current desk dictionaries such as those published by G. & C. Merriam Co., The World Publishing Company, Random House, and American Heritage and Houghton Mifflin. What are the contents of each dictionary? What listings do you find in one and not in another? To what extent do the dictionaries seem to *describe* the language; to what extent do they seem to be *prescriptive*? How up-to-date is each one? To what extent does each publish slang, argot, jargon, obscene, or foreign words? What words do you find in current newspapers or magazines that you don't find in these dictionaries? What do you do about the meanings of these new words? Why should we keep a dictionary on our desk when we write? Compose an essay of 500 or 600 words in which you consider one or more of these questions.

Further Reading

Laird, Charlton, *Thinking About Language*, Rinehart & Company, Inc., New York, 1959 (Rinehart English Pamphlets).

Jespersen, Otto, *Growth and Structure of the English Language*, Doubleday & Company, Inc., Garden City, New York, 1955.

Bloomfield, Leonard, *Language*, Holt and Company, New York, 1933 (1956).

Baugh, Albert C., *A History of the English Language*, Appleton-Century Crofts, Inc., New York, 1935 (1957).

McLuhan, Marshall, *The Mechanical Bride*, Vanguard Press Inc., New York, 1951; *The Gutenberg Galaxy*, Signet, 1969; *Understanding Media*, Signet.

Kottler, Barnet and Martin Light, *The World of Words*, Houghton Mifflin Company, Boston, 1967.

Evans, Bergen and Cornelia, *A Dictionary of English-American Usage*, Oxford University Press, New York, 1957.

Whorf, Benjamin Lee, *Language, Thought and Reality*, Technology Press, Cambridge, Mass., 1956.

Johnson, Wendell, *People in Quandaries: The Semantics of Personal Adjustment*, Harper & Row, New York, 1946.

Hayakawa, S. I., *Language in Thought and Action*, Harcourt, Brace and Company, New York, 1949.

Huxley, Aldous: *Words and Their Meaning*, The Ward Ritchie Press, Los Angeles, 1940.

Chase, Stuart, *The Tyranny of Words*, Harcourt, Brace and Company, New York, 1938.

Desk dictionaries: *Webster's New World Dictionary of the American Language* (World); *Webster's New Collegiate Dictionary* (Merriam-Webster); *The American College Dictionary* (Random House); *The American Heritage Dictionary of the English Language* (American Heritage and Houghton Mifflin).

4

Words
at Work

The thesis of this text is that a writer must nave a point to make and must make it. I am not alone in this conviction. Nevertheless, there are those who have another attitude. Here is the voice of one of those:

To the man with an ear for verbal delicacies—the man who searches painfully for the perfect word, and *puts the way of saying a thing above the thing said* [italics mine]—there is in writing the constant joy of sudden discovery, of happy accident.[1]

Although I am as happy as anyone with the felicitous expression—"what's oft been thought but ne'er so well expressed"—I don't agree with Mencken. However, in this chapter I am going to give the advocates of stylistic niceties (and others) their day in court.

[1] H. L. Mencken, *A Book of Prefaces*, Alfred A. Knopf, 1925, p. 85.

The "Power" of Words

There has always been the popular notion that words have certain powers. This device was often worn on amulets to ward off disease, for instance:

Such beliefs range from superstition to magic and religion—and often on to science! *Superstition* is primarily a belief in something that runs contrary to fact—the notion that Friday the thirteenth is unlucky, or that hotels should not have a thirteenth floor. *Magic* is a belief in the power of man to change natural forces, and it is of two kinds. *Contagious magic* is a belief in the efficacy of direct touch. As far as words go, it is illustrated by the command "Open sesame" in *Ali Baba and the Forty Thieves* —the command that opened the door to the cave where the gold was hidden. *Contiguous magic* is illustrated in such childhood folklore as the avoidance of walking on cracks in the street—"Step on a crack and you'll break your mother's back."

Superstitious belief in the power of words partially accounts for the use of *euphemisms* and the classification *taboo words* (although euphemisms and taboo words also exist because of a human desire for less offensive or suggestive words). Euphemisms are used in social situations where it is felt that they will do less harm or improve the status of something. "Realtor" was coined as a euphemism for "real estate salesman" because many unethical persons were calling themselves by the latter title. ("Realtor" is copyrighted.) The Coca-Cola Company waged a long campaign against popular use of "Coke" as a nickname, but finally gave up the fight and obtained a copyright.

Taboo words are words that are social outcasts (the so-called four-letter Anglo-Saxon verbs that are thought of as obscene or pornographic are examples), forbidden for religious reasons (the sacred unprintable unspeakable Hebrew word for God, for instance), or forbidden because of their assumed magical powers. Taboo words owe their prohibition to several ideas: (1) the subject is too unpleasant to contemplate or discuss, (2) the word is the thing, (3) the thing either doesn't exist or will disappear if the word is not spoken, (4) the thing will harm us if the word is spoken.

Nevertheless, there are levels of acceptance for taboo words. They manage to exist in a "secret language," being preserved in spite of all attempts to suppress them or deny them space on the printed page. This secret language is largely preserved by males of certain types; seamen with their "strings of oaths"; mule-skinners and other hard-working laborers; military men, particularly of the enlisted category; traveling salesmen; and many others. (At least that is how the folklore would have it.)

Assignment for Discussion

Look up "tetragrammaton," *YHVH* or *JHVH* or "Yahweh (Jehovah)" in an unabridged dictionary, a general encylcopedia, or an encylcopedia of religion, and report your findings to the class. Perhaps an orthodox Jewish member of the community would be willing to discuss the concept of the sacred name for God. Look up "taboo" in an encyclopedia of social sciences. Look up "magic" in Sir James Frazier's *The Golden Bough*. Read the preface to Harold Wentworth's and Stuart Bergl Flexner's *Dictionary of American Slang*. Discuss your findings in class.

The power of the taboo word to harm is seen in our attitude toward its application to our persons. "When you say that, smile," said the Virginian. We resent name-calling or *invective* (a string of modifiers aimed at a personal referent) because we believe that the power to name is a real power—deriving our belief, partially at least, from the passage in *Genesis* where God gives Adam the power to name the animals:

Primitive people, authorities assert, imagine the word to have power over the thing. Do civilized people believe otherwise? When Harriet Pick, for instance, marries Kenneth Shovel in Oklahoma City, papers in Toronto and Miami carry the news, and *Cornet* and *Time* find space in one of their jocular departments, and Mr. and

Mrs. Shovel must begin to wonder if in truth they are, as they seem to each other, flesh and blood, and not a pair of implements.[2]

"What's in a name?" muses Juliet. "A rose by any other name would smell as sweet." But would it? What about words beginning with *sn-*: snide, snarl, sneer, snake, snot, snicker, snip? What happens when the Good Samaritan Hospital becomes known as "Good Sam"? What happens when Governor Will Hogg of Texas names his two daughters Ima and Etta? Who is prettier—Norma Jean Mortenson or Marilyn Monroe? Who is handsomer—Spangler Arlington Brugh or Robert Taylor?

Here is a current list of names of drugs: marijuana, mary jane, grass, hemp, acapulco gold, strawberries, blue heavens, peyote, mescaline, hashish, dream stuff, horse, orange-babies, yo-yo, heroin, cocaine. Does a drug become less sinister when its technical name is replaced with a familiar name or nickname? Given a choice, would you rather be Clarence, Buster, Clancy, or Clare? Candace or Candy? Dorothy or Dee? Why?

Name-calling often replaces logical argument because people know it often is easier to defeat an opponent by naming him than by presenting facts. Here are two instances taken from newspapers published as I write:

. . . a new generation of the greatest conglomeration of hippie, happy, revolutionary boneheads and dopeheads this country has ever known . . .

. . . peace marchers: hippies, Yippies, beatniks, peaceniks, yellow-bellies, traitors, Commies and their agents and dupes . . .

The process of understanding and identifying an object or concept and the process of naming it or establishing a *referential* word for it should be the same—but often they are not. We do not usually comprehend unless we can verbalize or create symbols—but usage does not necessarily correspond to understanding. The process of naming often involves no comprehension at all on the part of the namer. There is only an illusion of understanding to give comfort. Unfortunately, the comfort is deceptive—for such naming or labeling often does us a disfavor by blocking our logical processes of thought.

We do not, however, engage in name-calling to block our own

thought processes. Our real aim is to block the thought processes of others. We accomplish our goal because name-calling appeals to prejudice, to custom, to convention, to habits of association—all of those behavioral activities in which we engage because we are mentally lazy or afraid to offend.

You can, of course, justify name-calling:
1. First define the name.
2. Show that the referent is identified or classified by the definition.
3. Show that the identification or classification in a particular situation is necessarily desirable or undesirable.
4. Repeat the process for every new specimen to whom the name is applied.

Even for the logical minded, naming is not easy. College professors, in basic agreement over an issue or a concept, disagree over the terminology. In a discussion, we often shift the meaning of key words. Currently in the United States there are several groups who want "peace," but there is no agreement over the meaning of the term.

E. B. White shows how a word can change in its meaning, quoting from an unintentional slip by Henry Seidel Canby:

. . . the makers of textbooks who are nearly always reactionary, and often unscholarly in denying the right to change to a language that has always been changing . . . (*The Second Tree from the Corner*)

The focal word is "change." Is it a noun or a verb? If it is a noun, the quotation may be paraphrased as follows:

. . . denying to a language (that has always been changing) the right to change . . .

If "change" is a verb, the paraphrase is:

. . . in denying to the textbook readers the right to switch to another language . . .

The belief in the power of words leads some word-mongers to search for "the ten loveliest words" or "the ten ugliest words." When I was young, I was a word-monger, and I used to mouth this phrase and dream of someday using it in a fiction:

As she strolled on the Bubbling Well Road, a sudden mistiness crept into her lovely azure eyes.

Our belief in the power of words leads to the establishment of "ultimate terms" in the words of Richard Weaver.[3] If they acquire charismatic qualities, they become "god" terms; if the opposite holds, they become "devil" terms.

What are "god" terms for one become "devil" terms for another. Liberal, conservative, war, peace, communism, democracy, Democrat, Republican, hair, ROTC—various individuals and groups tend to place ultimate values on words that are otherwise only abstractions.

Assignment for Writing

Take as your subject words you like or dislike, or a situation in which naming or name-calling played a part. You may want to describe an incident in which there was a quarrel over the meaning of a word. In any case, try to analyze the experience you describe. Why are certain words appealing or unappealing to you? What have been your reactions to situations involving words? Do people disagree over words or over something else?

Connotative Words

The quality or attribute I have been discussing is the *connotative* aspect of words—their tendency to take on a "halo" effect, so to speak, to point to some quality or qualities in a referent. Because connotations are often subjective or internal or limited to small groups, connotative words are not adequately treated or explained in dictionaries. Connotations are shifting, vague areas of meaning that do not lend themselves to precise definition any more easily than sand dunes lend themselves to contour mapping.

Connotative words especially appeal to those commercial interests that seem to be always trying to name a product so that it appears to be something more than it really is. *Time* comments:

Finding names for all the products is becoming a major preoccupation. More than 370,000 trademarks are registered with the U. S.

[3] Richard Weaver, *The Ethics of Rhetoric*, Henry Regnery Company, 1953. He explores the subject in Chapter IX.

Patent Office, and the number is growing by 20,000 a year. Having all but exhausted the dictionary, marketers are increasingly turning to the computer to produce suitably short, evocative non-words. A typical computer printout reads: EMBO, EMBU, EMCA, EMCE—and so on and on.

At Du Pont, finding one name can tie up the talents of a team of marketers, lawyers, advertising men and psychologists. They comb the computer lists, eliminating those words that are difficult to pronounce, look bad in print, or are too similar to existing trademarks. The left-overs are tested for general appeal and memorability. With so many names floating about, no marketing man can be sure of avoiding a conflict. General Foods recently test-marketed a snack product called Pringle's Pop Chips only to discover that Proctor & Gamble was simultaneously testing Pringle's Newfangled Potato Chips. Even greater risks lurk in the slang of foreign languages. A leather-preservatives manufacturer tried to market a product called Dreck—until he discovered that the name means dirt (or worse) in German and Yiddish.[4]

Benjamin Whorf asserted that the environment of a culture or its interests dictated its vocabulary, adding a comment on the very large stock of Eskimo words relating to snow and cold, and the very large stock of Arabic words concerning the camel. You might test this in your own environment by making a list of words that apply to the automobile (including the trade names Mustang, Maverick, Camaro), and then comparing it with the list of words you have for "man." On that subject you might look at this list of Black words for man—ofay, arnchy, blue, buckra, brick-presser, charcoal, creeper, daddy, dinge, Eastman, fagingy-fagade, high yellow, jig, jig-chaser, mama, Miss Annie, Mr. Eddie, monkey-chaser, mustard-seed, shine, spagingy-spagade, and, of course, "the man."

Figurative Language

Words such as these are a part of the *figurative language*—a language created by all of us to express the relationships (analogies and similarities) between two concepts. The figurative word may serve either to define or to express an emotional mood:

He knows that dark time is flowing by him *like a river*. (Thomas Wolfe)

[4] *Time*, October 24, 1969, p. 93. Reprinted by permission from *Time,* The Weekly Newsmagazine; Copyright Time Inc.

. . . snowflakes . . . *like dim soft little stars.* (Ruth Suckow)

Because of deep-seated beliefs, we create figurative language by direct statement:

Nature speaks to us . . . things are in the saddle . . . Death reaches out his bony hand . . . raining cats and dogs . . .

Striving for emphasis, to make a point, or for clarity, we compare one thing to another:

A man casts off his years as a snake his skin . . . aiming the car down the straights like you would aim a gun . . . I'm talking like a press agent . . .

In the direct statement we convert the inanimate or the abstract to human form. One term for this is *personification—* another is *anthropomorphism,* meaning in the shape or image of man. The term for the comparison is *simile* or *similitude.* Sometimes we compare one whole to another; sometimes only a characteristic. We use the known to make the unknown clearer.

Or we use a part to represent a whole: a car is a set of wheels, a man is a loud-mouth. Or we do the opposite—we use the whole for the part: he sets a good table (meaning he serves good food).

Figurative language may be created by using a quality as a term for the whole. The result is that characteristic of language called *semantic growth,* that is, the creation of new meanings for an old word through an analogous transfer (see page 66). For example, a familiar household appliance was originally heated over a fire and then used to remove the wrinkles from clothing. Because originally many of these appliances were made from iron, the word for the quality of the appliance became the name for the appliance: *iron.* The removal of the wrinkles came to be called *ironing* (another instance of semantic growth, where a noun is transformed into a verb). Later, because of advances in the technology, the appliances came to be made of steel and coated with a chrome- or nickel-alloy surface; an electrical resistor within the appliance provided the necessary heat. Yet the name of the device continued to be *iron.* Later the concept of *ironing* was transferred to other operations having nothing to do with the appliance or the household appliance, and we speak of *ironing out the wrinkles* in a new process.

The learning writer is often cautioned against mixing his examples of figurative language, and it is probably good advice. To show you what can happen if one is not careful, I culled these examples from one essay:

their noses had not been rubbed in the drudgery . . . teachers' pets . . . an academic crown of laurel . . . convalescing from overexposure to products of the academic mind . . . deathless prose [a cliché as well] . . . explorers into the wilderness of statistics . . . cream-skimmer . . . literary treat . . . forest of words . . . . my weapons were several batteries of pencils . . . my armor was a thesaurus . . . instead of big trees I found underbrush . . . lumbering sentences . . . verbal burdocks . . . cat-chasing-its-own-tail-verbosity . . . tone deaf to words, a lighthouse of clarity . . . members of a caste so used to taking in each other's literary washing that it has become a habit for them to clothe their thoughts in the same smothering verbal garments [5]

What is your reaction to this potpourri?

Assignment for Discussion

Magazines and newspapers often use figurative language in order to create a mood, make a point, or define a concept. Bring in examples that you think work—or don't work. Discuss their function, the kind of figure, and the reasons why you liked or disliked them. As a partial aid to the discussion you might want to look up these terms in an unabridged dictionary: metonymy, synedoche, simile, metaphor, analogy.

An extension of figurative language is the *symbol.* Symbols can, of course, be something else than language: the American flag, the Statute of Liberty, a Rolls-Royce. But my concern here is with symbolic language.

Symbols are stimuli that come, somehow, to set up the same kind of physical, logical, or emotional reactions as the particulars with which they are associated. Pavlov's dogs, for example, came to associate the ringing of a bell with the idea of food, so that the sound of the bell became a symbol for food, and their

[5] Samuel T. Williamson, "How to Write Like a Social Scientist," *The Saturday Review of Literature,* October 4, 1947.

mouths watered whenever they heard the bell. (So, perhaps, did Pavlov's!) Word symbols, initially at least, are usually arbitrary conventions—the English *man,* the German *der mann,* the French *l'homme,* the Spanish *el hombre,* are all word symbols for the same concept.

Some word symbols are public: cow, tree, man, 1984, and the like. Some symbols are private. If your eyes moisten whenever you hear the word *tree* because your favorite poem begins:

> I think that I shall never see
> A poem lovely as a tree,

then *tree* is a private symbol for you. We each have our own stock of private symbols, some so significant that we keep them quite to ourselves.

All public symbols (in addition to having potential or actual private symbolic meanings) are potentially ambiguous. They may affect you for one reason, affect someone else for another. For example, what does the word *ring* symbolize for you? A wedding or engagement *ring* with its attached significances? A *ring* around the moon—or a *ring* around the bathtub? Or a *ring* of children playing ring-around-the-rosey? Does it appeal to your sense of sound—the *ring* of a telephone or alarm clock, the *ring* of a church bell, or the *ring* of the human voice? Or does it have some other meaning, as in the Tweed *ring*?

When speaking or writing we must always establish the referent for our symbols, unless we are being deliberately ambiguous as is Ring Lardner when he writes:

> What road do I take for Grenitch Conn quired my father with poping eyes.
> Take the Boston post replid the policeman.
> I have all ready subscribed to one out of town paper said my father.[6]

In a composition, a scene or an incident may become a symbol for some theme in the composition. For example, in Chapter VIII, Book Two, of one version of F. Scott Fitzgerald's *Tender Is the Night,* the hero, Dick Diver meets Nicole Warren (whom he eventually wins and loses) in a "funicular train" that is taking both of them to the top of a Swiss mountain. The train is pulled to the top of the mountain by the weight of another similar train going down. At one point the two trains pass:

[6] Ring Lardner, "The Young Immigrunts," Charles Scribner's Sons.

When the funicular came to rest those new to it stirred in suspension between the blues of two heavens. It was merely for a mysterious exchange between the conductor of the car going up and the car going down.[7]

This incident, brief as it is, is a symbol for a theme of the book —Dick Diver's rise and fall, Nicole Warren's rise from the depths of insanity. Fitzgerald, a few pages, later makes his symbolic intent clear:

A ride in a train can be a terrible, heavy-hearted or comic thing; it can be a trial flight; it can be a prefiguration of another journey.[8]

Sometimes, as in the *leitmotif* or thematic usage, figurative language may not seem to be figurative at all unless its total effect is weighed. Fitzgerald's *The Great Gatsby* offers several examples (as does E. B. White's "Once More to the Lake"—see pages 317–322 of this text). One set of language figures relates to the theme of money and wealth:

It was full of money—that was the inexhaustible charm that rose and fell in it, the jingle of it, the cymbals' song of it. . . . High in a white palace the king's daughter, the golden girl . . .[9]

The motif *yellow* is also used in the novel. The building in which George Wilson has his garage is "a small block of yellow brick." Gatsby's station wagon "scamper[s] like a yellow brisk bug to meet all trains." At Gatsby's party the orchestra plays "yellow cocktail music," and two girls "in twin yellow dresses" are present. Gatsby buys "twelve lemon cakes" for his rendezvous with Daisy. Gatsby's murder is precipitated by the "big yellow car" that strikes Myrtle Wilson down.

Assignment for Discussion

Read E. B. White's "Once More to the Lake" (pages 317–322), looking for thematic words (those having to do with time, for instance). Later, when you read the essay again, you may want to discuss the potential symbolic qualities of these words.

---

[7] F. Scott Fitzgerald, *Three Novels of F. Scott Fitzgerald*, Charles Scribner's Sons, pp. 41–42.

[8] *Ibid.*, p. 50.

[9] *Ibid.*, p. 91.

Allegory

Allegory is another means by which figurative language is extended. Allegory is a literary device by which one symbol or set of symbols comes to represent two sets of concepts. The Statue of Liberty is both a statue of a woman holding a torch and a book and an allegorical representation of the concept of liberty. (It was originally planned as a token of the goodwill existing between our nation and the French nation.) The word "nature" (with a small "n") has as one of its meanings the natural world of landscape, plants, and animals. When the word is written "Nature" (with a capital "N") it also comes to refer to the goddess Nature. In that double meaning the word becomes allegorical.

Allegory often uses the device of *personification* as these examples show. Personification, as noted earlier, is the device by which we give animation to the inanimate. Sometimes we do this almost unconsciously as when the Iowa farmer says: "The horse went and died on me," thus implying that nature has a conscious will.

Language may be used in many other ways. Following is a discussion of some of them.

Irony

Irony is intended to be witty or humorous. In its various degrees it may take the form of sarcasm or ridicule. Its purpose is to persuade us to accept the writer's point of view toward the subject he has aimed his barbs at. Its true intention is something more than the denotative meaning of the words; therefore, we must be on our guard when we are reading, for irony is omnipresent. The ironic "voice" is one "voice" the writer may use.

Mark Twain was a master ironist. Here are some examples of his technique from "Cooper's Literary Offenses":

[About a man who had praised Cooper's work as "pure art"] It seems to me that it was far from right for the Professor . . . to deliver opinions on Cooper's literature without having read some of it. . . .

Cooper's art has some defects. In one place in *Deerslayer,* and in the restricted space of two-thirds of a page, Cooper has scored 114 offenses against literary art out of a possible 115.

Cooper describes the ark, but pretty obscurely. In the matter of dimensions "it was a little more than a modern canalboat." Let us guess then that it was about one hundred and forty feet long. "It was of greater breadth than common." Let us guess, then, that it was about sixteen feet wide. This leviathan had been prowling down bends which were but a third as long as itself, and scraping between banks where it had only two feet of space to spare on each side. We cannot too much admire this miracle.

Irony accomplishes its effect by focusing our attention on itself and on the laughter that it produces, thus taking our minds off the true issue.

Assignment for Reading

Read Ring Lardner's "How to Write Short Stories" (pages 323–326 of this text) and try to identify instances of irony in it. You might also look for instances of some of the other techniques described in following sections of this chapter.

Assignment for Writing

Write a brief essay about something that displeases you or otherwise makes you unhappy. Try to use irony as your persuasive device, and try to keep your attack witty and humorous rather than bitter.

Paradox

Paradox is a device that presents seemingly contradictory facts—that is the facts may seem to contradict themselves or they may seem to contradict common sense.

Here are some examples of paradox from the same Twain essay:

If Cooper had any real knowledge of Nature's ways of doing things, he had a most delicate art in concealing the fact. . . .

The reader will find some examples of Cooper's high talent for inaccurate observation in the account of the shooting match in *The Pathfinder*.

Cooper deals freely in important omissions.

Understatement

The purpose of understatement is to say less than necessary and thus persuade by the apparent sincerity or irony as in this example from Twain:

A work of art? It has no invention; it has no order, system, sequence or result; it has no life-likeness, no thrill, no stir, no seeming of reality; its characters are confusedly drawn, and by their acts and words they prove that they are not the sort of people the author claims they are; its humor is pathetic; its pathos is funny; its conversations are—oh! indescribable; its love-scenes odious; its English a crime against the language.
Counting these out what is left is Art. I think we must all admit that.

(A word about this quotation; along the way it uses some of the other figurative forms I have already described, but it was necessary to quote the whole to demonstrate the understatement in the last two lines.)

Hyperbole

The opposite of understatement is overstatement in the form of exaggeration; literary extravagance for effect. One form of hyperbole is invective:

They require that when a personage talks like an illustrated, gilt-edge, tree-calf, hand-tooled, seven dollar Friendship's Offering in the beginning . . . (Mark Twain)

Another form is simple exaggeration:

Cooper wore out barrels and barrels of moccasins in working that trick. (Mark Twain)

. . . that particular statement needs to be taken with a few tons of salt. . . . Cooper hadn't any more invention than a horse; and I don't mean a high-class horse either; I mean a clothes-horse. (Mark Twain)

Mimicry

Direct quotation of a familiar literary statement is a device often used. If one does not have a large acquaintanceship with such statements, a collection such as *Bartlett's Familiar Quota-*

tions can be used. These books are indexed by topic and author so that quotations can easily be found.

A variation of the direct quotation is *mimicry,* a statement in which the original is echoed but with some play on the words, or some inversion, to produce a slightly different and perhaps humorous or ironic effect. Here are two examples, again, from Mark Twain:

He saw nearly all things as through a glass darkly.

There are nineteen rules governing literary art in the domain of romantic fiction—some say twenty-two.

Paronomasia (Punning)

Playing on words is the great human game—most of us enjoy a pun now and then. The pun is actually a speech tradition for it usually depends on the sounds of words on which the play is based. Often the effectiveness of the pun is due to the special knowledge of the people engaged in the play. *Chacun a son gout* requires a knowledge of French as well as an awareness of the bilingual pun, and *tout le monde est megilloth-mane* requires a knowledge of French, Hebrew, and the circumstances surrounding the finding of the Dead Sea Scrolls (or "dead sea gulls" as my son once called them).

Punning owes part of its effect to the *homonymic* quality of the language—the fact that words with different spellings and different meanings are pronounced the same: *fare* and *fair, colonel* and *kernel, tail* and *tale;* and James Thurber's immortal dog, "a Peke named Darien" (which is also an example of mimicry). Sometimes there is a slight difference in pronunciation; sometimes the pun is visual as in "mall adjusted," a pun on "maladjusted."

Punning owes another part of its effect to the differences in meanings in one word as in these examples from Ring Lardner:

He passed in rhetoric and out of college in one semester.

[Talking about the girl who married a young man she met on the subway and who lived on 35th street, Lardner wrote:] She married beneath her station. She usually got off at 42nd street.

I leave it to you to find your own examples, but if you have trouble, here is one clue: turn to the speeches of Romeo and Juliet in the scene in Shakespeare's play where they meet.

A form of the pun is the *double entendre* (or sometimes *double entente*). This is a phrase, sentence, or paragraph that is ambiguous in the sense it has a double intention, one of which is, as *Webster's* puts it, "indelicate." In a current advertisement, for instance, there is a photograph of an attractive girl staring directly at the viewer. Under the photograph is this caption:

Joan Daly likes it when guys wear Old Spice

The Catalog

Since the time of *The Iliad* the catalog or list of names has been a favorite literary device. Here are two examples:

Richard Burton, Elizabeth Taylor, Marlon Brando, Gregory Peck, Rock Hudson, Kirk Douglas, Burt Lancaster, Julie Andrews, Sidney Poitier, Shirley MacLaine, Michael Caine, James Coburn, Rex Harrison, Frank Sinatra, David Niven, Peter Sellers, Jack Lemmon, Yul Brynner, Lee Marvin, Robert Mitchum, Vanessa Redgrave, William Holden, Dick Van Dyke, Anthony Quinn, Kim Novak and Faye Dunaway to name an outstanding few.[10]

Hops from Cowiche, Grandview, Prosser, Yakima, Mabton, Roy and Moxee, Grants Pass, Salem, Wilder, Parma, Sloughhouse, and Elk Grove.
Barley from Fargo, Camas Prairie, Colfax, Dayton, Corvallis, Newberg, and Klamath Falls, Woodland, Paso Robles, Montpelier.
Water from Tumwater. (Olympia Brewing Company advertisement)

These two examples illustrate the popularity and attractiveness of the catalog as a persuasive device. In the first place (because it can be seriously doubted that anyone reads the entire list) it is the sheer verbal weight of the list providing authority for the writer's statement that the day of the movie star is past. In the second there is the obvious fun provided by some of the names (Cowiche, Moxee, Sloughhouse, Tumwater) for one thing; for another there is the contrast between the list of suppliers of grain and hops, and the one supplier of water. This contrast is used to advantage by the advertiser when he later emphasizes that "It's the Water" that makes his product tasty.

[10] Wayne Warga, *The Los Angeles Times,* November 23, 1969.

Other Fun with Words

Some writers deliberately use language in an outrageous fashion to attract attention, create fun, and perhaps persuade as well. Here are some examples:

Aldiborontiphoscophornio!
Where left you Chrononhotonthologos? . . .

His cogitative faculties immersed
In a cogibundity of cogitation.
(Henry Carey, *Chrononhotonthologos*)

Then a sentimental passion of a vegetable fashion must excite your
    languid spleen,
An attachment a la Plato for a bashful young potato, or a not too
    French French bean!
Though the philistine may jostle, you will rank as an apostle in the
    high ascetic band,
If you walk down Picadilly with a poppy or a lily in your medieval
    hand . . .

Francesca di Rimini, miminy, piminy,
Je-ne-sais-quoi young man! . . .

A greenery-yallery, Grosvenor Gallery
Foot-in-the-grave young man!
(William S. Gilbert, *Patience*)

A rarely used type of the play on words is the *palindrome:*

Able was I ere I saw Elba (said of Napoleon)
Lewd did I live; evil I did dwell (*Webster's*)

More common are *alliteration:*

"Oh, of course the Grace of God," George hastened in common cour-
tesy conventionally to adjoin. (Frederick Rolfe, *Hadrian the Seventh*)

assonance and *consonance:*

The splendour falls on castle walls
And snowy summits old in story
The long light shakes across the lakes
(Alfred, Lord Tennyson, *The Princess*)

While, as these latter examples indicate, these last three de-vices tend to appear more often in poetry than prose, nevertheless they are used in prose compositions. But because they do have either the poetic or comic ring about them, you must be careful when you use them for they can cause an unwanted change in your narrative voice. And, too often, they attract undue attention to themselves as they do in the *Hadrian the Seventh* example.

The *"undecidable sentence"* is a form of *paradox:*

This statement is false. Don't miss it if you can. Disregard this notice.

Assignment for Discussion

Bring in examples of the above techniques that you have found in books or magazine or newspaper articles. In what contexts do they seem to be the most commonly used? Do you ever find any instances in scientific reporting? How and why do you find them effective or ineffective as persuasive devices?

Apostrophe

The apostrophe is a deliberate turning away from one's audience to address someone directly:

O death, where is thy sting? O grave, where is thy victory? (I Corinthians, XV, 54)

Rhetorical Questions

The rhetorical question is one that the author asks, either with intent to answer the question himself, or else (as in the following example) with an implied answer:

Was he sincere when he opposed imperialism in the Philipines, or when he fed it with deserving Democrats in Santo Domingo? Was he sincere when he tried to shove the Prohibitionists under the table, or when he seized their banner and began to lead them with loud war whoops? Was he sincere when he bellowed against war, or when he dreamed of himself as a tin-soldier in uniform, with a grave reserved among the generals? Was he sincere when he denounced the late John W. Davis, or when he swallowed Davis? Was he sincere when he fawned over Champ Clark, or when he betrayed Clark? [11]

[11] H. L. Mencken, "In Memoriam: William Jennings Bryan," *The American Mercury Reader*, p. 35.

The rhetorical question is an economical way of making a point since questions are easily asked but answers may become long and involved, or may not be possible. Moreover, statements require proof; questions don't.

Satire

Satire, like irony, is a way of saying one thing while intending another. Here is an expert:

Has it been duly marked by historians that the late William Jennings Bryan's last secular act on this earth was to catch flies? A curious detail, but not without its sardonic overtones. He was the most sedulous flycatcher in American history, and by long odds the most successful. His quarry, of course, was not *Musca domestica* but *Homo neandertalensis*. For forty years he tracked it with snare and blunderbuss, up and down the backways of the Republic.[12]

The satire here derives from the fact of Bryan and his fly-swatter in the Tennessee courtroom during the "monkey trial" in Knoxville, from the play on "Neanderthal," from the reference to people as flies, and from the reference to "snare and blunderbuss," archaic weapons.

Here is a second expert:

> A man so various, that he seemed to be
> Not one, but all mankind's epitome;
> Stiff in opinions, always in the wrong,
> Was everything by starts, and nothing long;
> But in the course of one revolving moon,
> Was chymist, fiddler, statesman and buffoon.
>
> (John Dryden, *Absalom and Achitophel*)

Aphorisms

The aphorism is a short pithy statement that seems to have the ring of truth about it; it appeals often to common sense. Here are a few examples:

Don't squirt half the house in order to water a single rosebush.[13]

We must not herd ourselves under the authority of the past and lie down like sheep in the shade of a hedge.[14]

---

[12] *Ibid.*, p. 34.

[13] Virginia Woolf, "How Should One Read a Book?" *The Second Common Reader,* Harcourt Brace Jovanovich, p. 28.

[14] *Ibid.*

Better make a weak man your enemy than your friend. ("Josh Billings")

Cliché

The aphorism passes into the common language ("folklore") of a culture where it serves a purpose as a common-sense generalization about our behavior. There is a similar tendency on the part of many users of the language to repeat many words or phrases in repetitive situations—"it's raining cats and dogs," for instance—and as a result the beginning writer is often warned against the use of clichés. But something needs to be said for clichés—not everyone is as facile with language as the poet or professional author. Moreover, the cliché does facilitate communication, especially if there is some understanding of its application on the part of user and reader or listener. Furthermore, we must ask, "cliché for whom?" Perhaps to the English teacher the advice of Polonius—"This above all, to thine ownself be true"—is a cliché, but I can remember how fascinated I was by the words when first I saw them—and they still tease my mind.

Perhaps the English teacher ought to be reminded of the frequency with which even our best authors use clichés. In one essay by Virginia Woolf, I find these:

lives of great men . . . to throw light on literature . . . the cat is out of the bag . . . the dust . . . to settle . . . from start to finish . . . the Day of Judgment dawns [15]

Jargon, Argot, Cant, Slang

A characteristic of human groups is the development of a "private" language with its own esoteric terms. These differ from dialect in that dialect is the term applied to a larger language pattern. Dialect is primarily a matter of pronunciation rather than spelling: thus *father, car, comedy, cow* may have a common spelling in England and the United States, but the pronunciation is not the same across these areas. Some dialects, it is true, incorporate their own special terms; *bag, sack, poke* are three dialectal variants for the same thing.

Jargon is the term applied to a small-group language (relatively small group, that is) that has a high percentage of words

[15] *Ibid.*

used only within the group, or that has particularized meanings for members of the group:

In the long run, developments in transportation, housing, optimum size of plant, etc., might tend to induce an industrial and demographic pattern similar to the one that consciousness of vulnerability would dictate. Such a tendency might be advanced by public persuasion and governmental inducement, and advanced more effectively if the causes of urbanization had been carefully studied.[16]

The danger signs of jargon are these:

• The use of the passive voice. As Sir Arthur Quiller-Couch says "when you write in the active voice, you write like a man." "He won first place" is to be preferred over "He was designated as the winner of first place."
• The abstract noun. Don't write:

One of the most important reforms mentioned in the rescript is the unification of the organization of judicial institutions and the guarantee for all the tribunals of the independence necessary for securing to all classes of the community equality before the law.

Write:

Court reform is one of the most important. The Courts need a uniform system and to be made independent. Then all men can be assured that they are equal before the law.[17]

• The use of *circumlocution*. Circumlocution can be recognized when "adverse climatic conditions" replaces "bad weather," when someone instead of saying "no" says "the answer is in the negative." The danger signals of circumlocution are "case," "instance," "character," "nature," "condition," "persuasion," "degree."
• The use of *the elegant variation*. As students you have been warned and even scolded about "repetitive writing" or repetition. You therefore avoid the duplication of a word or phrase as you would avoid the plague. The result is either ambiguity or the elegant variation. You write a sports story about an outstanding player on your football team whose name is John Brown. Because of your "thing" about repetition, the story comes out like this:

[16] Samuel T. Williamson, "How to Write Like a Social Scientist," *The Saturday Review of Literature*, October 4, 1947.

[17] Sir Arthur Quiller-Couch, *On the Art of Writing*, G. P. Putnam's Sons, 1961.

John Brown carried the ball five times against the Hagiocrats and scored each time. In the first quarter, the fleet footballer, on a fourth and nine situation, raced in 28 yards. In the second installment, the mustachioed marvel scrambled for 16 and 22. In the third period, the Denver Dynamo fought his way for 39 yards. In the final stanza, the Rapid Rabbit gamboled for 23 yards.

• Finally, keep your blue pencil ever on the alert for: "as regards," "with regard to," "in respect of," "in connection with," "according as to whether," and so on. In the words of Quiller-Couch, from whom I got these, "it is not enough to avoid them nine times out of ten, or nine-and-ninety times out of a hundred. You should never use them."

Argot is a term applied to a language used by a clique or set:

The pitch is long and wide 120 x 100, no slope, no divots, high grass and the air is heavy so watch for short falls. Not much chance for flight balls today.

Excellent wing men and you backs are going to have to ghost them constantly. Center half, you are to play stopper today and plug up the middle.

They learned from the Muscle Christians, so they play fundamental which should make them a natural for the schemers to hit the strikers early.

Once we get ahead, stopper, you change to sweeper and you backs play them off. At the same time, forwards, jockey your men but watch the ref because he likes to pull the book early in the game.

Their backs are choppers so don't rely on dribbles. When you get within range—blast, powder, power that ball because their goalie is quick but gun shy.

In the second half when we are ahead you backs become boomers and if we are not ahead then play heavy with inside men coming back to help out.

On free kicks near goal let the stopper try his banana on alternate shots.

Whenever possible center forward use your scissors as these cave men have never seen one.

Remember the rest of the week you are dagos, krauts, polacks and spics but today you are all Hibernians. Play as a team.

Now any questions?   (Harold T. Conley)

At this point you probably have some. I'll answer two—the game is soccer, and a "Muscle Christian" is probably a member of a Young Men's Christian Association or similar group.

Cant is the term applied to a special language that has become stereotyped through usage so that the speaker seems to be reciting rather than advocating ideas of his own. Cant is difficult to illustrate; one man's cant is another man's elegance. But its presence can be suspected if the sound of a piece is platitudinous:

The importance of people cannot be overemphasized, for only through their personal pride can Outfield continue to meet the challenges of an increasingly competitive age. *People are Outfield's most important asset.*

Slang is the term applied to popular innovations of a faddish kind. Through recorded history there have been two types of language—the so-called "vulgar" language of the streets and the schoolbook or formal language. Romans, for instance, had two words for *horse*—the classical "equus," which is taught in public school Latin courses, and the popular "caballus." "Equus" survives in such rarely used words as "equestrian." "Caballus" survives in "cavalry," "chevalier," "caballero," "chivalry," "cavalier," and so on.

The advocates of slang and the advocates of schoolboy English have had and will continue to have their differences. The latter, in their obvious displeasure with slang, overlook the fact that many words that are good English today began as slang: "row" (in the sense of a quarrel or disturbance), "boom," "slump," "crank," "fad," "grit," and "pluck" are some examples. One fact you must not overlook, however—social distinctions are made on the basis of language usage. If you are happy with your gang and if your gang uses slang (as all gangs do, slang often serving as a private signal of membership, you know), you would probably find yourself ostracized if you began speaking schoolhouse English seriously while you are with your gang.

Some indication of the quarrel can be seen in this bit of current comment:

I believe that the purpose of schools is to teach the standards of a society in language, arithmetic, social studies. I do not believe that you can make the deviations and the variants the standards.

I am also opposed to what I understand is the new style among grammarians, that anything goes as long as it is used. If one were to translate that permissiveness into arithmetic, for instance, you would have chaos.[18]

[18] Dr. Kenneth B. Clarke, *The Arizona Republic*, November 25, 1969, p. 48.

I am on the other side of this row. Without protesting against the logical fallacies that I find in the comment, and merely taking the statement in the spirit in which it was made, I believe what the student needs to be taught is the truth about language usage—and not merely one standard that may be used in one place and nowhere else. That is the philosophy in which I believe and I am willing to man the barricades to support it.

Now you have seen both sides of the quarrel.

Assignment for Discussion

Discuss the effectiveness of: irony, paradox, understatement, hyperbole, mimicry, paronomasia, the catalog, word play or word fun, apostrophes, rhetorical questions, satire, aphorisms, clichés, jargon, argot, slang, cant, and other kinds of language usage in making a point. Bring in examples to document your argument.

Assignment for Writing

Take a side in the quarrel mentioned in the section on slang. In a brief essay argue for your point of view. If you advocate slang, try to use slang in support of your argument—either directly or in examples. If you come out against slang, do not use it in your essay except as a horrible example.

Or, write a persuasive paper on some subject on which you feel strongly. You may want to attack or support the Establishment, come out for or against some political party or philosophy, or simply argue for some personal idiosyncrasy. In your paper use some of the devices discussed in this chapter.

Denotative Language

If people are to communicate through language, particularly the written language where there is no immediate opportunity for feedback or give-and-take, then words must have closely similar meanings for all parties to a communication. I do not mean here only that all parties must have access to the same dictionary, although that would help; I mean also that in terms of experience and background the parties must see similar meanings in words.

Such communication is helped by the use of *denotative* words,

words that refer to limited fixed characteristics of a referent. *Connotative* words are words whose meanings take on a halo or suggestive quality; *denotative* words are words whose meaning is limited to a specified characteristic or set of characteristics. Sometimes the denotative meaning of a word is said to be that meaning which is given in a dictionary.

The referent of a denotative word may be concrete or abstract, known or unknown, tangible or ideal. A denotative word is one or the other of two types—*referential* (or *presentational*) or *relational*.

Referential Words

Referential or presentational words *refer to* or *present* known or specified characteristics of their referents.

The characteristics may be *logical*—that is, those characteristics of a referent that have been arbitrarily agreed upon or named. Logical words include: inch, yard, meter, pound, gram, liter, quart, and the like.

The characteristics may be *sensory*—that is, those characteristics that result from the use of our senses: light, dark, sweet, sour, bitter, loud, rough, acrid, and the like.

The characteristics may be *affective* or *emotional* (as long as they remain non-suggestive): lovely, ugly, pleasant, homely, fragrant, and the like.

Denotative words may apply to facts: cow, dog, horse, mountain, rain.

Denotative words may apply to generalizations: family, mankind, animals, vehicles, weather.

Denotative words may apply to intangible generalizations: truth, beauty, religion, philosophy, knowledge.

Denotative words may apply to the Ideal or its opposites: God, Heaven, Hell, the Devil, Nature, Justice.

Denotative words may name things: the United States, North America, John Smith, Fido.

Denotative words may apply to actions: run, jump, swim, leap; or to actions of a less visible kind: think, hate, love, wish.

Assignment for Discussion

Bring to class various examples of prose from the worlds of sport, business, politics, religion, entertainment, education, advertising, and so on. Select at random 300 to 500 words from each example; count the number of denotative words, calculate the percentages. Can you arrive at any generalizations from such analysis? For instance, what is the relationship between the amount of information furnished in a given sample and the percentage of denotative words?

Assignment for Writing

Write a 300- to 500-word essay on some personal experience. Limit your word choice to denotative words. What problems do you have?

Or, write three 150-word paragraphs describing a flower, an encounter, an object such as a favorite piece of clothing. In the first paragraph limit yourself to logical words. In the second limit yourself to sensory words. In the third limit yourself to affective words.

Do you have any problems as you write? Of what sort are they? What differences do you discern among your paragraphs? What happens if you put the three paragraphs together to form one essay about your topic? Does this exercise offer you any clues as to means of improving your writing?

Relational Words

As you wrote the above assignment you were forced to use some words that are not referential but that, rather, establish relationships among the referential words. These are relational words: of, the, an, a, to, among, with, as, at, on, where, who, and the like. They refer to no specific referent, except perhaps as they are used. "Who" becomes a referential word if it refers to someone specifically as in the sentence "Who is your brother?"

Relational words can indicate almost any kind of a relationship that can be imagined and thus are very difficult to classify in a grammatical scheme. Consider the following relationships indicated by the common word "and":

One and one equals two, Mary and I, swimming and diving, shoes and socks, bread and butter, eating and sleeping, reading and thinking, arithmetic and English are favorite subjects, and so on, living and dying, now and then, on and on, truth and beauty, two and two, there are women and women, your fair and outward character, sweet and lovely, try and stop me, he sat and smoked, sit and wait, I said go and he went, he promised to come and he didn't, he would not want both you and me to come, he and he alone, First Avenue and Third Street.

If you need some help with this list, I refer you to an unabridged dictionary, one of which is my authority here.

A kind of relationship is established by the use of *transitional words* or *phrases:* first, second, as another example, meanwhile, moreover, however, on the other hand, and the like. The essay, "A Philosophy of Handicap" (see pages 309–316), has many good examples. Transitional words and phrases are to writing what the highway traffic sign is to the motorist. Without them, we are dead.

Transitional phrases are used to establish subordination, co-ordination, antithesis, spatial relationships, temporal relationships, functional relationships, and the like.

Writing Assignments

1. It is possible to write titles without relational words: "Hub Fans Bid Kid Adieu." Try writing a paragraph of 150 to 300 words without any relational words.
2. "God" terms and "devil" terms are sometimes called "slur" words and "purr" words. "Slur" words are sometimes called "snarl" words. Scholars also conceive of neutral words in the middle of a continuum at one end of which is a snarl word and at the other a purr word. Make up a list of ten or twelve sets of concepts in a table such as this one:

Concept	Snarl word	Neutral word	Purr word

3. A teacher was recently reprimanded because he gave his students an assignment similar to the one above in which he listed some snarl words that are ordinarily conceived as obscene or pornographic. Discuss this issue as you see it, trying to present opposite points of view.

Questions for Discussion

1. If language is a demarcator of social classes, how do you account for the popularity of the following people:

Al Jolson: "You ain't heard nothin' yet, folks."

Joe Jacobs, boxing impresario: "I should of stood in bed."
                                            "We was robbed."

Will Rogers: "People who ain't saying ain't ain't eating."

Samuel Goldwyn: "In two words: im-possible."
                          "For years I have been known for saying 'in-
                          clude me out,' but today I am giving it up for-
                          ever. From now on let me say: 'Oxford and
                          Balliol, 'include me in.' "

Fiorello LaGuardia: "Ticker tape ain't spaghetti."

2. Defend or attack this statement:

   I believe that the purpose of schools is to teach the standards of
   society in language.

3. Who should determine the standards of your language? Who
   is your model for "good" language usage? Why?
4. Assume that you have been employed as a "marketer" of
   products for young people. Make up a list of product names.
5. List phrases that have a common term:

   coffee break   circuit break   break for lunch
   football play   dramatic play   he made a play for her

   Discuss differences and similarities in the meanings of the
   common terms ("break," "play" in the above examples).
6. From the library get novels by Hamlin Garland, William
   Dean Howells, Charles Dickens, and Henry James. List names
   of characters and compare with names found in wedding
   and engagement announcements in a newspaper. Can you
   account for any differences you find? What seem to be the
   sources for the names? (Use a dictionary.)
7. Here is a list of Iowa place names: Rabbit Hill, Brown Jug,
   Cockleburr, Little Flock, Log Chain, Kniffin, Calathump.
   Make up a list of "odd" place names found in your own community. Why are they "odd"?
8. Comment on this passage from a 1925 American novel:

   Steve, eh? Well, that's a good old-fashioned name. No frippery
   about it. By gracious, Anthony, if you'd named him Clarence I'd
   have cut you out of my will.

9. Phil Stong noted that a great many nineteenth-century men were named Ivanhoe. Herbert Quick reported the popularity of Helen Mar and William Wallace, deriving from Jane Porter's *Scottish Chiefs* (1810). What will you name your children?

5

Order
and
Knowledge

In the act of denotating, words make classifications. These classifications are often unsystematic and illogical. (This may not be true in scientific terminology where the classifications, because they are based on Greek roots and stems, are likely to be systematic and logical—although scientists have a great deal of trouble agreeing on the systems, the logic, and the terminology!) As I have already demonstrated a word may often designate a very large number of objects or concepts with only the most tenuous idealogical quality in common—the idea of a *circle* in a diamond ring and in a political organization ("Tweed ring") is not present in the meaning of *ring* in the sound of a bell. A word may therefore refer to objects or classes of objects with infinite or indefinite boundaries or qualities. Or a word may be ambiguous in its one indicated meaning:

> Beauty is truth, truth beauty . . .

All of this may imply that words are at fault—not at all. The fault lies with us who create them and use them.

Words classify through their similarities of meaning. Such words are called *synonyms* from the Greek prefix *syn-* meaning "like," and *onyma,* "name." (Our word "name" derives from the Anglo-Saxon *nama,* but this word and the Greek word both have their common origin in the Indo-European family of languages.) Synonyms classify words according to *nuances of meaning:* thus deny, gainsay, contradict, negative, traverse, impugn, contravene all come in the category of declaring untrue or of going counter to the truth. Within these general categories, each has a special sense.

The nuances of synonyms are set forth in good dictionaries. Synonyms are listed according to categories (classifications) in a *thesaurus* or dictionary of synonyms. The most useful function of the thesaurus is not in broadening one's vocabulary (which it helps do); it is rather in helping us to break through a mental block, or to help us find the one word that has the specific sense we are looking for. But we must be sure to check the dictionary to insure we have the best term.

Classification Processes

You use classification processes all of the time. When you are working out your annual federal or state income tax report, you are classifying. You first categorize everything as either receivables or expenditures. Receivables are further classified as taxable receivables and nontaxable receivables. Expenditures are classified as deductible and nondeductible (notice how much we classify words rather than things). The government requires that deductible expenses be classified according to their types: taxes, interest, medical, educational, and the like.

In business there are three broad items: income, expense, profit or loss. Income is classified according to source: sales, repairs, rents, labor. Expense is classified as merchandise costs, operating costs, labor costs, rentals, interest, depreciation, burden. Even profits are classified: those that are to be distributed to owner, partners, or shareholders, and those that are to be plowed back into the business or placed in reserve for future contingencies.

At its simplest, classification is the indexing of an object by a single quality or group of qualities. Actually we index ("pigeon-hole" if you will) words that refer to the qualities. If I say a piece of metal is iron, I am classifying it by one quality. If I say the piece of metal is heavy, I am classifying it by another quality. In either case, I select a familiar quality and ignore others that might refer to its feel, its color, its chemical components, and so on. If I point at a passing animal and call it a dog, I am classifying that animal by a term that incorporates all of the qualities possessed by the species *dog*.

Or we can classify by a generalization that can be at either a high level of abstraction or a low level. Something passes us and we can point at it and use any one of these terms: animal, mammal, vertebrate, canine, carnivore, dog, St. Bernard, "Butch." "Animal" is the highest level of abstraction in that set.

Levels of Abstraction

At this point a digression on levels of abstraction may be useful. Here is a set of abstractions that begin at a low level and range to a high level:

Windsor dining-room chair. Although several variations in the style of this chair are possible, it is basically a wooden chair, popular in the eighteenth century in England and the American colonies. Specific features are a curved spindle back, turned raking legs, and a saddle seat. Some models have arms, some do not, but in any model, the Windsor chair is a distinctive type.

Dining-room chair. The most that can be said specifically about this chair is that it is usually part of a dining set, and it is usually found in that part of the house set apart for dining. It may be of wood or metal, with or without arms, without upholstering or with some degree of upholstering.

Chair. Any device, wooden, metal, plastic, or of other material, upholstered wholly, partially, or not at all, sometimes with four legs, sometimes mounted on a pedestal, sometimes with no legs, with a seat and back support, designed for seating an individual. The term is so general as to permit an extremely wide range of designs.

Furniture. Utilitarian objects, including chairs, usually movable, designed for household, office, and other public or private places; intended for seating, housing, storing, placing, illuminating, holding, sleeping, and including beds, desks, tables, cabinets, lamps, and the like.

Household goods. Items needed in the establishment and maintenance of a home. The term includes furniture, but it also refers to dishes, bedding, linens, rugs, pictures, appliances, and the like.

Chattels. Personal property, including household goods, but also including jewelry, clothing, automobiles, boats—anything movable. The term does not include real estate. With *chattels* we have reached a comparatively high level of abstraction—so high that in legal matters, chattels often have to be defined or enumerated.

The lower the level of abstraction, the more *concrete* the term—but any term is still an abstraction.

Assignment for Writing

Take some personal object and use it as the basis for a set of abstractions similar to the above. What problems do you encounter?

At a more complex level classification becomes the indexing of an object by multiple qualities and groups of qualities. In such a process two schemes of classification are at work at once. One has to do with the object being classified. The other has to do with the classification of the qualities and groups of qualities. The process is similar to that of logical definition. The subject to be classified becomes the specimen. The specimen is one in an almost infinite group and is according to kingdom, family, class, and species.

The classes of qualities are logical, emotional, and sensory. When we have selected our specimen we must decide from which broad group our qualities are to be selected; we may choose from one, two, or all three. Our broad choices and our subsequent choices will depend upon our purpose.

The classification process works in one of two ways—either we have the category (pigeonhole) and we go looking for the precise object to fit it, or we have the object and we look for the category in which it belongs. The first or deductive process is illustrated by a classified employment advertisement in a newspaper. The second or inductive process is illustrated by the case of an insect found in the desert.

In the first case we select criteria for an ideal specimen. Because we are trying to be objective we use logical qualities. These would include the physical, intellectual, educational, experiential, and characteristic attributes of our ideal. He must pass our organization's physical examination as specified by our physician. He must have at least two years of college and have taken courses in accounting and office management. He must not have incurred a felony conviction, and he must present two character references. He must have had at least two years of accounting experience in our field. He may be either male or female.

In the second case we follow standard procedures for identifying animals. What is his breathing apparatus? How does he reproduce? Does he have a backbone? Does he have wings? How many legs? What about his thorax? What is his color and size? The answers to these questions are classifiers.

We might look at classification as a logical process in which two mental operations take place simultaneously. Diagrammed, the process of categorizing and selecting a new employee might look like this:

Classes of criteria	Specific instances
Title of position	Junior accountant and assistant office manager
Job class	Eight
Salary range	$800–1000 monthly
Physical qualities	Pass physical examination
Sex	Either
Education	Two years college, courses in accounting and office management
Character	No felony conviction, two recommendations
Experience	Two years in our field
Person selected	Mary Smith, SSN 481–03–8057

In this classifying process a third column comes into being— the specific qualifications of Miss Mary Smith: an Associate of Arts degree from Centerville Community College, two and one-half years of experience as an accountant with the Centerville Cooperative Supply Company, for example.

A similar table would be set up for the desert animal.

Logically the process is like that demonstrated in the table of abstractions or in the levels of generalities in sentences. Although this subject is discussed in some detail in Chapter 10, here is an example of what I am talking about:

But on our southern coasts, the wall-sided cliffs, many hundred feet high, with vast needles and pinnacles standing out in the sea, sharp and solitary enough to serve as perches for the wary cormorant, confer a wonderful beauty and grandeur upon the chalk headlands. (Thomas Henry Huxley, "On a Piece of Chalk")

In that sentence we have two high-level abstractions operating side by side—the noun "cliffs," and the verb "confer." Everything else in the sentence serves to modify one or the other of these terms and thus to reduce them to fairly specific low-level generalizations. The process is one of classification, as this table will help demonstrate:

Word or phrase	Level of abstraction	Grammatical class
But	not applicable—relational word	transitional function
on our southern coasts	2	subject modifier
the wall-sided cliffs	1	subject
many hundred feet high	2	subject modifier
with	relational word	
vast needles and pinnacles	2	subject modifier
standing out	3	modifier of modifier
in the sea	4	modifier of modifier of modifier
sharp and solitary enough	2	subject modifier
to serve	3	modifier of modifier
as perches	4	modifier of modifier of modifier
for the wary cormorant	4	modifier of modifier of modifier
confer	1	verb
a wonderful beauty and grandeur	2	direct object
upon the chalk headlands	3	indirect object

Within a phrase such as "the wall-sided cliffs, another set of abstractions occur:

the	2	subject modifier
-sided	2	subject modifier
wall	3	modifier of modifier
cliffs	1	subject

Modifiers such as "the" and "wall-sided" are described by grammarians as "bound" or "fixed"—that is, they cannot be moved freely in the sentence without distorting the meaning. Modifiers such as "on our southern cliffs" are termed "free"— they can be moved about in the sentence (in order to secure a more rhythmic sentence, for instance) without disturbing the meaning. The obvious function of either type of modifier is to help create more specific or concrete sentences.

I apologize for this awkward table, but at the same time I marvel at what it represents—the ability of our logical, emotional, and sensory mental processes to select subjects and to relate them to each other, to particularize them, and to communicate them to other people in meaningful ways.

You might appreciate these mental processes even more— and thus be motivated to improve your own—if you see clearly that the above classification processes are only a part of the total mental process. For instance, the term "cliffs" might have been classified in terms of geography, geology, mineralogy, aesthetic values, or ecology. Examining our sentence we can see the classes of choices that were made:

Geography
    Location   southern coasts, sea
Geology
    Contours   needles and pinnacles, wall-sided
Ecology
    Habitats   perches
    Animal   wary cormorant
Aesthetic qualities   beauty, grandeur
Other logical qualities
    Vertical qualities   wall-sided, standing out, hundred
                                        feet high
Sensory qualities
    Visible   high, vast

This outline may also seem cumbersome and unnecessarily complex to you, and that it is. But it is an attempt to illustrate for you the way your mind functions when you compose sentences. The composition process happens so fast most of the time that we are not aware of its workings. But when composition comes slowly and painfully you might keep this outline in mind. Ask yourself: What is my major generalization (my point)? What are its chief components? Are they logical, sensory, emotional, idealogical? Are they geographical, ecological, demographical?

Outlining

This kind of analytical or classifying process leads logically to the *outline*. Most of us pale at the word, dread the subject. Yet whether we put the outline down on paper or keep it snugly in our heads, if we are to produce any kind of composition at all, we need some sense of organization, of the direction we are going. Topsy may have just "growed," and Coleridge may have honestly believed he wrote "Kubla Khan" as he described, but common sense and John Livingston Lowes have taught us otherwise.

Suppose you were to write an essay on "Philately—Stamp Collecting to You." How would classification work and why would an outline naturally result?

The subject is a very broad one, so you might have to narrow it somewhat. Under "philately" we might expect to find these subclassifications: History of stamp collecting; How one goes about collecting stamps; Why one collects stamps; Some famous philatelists; The economics of collecting stamps; Kinds of stamps. But let's say I am writing an encyclopedia article and so I want to treat each of these subjects. I think about them a minute and then list them in this order (using Roman numerals to indicate they are my chief subclassifications):

      I. Some famous philatelists
     II. History of stamp collecting
    III. Kinds of stamps
     IV. Why one collects stamps
      V. How one goes about collecting stamps

You will have noted that this outline leaves out "the economics of stamp collecting." Further reflection led me to see that this subject and "the pleasures of stamp collecting" are parallel and belong under heading IV. So I number them:

    IV. A. The pleasures of stamp collecting
        B. The economics of stamp collecting

Under III, "Kinds of stamps," I would place these headings:

    A. Revenue and semi-postal stamps
    B. Commemorative issues
    C. Christmas issues
    D. Airmail stamps
    E. Special purpose stamps

Under III, E, I would place these headings:

    1. Special delivery stamps
    2. Postage due stamps

Under III, E, 2, I would add these headings:

    a. United States postage dues
      i. Nineteenth-century issues
     ii. Twentieth-century issues

In the course of your education, you have undoubtedly been taught that each item in an outline should be a "sentence"— that is, it should contain a subject and predicate (verb). But notice that in a "subject-oriented" outline such as this one there is no need for the predicate or for a verb. The predicate is stated in succeeding subheadings, and the verbs (which would be "is," "are," "include," and the like) are implied in the outline form.

Thinking about levels of abstracting, levels of generality, abstract terms and concrete terms, and outlines, you will come to see that outlining as a system of classification is a means of moving from the high-level abstraction to specimens. Our title is often our highest level of abstraction, and an explanatory note placed under the title is the second highest level of abstraction.

Professional writers often prepare an outline after their first draft is written. In such cases, the outline serves as a basis for reclassifying (restructuring) their materials. The control for the outline may well be one of the organizing principles discussed in Chapter 7.

The outline discussed above is based on the deductive process of classifying. In the inductive process, we begin with the specimen and "move back up" the outline, reversing the illustrated process. In the case of the unknown desert animal we mentioned earlier, our purpose in classifying will determine the headings and subheadings of our outline. If our purpose is to place him in the family of insects, we look at the characteristics (these will become our headings and subheadings) by which we can compare him with other insects whose identity we have already established. If we are interested in him as a desert dweller, we study his living habits—the type of home he builds, his family or tribal habits, the kind of food he eats, the way he reproduces. If we are interested in exterminating him, we look at his digestive system, his nervous system or his reproductive system.

Assignment for Discussion

Assume that you have gone to work for a paint company that is building a new storage warehouse. You are asked to organize the warehouse so that paint may be easily stored and taken out of the warehouse as demand and supply dictates. (There's your purpose.) You learn that paint comes in barrels, drums, five-gallon cans, one-gallon cans, quarts, pints, and tubes. Paint comes in various colors. It is sprayed or brushed on. It is applied to metal, wood, plaster, cement, interiors, exteriors. It comes in three different qualities. Assignment: Deploy the paint containers for most efficient handling.

Assignment for Writing

Make a list of 50 objects found in your room. Classify them three different ways: according to their use, according to the source of supply, and one other way which I leave to your ingenuity. When you have finished write a brief description of your procedures and the differences in your three lists.

Static Analysis

Did it occur to you while you were working on the paint problem that you were not actually classifying paint containers; you were classifying words? Every work process, every set of objects is reducible to a set of words.

This is true even of scientific research. Benjamin Whorf has noted that:

It is the use of *language upon data* that is central to scientific progress. . . . Science begins and ends in talk . . . such words as "analyze, compare, deduce, reason, infer, postulate, theorize, test, demonstrate" mean that whenever a scientist does something, he talks about the things he does. . . .[1]

And Leonard Bloomfield has said:

Scientific research begins with a set of sentences which point the way to certain observations and experiments, the results of which do not become fully scientific until they have been turned back into language, yielding again a set of sentences which then become the basis of further exploration into the unknown.

The process of *static analysis* is also a problem in word manipulation, although it is true that in this process, as in the process of classification, there may come a time when we have to set words aside and engage in the dirty hard work of lifting and moving objects such as paint containers. Even then, though, we must still continue to reason as we go, and reasoning requires words.

Static analysis is a process of dissection of an object or concept that is not changing in time or space. A house that is unoccupied or yet to be built, an automobile either on an assembly line, in a repair shop, or sitting at the curb, a city in the abstract, a government, a planned production line, an institution or an industrial plant—all of these are subject to static analysis.

Static analysis is concerned with wholes, parts, joints, and the purpose for analysis. Other names for parts are: components, assemblies, subassemblies. Any object may be thought of either as a whole or a part; an automobile is a whole in itself, but in a dealer's showroom it becomes a part of his inventory. The battery is a part of the automobile, but on a dealer's shelf or on a production line it becomes a whole. Joints are of various kinds. They may be pure abstractions as the boundary between two states or the line that separates the ocean into continental and international waters. A good example of this is the summer home of the President of the United States on the beach at San Clemente, California. Ordinarily in that area the high-water line is the joint (line of demarcation) between private property and the ocean. When the President is in residence the joint is moved several miles out into the Pacific. Question: How

[1] Benjamin Lee Whorf, *Language, Thought and Reality*, The M.I.T. Press, 1956, pp. 220–221.

close might a foreign warship approach that beach without causing serious international problems?

A joint may be a place where two components are welded, glued, bolted, nailed, or otherwise fastened together. It may be a place that has been arbitrarily agreed upon—by law or habit or custom or convention.

The purpose of static analysis must be clear. Are we assembling or disassembling (once two components have been welded together, it is not easy to separate them)? Are we planning or legislating? Are we enforcing a law or manufacturing? Are we buying or selling? Are we pricing or describing?

The steps in static analysis: Decide upon the purpose; locate all joints and establish the boundaries for divisions, subdivisions, and so on; identify the whole and the parts; then decide upon a sequence.

The sequence may be functional, economical, logical, sequential, temporal, or spatial—or perhaps something else. An automobile may be analyzed according to its functions—locomotion, braking, ignition, carburetion. A budget is analyzed on the principles of economics. A concept—philosophy, religion, honesty—may be analyzed along logical lines. A trip across country may be analyzed in sequences (state by state, airlines and terminals) or in terms of time (one day at a time or hour by hour). A production line, in its planning stages, may be analyzed in terms of space and sequence of operations. A day is analyzed according to time—a map according to space. A political institution is analyzed by functions, by methods of election and appointment, or by job classifications.

Once the sequence is selected you must still decide where to start. A trip begins here and ends there. If you are describing the geography of the United States, you probably begin with the New England states—why? If you are analyzing an automobile, where do you begin?

You must establish your terms and stick to them. Here is one time where the "elegant variation" must certainly be avoided. Budgets are analyzed in terms of assets and liabilities, expenditures and receipts, expendables and nonexpendables, capital and expenses. A car is analyzed in terms of parts—battery, carburetor, spark plugs, gas tank. A kitchen is analyzed in terms of function—food storage, food preparation, cooking, dish washing. Days are divided in hours, minutes, seconds, forenoons, noons, and afternoons.

Assignment for Writing

Prepare a static analysis of your city, college, or church. Determine components and joints and select the terminology. Decide upon a purpose for the analysis (other than the fact it is assigned) and select a sequence.

Dynamic Analysis

Cars move on the streets, people live in cities, governments govern, industrial plants operate, athletic teams engage in contests. If we are to understand our world in motion, we must have a system of analysis that can deal with motion.

Dynamic analysis, as an intellectual exercise, is parallel to static analysis. As a matter of fact dynamic analysis may require that a static analysis first be made. If we are to understand what takes place within an automobile as it moves along the street, we must know its parts.

Dynamic analysis requires identification of operations and stages in the operation. The junctions between stages must be designated.

An operation may be a total operation or it may be a stage in an operation. Using the voyage of Apollo 12 as an example, the operation may be identified as the series of events that took place from liftoff to splashdown. The stages would be: liftoff; second stage, earth orbit, interplanetary travel, moon orbit, separation of LEM from command module, landing of LEM, moon walk, LEM takeoff, rejoining of LEM and command module, movement back into earth orbit, interplanetary travel, and splashdown. But the moon walk itself became an operation, divisible into two stages separated by a return to the LEM. And the Apollo 12 flight is but a stage in the whole Apollo program; the program is but a stage in our whole space operation.

Junctions on the Apollo 12 flight would be: firing of the engines on the first stage, discard of first stage and firing of engines on second stage, firing of engines to start interplanetary travel, and so on. But note that even a stage can become so complex as to become an operation in itself.

We must establish terms for the various stages and junctions, and the terminology must be fixed. If you are giving a com-

mand to a man operating a highly complex device a quarter of
a million miles from earth, you and he had better not be playing
games with terminology.

You must have a purpose for analysis. The purpose of the
above example is to identify the operation, its stages and junctions. But we could have analyzed the Apollo 12 flight in terms
of functions of personnel: this group responsible for voice contact, that group responsible for instrument control, a third
group responsible for physical welfare of the astronauts, and
so on.

You must establish a sequence for analysis. The chronology
of the Apollo 12 flight is obvious; but what about the functional
analysis of the flight? Which function do you analyze first and
why? Again, the sequence can be logical, functional, economical, sequential, spatial or temporal—or perhaps something
else.

Assignment for Writing

If you are a girl, write a functional analysis of something
ordinarily regarded as a "masculine function"—perhaps flying
an airplane or loading, firing, and cleaning a gun. If you are a
boy, write a functional analysis of something that seems to be a
feminine prerogative—such as cooking a meal or tailoring
a costume (which used to be called "dressmaking"). Then present your paper to a member of the opposite sex for his or her
approval.

Opinion, Assertion, Projection, Hypothesis

Any piece of prose, other than the rhetorical question, is
likely to be a *statement* of some kind. The kind of statement is
or ought to be of concern to us as we read; and certainly we
should know what kind of statements we are making as we
write.

Opinion represents a venture, a guess, an estimate, the result
of the application of one's common sense or perhaps even judgment to a situation or problem. When an opinion is offered, it
ought to be identified as in this paragraph:

Finally, I wish to emphasize once more that what has been said here in a somewhat categorial form does not claim to mean more than the personal opinion of a man, which is founded upon *nothing but* his own personal experience. . . .[2]

Technically, an opinion is a statement that is either not directly supported by evidence or that is not framed in such a way that it can serve as a basis for research or investigation.

Opinions need not be accepted as fact, but the authority and experience of the speaker or writer ought to be taken into consideration. On the other hand, one ought certainly to reserve his judgment on a matter when it is phrased like this:

. . . the Department of Health, Wealth, Sex Education and Welfare has to do something to justify its existence, but regardless of whether they are for or against the issue is fundamentally as baseless, as is the issue itself—for how in the devil are you going to teach a kid something that nature will adequately teach him and at the proper time? (From a column in a daily newspaper)

An *assertion* is a statement offered as if it were fact when its factual quality has not been determined:

His place in the Tennessee hagiocracy is secure. If the village barber saved any of his hair, then it is curing gallstones down there today.

Projections are statements based upon the writer's estimate of his own behavior in the other person's situation; the statement is made, however, about the other person's behavior. Some years ago a French film labeled projection as the "eighth deadly sin," and charged all of us with being guilty.

Hypothesis is a statement made to be proved. It sets up a test situation with a reasonable number of alternatives to be tested; many scientific hypotheses test one alternative at a time. The hypothesis is phrased in non-ambiguous language; each word in the hypothesis, as it is used in that context, is capable of but one meaning or interpretation. It usually aims at a problem to be solved.

The hypothesis must not be open-ended; instead it must present go/no go kinds of alternatives. A sentence which states, for example, that the quality of drinking water in a given municipal

[2] Albert Einstein, *Out of My Later Years*, 1950. By permission of the Estate of Albert Einstein.

corporation can be improved is an assertion, not a hypothesis; a hypothesis in the situation would be like this:

That an addition can be constructed on the Balltown Water Plant to cost not more than $25,000, and to be capable of reducing the hardness of the present water supply from 25 grains per thousand gallons to seven grains per thousand gallons.

Fact

An important function of language is to establish or identify fact. A fact is an agreed-upon condition of some particular which we all accept for the present so that we may get on with our daily work. It is the result of the suspension of investigation or research for the present.

An example. For years the "noble" gases—krypton, neon, argon, xenon and helium—were assumed by scientists to be "inert"—to be incapable, that is, of combining with other elements to produce compounds. Their inertness was a fact, and this fact was duly recorded in the textbooks and taught in the schools.

Then, research demonstrated that xenon and fluorine could be combined to produce xenon tetrafluoride—and the facts in the matter had to be changed.

Here are some of the ways by which facts are established:

1. Facts may be established by analysis or classification.

2. Facts may be established by experimentation or research.

3. Facts may be established by measurement based on arbitrarily determined standards. Such facts have no existence at all except as a convenience to man. Such measurements are applied to height, weight, breadth, distance, volume, mass, time, speed, and the like.

4. Facts may be established by the differences from or the resemblances to other facts or standards.

5. Facts may be established by verbalization or definition. Thus the calculus came into being on the basis of Newton's description of it.

6. Facts may be established through the process of repetition. If one or more of us performs an experiment and achieves certain results, and the same experiment achieving the same results is duplicated by another or others, the experiment and the results become factual.

7. Facts may be established by verification of a hypothesis.

8. Facts may be established through the use of syllogisms, provided our original premise is valid.

9. Facts may be established through the use of common sense or the application of good judgment based on our experience.

10. Facts may be determined through the use of the senses or through the use of adjuncts to the senses—the microscope, the oscilloscope, the telescope, listening devices, radar, the motion picture.

11. Facts may be established by reference to authority. However, we must be cautious—authorities do become discredited or obsolete.

12. Facts may be established by our experience. But we must not forget the lesson in the fable of the seven blind men, each of whom grasped a different part of an elephant. This fable must also be kept in mind when we are depending on our senses.

What I have been describing has been called "objective" or "external" fact. There is another type—the "subjective" or "internal" or "demonic" fact, as this newspaper account demonstrates:

If those Apollo 12 fellows get the moon all riled up again, they'll have the angry masses of Eggbornsville to deal with when they get home.

This isolated mountain community's entire population of 50 is preparing for the worst. After all, they'll tell you, after that Apollo 11 landing on the moon, Eggbornsville had the worst rains and floods in its history. . . .

One elderly Eggbornsville woman paused as she carried firewood into her house and voiced angry disapproval of America's space scientists. "They don't know what they're doing," she growled. "They're fooling around with things that don't concern them."

Not far down the road her neighbor was also stocking her house with provisions. "If them nastynauts keep messing around up there, they're going to set the world on fire," she predicted.

We may smile at this account but each of us has his own stock of private facts in which he believes, and which either inhibit him from doing certain things or motivate him to do other things. Be honest with yourself—what are your private facts?

Another type of fact is the "hypothetical" or "analagous" fact —those facts which pertain to speculative situations where, for one reason or another, close determination is not possible. For instance, before the Apollo 11 and Apollo 12 flights were made, the crews were given training on earth in situations which it was expected would be duplicated in space and on the moon.

All of the methods for determining fact are constantly in use; the growth of factual information is pyramiding at an increasing rate. As Dr. J. Robert Oppenheimer noted:

Nearly everything that is now known was not in any book when most of us went to school.

A final class of fact is the literary or poetic fact. These are statements of apparent fact, presented in all seriousness by their authors:

The Assyrian came down like a wolf on the field

The hare limp'd trembling through the frozen grass

Mr. Howard McLane in his chair let his newspaper fall on his lap and gazed out . . . with dreaming eyes. [The scene] had a certain mysterious glamour to him; the lakes were cooler and brighter to his eye, the greens fresher, and the grain more golden than to anyone else, for he was coming back to it all after an absence of ten years. It was, besides, *his* West. He still took pride in being a Western man. (Hamlin Garland, "Up the Coulee")

Grammar

It seems that every time I meet someone new and he learns that I am an English teacher, he responds: "An English teacher! I'd better watch my grammar!"

His response indicates the seriousness with which people take a subject that everyone professes to have trouble with. Not only are we conscious of our own shortcomings; we are quick to condemn the grammatical miscalculations of others:

It may sound presumptuous for a person with only the background of a high school education to criticize the contents of a letter which . . . carried the prestigious signature of an associate professor. . . .

In his letter I found the following sentence: "Evidently the trail ended near the charming couple's house who so courteously informed us we couldn't read." Was it the house which informed them they couldn't read? . . .

When . . . grammatical errors such as these occur in a letter written by a Ph.D., I think his educational background could stand some scrutiny. (*The Arizona Republic*, November 17, 1969)

Grammar is the study of the arrangement of words in a sentence and of the function of words in a sentence. Because that definition may seem a bit too inclusive, let me offer an example as a way of saying what grammar is not:

One Sunday afternoon, a circus horse balanced himself on the point of a needle of gold.

Grammatically, that sentence is fine. We expect that a sentence might begin with a phrase such as "one Sunday afternoon" —that is phrases indicating place, time, condition, causality, sequence, consequence, and the like. We expect that this phrase might be followed by one on the order of "a circus horse"— phrases beginning with words such as "a," "an," "any," "some," "each," "both," "one," "two," followed immediately by words such as "circus," "hungry," "black," and succeeded by words such as "horse," "dog," "man," "woman." In other words a term indicating a quantity followed by a modifier followed by a substantive. Following this second type of phrase we expect a word or words such as "balanced," "balances," "is balancing," "has balanced," "will balance."

Something inherent in us or something educated into us by long custom tells us there is a propriety about the placement of certain words and phrases in a sentence. We know that as logical as this set of words is:

a   a   afternoon   balanced   circus   gold   himself
horse needle of   of   on   one   point   Sunday   the

(the set is logical because the words are presented in alphabetical order as in a spelling list or dictionary), it is not right. In that order the words do not make sense, at least not easily. Furthermore, there seems to be no connection or relationship among the words, and the whole set seems pointless.

But you say—the sentence about the circus horse does not make sense either; a horse could not balance on a needle of any kind—and why is this needle of gold? My answer is—grammar is not about meaning. Grammar is about logical order, about the relationships among words, and about the function of words. Once order, relationship, and function are established, then we can worry about meaning. Meaning cannot exist without grammar.

Grammar is the means by which we establish the difference in intent in sentences such as these:

I saw a man-eating fish. (in an aquarium)
I saw a man eating fish. (in a restaurant)

Nero murdered Aquarius.

Aquarius murdered Nero.

Our real problems with grammar come because we get ourselves trapped into sentence-situations such as the one quoted
in the letter that criticized the Ph.D. We are actually talking
about two things at once—the end of the trail and the charming couple, in this case. Because the trail ends at the house and
the charming couple live within it, we get trapped trying to
make one sentence do what two ought to: "Evidently the trail
ended near a house. The charming couple who lived there courteously informed us. . . ."

Or, still trying to do two things at once, you write, "Climbing
up the mountain, my axe slipped from its carrying-case." What
happened was that you were climbing up the mountain, carrying an axe, and while you were climbing, the axe slipped. But
the sentence doesn't say that.

We all write ungrammatical sentences in rough drafts. Unless we are hopelessly lazy we read what we have written and
catch those errors—most of them at least (even a Ph.D. can
slip now and then)—and we correct them. We correct them,
that is, if we recognize what we have done wrong.

At this point I am going to do what I have done before—I am
going to leave you on your own. The kinds of grammatical
errors you can make are almost infinite, and I cannot illustrate
all of them. If you do not make them, there is no point in wast-
ing your time and mine on the subject. If you do make them,
your writing teacher will undoubtedly catch them, and he will
make some unintelligible red squiggles on the margin of your
paper or invite you in for a conference. And that is the way
your tendency to make errors of grammar should be handled.
Just think—if you do make errors in grammar, you will get to
know your writing instructor very well—and he is undoubtedly
a fine person to know. If you don't make such errors, you will
probably never make his acquaintance—and, unhappily, you
will never know what you have missed!

Usage

All languages and dialects have grammars. A student of the
language of an Indian tribe living north of the Arctic circle has

discovered that this language has a grammar as complicated as the English grammar. Others, observing and recording the speech patterns of seemingly illiterate children in the ghettoes of our big cities, have discovered a grammar as complex as the grammar you use.

For instance if you were asked about your father you might reply: He is sick. A week later the same question wondering about his continuing state of health would elicit the same reply: He is sick. The first answer means that the man is sick at the moment the question is asked; the second answer means that he continues to be sick.

A ghetto child asked the first question would respond: He sick. Asked the second time he would respond: He be sick.

The speech in both situations is grammatically correct for that child, if not for us, but yet we question it. (We would never, however, question the grammar or correctness of a French-speaking person with whom we came in contact.) We fail to see that the ghetto child's grammar is capable of making simply a distinction that requires a greater effort on our part; we would have to say, for instance: He continues to be sick. In other words there are probably very few cases of failure to use grammar "correctly." What we are actually complaining about in the case of the ghetto child is that his *usage* is not like ours.

No two speakers or writers use language exactly the same. For example, both of these sentences are grammatically correct:

> I know he's going to town.
>
> I know *that* he *is* going to town.

The distinction is one of usage. One pattern suits you; the other suits me.

It is possible to distinguish *levels of usage* in the speech patterns and writing patterns of Americans. Each of us uses several. At breakfast with the family we may use one; on the street with our friends another; in the science laboratory another; in the English classroom another; in applying for a job another.

For example, a study of girls who had been born and raised in the same area of New York and educated in the same public schools revealed that those who went to work as clerks for Macy's or Gimbel's department store continued to use language as they had at home, while those who secured employment in such Fifth Avenue shops as Sak's or I. Magnin's soon achieved a very close imitation of the language patterns used by their clientele.

The study implies another characteristic of language usage—the patterns of language we use are effective as social markers. Professor Kenneth Johnson of the Chicago Circle Campus of the University of Illinois grew up in the ghetto, but he has very effectively mastered the language usage patterns of the lectern and the professional world in which he works. But he smiles and says: "When I go back to where I grew up, I'd better cool that language quick and jive like the other cats, or they'd chase me off the streets. You know?"

English teachers, of course, would like to have the whole world talk as English teachers talk in the classroom. (But English teachers also have *their* levels of usage!) Such a Utopian state will never come about, and a good thing too. Nothing would make the language a dead and sterile language as quickly as that eventuality would.

Assignments for Discussion

Reproduce in class patterns of speech you use (or have heard used) in various social situations. You might report your experience with lawyers, ministers, businessmen, undertakers, athletes, teachers of various sorts. Can you recall any time when a speech pattern was confusing to you and you had to ask the speaker what he meant? What values are there in formal and informal speech patterns? Why can't the business of Standard Oil (for example) be conducted in jive?

Bring to class samples of usage as you find them in: catalogues and brochures issued by your college, annual reports of business firms, church bulletins, newspaper columns from various sections of the newspaper, advertisements. How many examples do you find of the language innovations of young people being taken over by the "Establishment"?

Anthologies such as Kottler and Light's *The World of Words,* Dean and Wilson's *Essays on Language and Usage,* Anderson and Stageberg's *Introductory Readings on Language* have many interesting essays on some of the subjects discussed in this and the preceding chapter.

H. L. Mencken's *The American Language,* while somewhat dated and sometimes in error, is a voluminous but fascinating discussion of the way we Americans use our language. You can open one of the volumes almost anywhere and read a few pages with fun and profit.

Dictionaries

A convenient and very good source of study of our language is a good dictionary—any of those listed at the end of Chapter 3. Dictionaries not only list words and define them, they also provide a history of the language, they indicate acceptable pronunciations, they provide a valuable commentary on our society and culture—and they provide a good source for topics on which you can write. For instance, using the old Vergilian *sortes* system (look up *sors* in your *Unabridged*) I put my finger down on *money.* The etymology of the word leads me to the Roman Goddess *Moneta,* thence to *mint, moidore, monetary.* Soon I am looking up *Joachimsthaler*—and before long I have more than enough facts for my essay.

In the past most dictionary makers were regarded as ultimate authorities—one turned to them not only to be exact but also to be proper. Dictionaries designed on that philosophy are termed *prescriptive*—the Second Edition of *Webster's New International Dictionary of the English Language, Unabridged,* is typical. More recently there has been a tendency for dictionaries to reflect the reality of language usage, on the theory that language is not created by lexicographers but by people. Such dictionaries tend to be *descriptive*—*Webster's Third New International Dictionary, Unabridged,* is typical. Both have their advantages. There are values in being able to refer to an authority when one is using words; too many of us use language all too carelessly. On the other hand words are not strait-jacketed into sentences; they are modified by their context, and the carefully chosen denotative word all too frequently becomes connotative. Then, too, language changes—its sounds change, new words appear, old words take on added meanings or change meanings or lose meanings or disappear, dictionary or no. There are advantages in having a fixed language, but there are also advantages in having a language that can grow, take on added power, keep up with our changing understanding of our public and private universes. Dictionary makers will have to live with these conditions—and you will have to live with the dictionaries.

Dictionaries begin with slips about four by six inches on which the staff collects examples of new words and new meanings for old words from newspapers, magazines, books, television, radio, the films—everywhere they find language being used. The word is listed in the upper left hand corner of the slip. Below that is written the phrase or sentence in which the word appeared, followed by the place and date of occurrence, and (if ascertainable) the name of the person who used it.

From the recorded context, the lexicographers determine the meaning of the word as it is used in that instance. Later, when the time comes to assemble the dictionary, the cards are grouped, first according to the word, then within each word-group, according to the meaning. Finally the staff selects the words that will be used in the dictionary, and the meanings for each word that will be listed.

Class Project

Elect an editor-in-chief who in turn will appoint departmental editors. Assign the balance of the class to departmental groups: sports, politics, science and medicine, business, education, home and family, fashions, and the like. Each group will search through magazines and books and listen to television and radio for new words or old words with new meanings. Once words are located according to the procedures described above, slips will be made. Finally the class will prepare a class lexicon. Perhaps the college newspaper would publish 10 or 12 of these each week for a period of time.

Topics for Discussion and Writing

1. Make a list of five subjects or objects, one chosen from each of the following representatives of our world: the natural world, buildings, organizations, concepts, and activities. Write three sentences about each. In the first sentence for each subject, describe the subject in *sensory* terms only. In the second of the three sentences, use *logical* words only. In

the third sentence use *emotional* terms only. You might, for instance, describe a rose in this way:

(1) The rose is *soft* to the *touch, fragrant* in *odor,* as it *waves* on its stem in the *warm* breeze. (2) Its petals are *red,* its stem and leaves are *green,* and it is about *fifteen inches tall.* (3) It is a *lovely* plant, but its loveliness is in strong contrast to its *ugly* thorns.

If, as you write, you keep this exercise in mind, you will find that you are writing sentences that are satisfying to your reader because of the amount and diversity of detail they present.

2. Make a list of 50 different hardware items or household items. Plan an efficient way of storing these items in your home, apartment, or room. Discuss your plan with your friends. Is there disagreement over it? Why?

3. Take a specific item such as your automobile, your type-writer, a book, an article of clothing. Construct a table of abstractions, using five levels of abstraction and placing your item at the bottom of the list. Define each level and be sure it categorizes the lower levels, is categorized by the higher levels.

4. Here are two sets of abstractions:

I. Furniture	I. Furniture
A. Overstuffed	A. Chair
1. Chair	1. Overstuffed
2. Sofa	2. Metal
3. Hassock	3. Wood

Why are "overstuffed" and "chair" at one level of abstraction in one list, in a reversed order of abstraction in the other? What sort of problems, therefore, might arise when you are classifying?

5. Select five words that your dictionary lists as synonymous. Write five sentences, using each word in one of the sentences so as to capitalize on the nuances of meaning in each word.

6. Make up an application blank for a job you hope someday to work at. On the blank ask the questions that you think a potential employer might ask. Sort the questions into logical groups and subgroups.

7. In what ways will the purpose for classifying *control* the collection of items to be classified? Is it possible that as we

organize or classify, we might change our purpose? Is this good or bad?

8. Analyze a static object: your car, your home, apartment, or room, your classroom or college building, your hometown. Be careful to identify the whole; define parts, subparts, and joints. (What is the joint between your room and the one next to it?) In an apartment building where each apartment is privately-owned, who is responsible for insects in the walls that separate the apartments? for the floors? Use an outline form for your analysis.

9. Analyze a dynamic process, again using an outline form. Where does the process begin and end? What are the stages and junctions?

6
Motion

In a letter to his daughter, F. Scott Fitzgerald wrote:

. . . all fine prose is based on the verbs carrying the sentences. They make sentences move. Probably the finest technical poem in English is Keats' *Eve of Saint Agnes*. A line like:

> The hare limped trembling through the frozen grass

is so alive that you race through it, scarcely noticing it, yet it has colored the whole poem with its movement—the limping, trembling, and freezing is going on before your own eyes.[1]

The American way of life is an active one. American prose tends strongly to reflect this active life. The verb is the form of language that reports action. The verb gives point to the pres-

[1] *The Letters of F. Scott Fitzgerald,* ed. Andrew Turnbull, Charles Scribner's Sons, 1963, p. 29.

ence of the subject. You should, therefore, pay attention to your verbs when you write.

Verbs

Because actions are so essential to our way of life, we have devised exceedingly complex variations upon the basic patterns. You may think that your experience consists simply of past, present, and future—but your language will betray you every time. Here is an illustration from Mark Twain:

When DeSoto stood on the banks of the Mississippi . . . Shakespeare was not yet born; a hundred long years must still elapse before Englishmen would hear the name of Oliver Cromwell.

Twain is aware that our minds telescope time so that it is difficult for us to conceive of vast antiquities of the past, and he is trying to give us some idea of the length of time in which the river has played a part in the affairs of Western Civilization. So he begins by taking us back to 1542, to the first recorded view of the river, and from that time he looks forward to a time that is future for DeSoto but past for Twain. The verb forms that are available to us:

elapse   elapsed   will elapse   will have elapsed   would
elapse   would have elapsed   will have been elapsed   would
have been elapsed   were elapsing   elapsing   have been
elapsing   had been elapsing . . .

make this and all other points of view toward action possible.

The verb as the word that carries action must deal with man's dilemma in time. Man thinks of himself as living in the present but it is a specious present, past as soon as it happens. Our "present" is like Xeno's arrow which flies from the bow to the target. It occupies a given space but the space it occupies consists of an infinite number of units of space between bow and target. Likewise the units of time of the arrow's flight consist of an infinite number, the sum of which is equal to the total time of flight. Man, too, occupies from moment to moment an infinite number of units of space and time. To the extent that man can comprehend such infinities his verbs are capable of describing his actions, as in this set:

pause   hesitate   waiver   stand   stop   rest   suspend   cease
break

More often, activities are conceived as continuing, and the verb can express degrees and kinds of continuing action:

> The Mississippi is always moving.
>
> The New Orleans *Times-Democrat* says . . .
>
> The President says he is as anxious for peace as any of us.
>
> Mary says she is going.

In the last three sentences, the verb "says" indicates three varying degrees and kinds of action. In the first case, the newspaper, although its story appears on one specific day, continues to "say" what is in the story as long as time goes on. If we wanted to indicate a point of view held at one time, we would write: On April 14, the *Times-Democrat* said. . . .

In the second instance, the speaker may have made his statement on a certain day, but until there is a public announcement of a position change, he continues to maintain his position—as the verb shows.

In the third sentence, "says" refers to the immediate moment.

> "What did Mary say?"
> "Mary says she is going."

The verb pattern may be repeated and mean something different each time:

> "Where are you going?"
> "I am going to the dance." (I've answered your question.)
> "You are not going to the dance."
> "I am going to the dance." (Try and stop me.)

The writer must make situations of this kind clear, either by underscoring the *am* (in this last case) or in some other way.

The context in which a verb appears will affect the verb's meaning:

> The quarterback called "Time," at the coach's signal. (using his voice)
>
> The coach called the quarterback to the bench. (perhaps with a hand signal)
>
> John called his brother on the phone. (by dialing)
>
> The model called the Camaro sells best. (in advertisements, for instance)

Jon called on his mother after the game. (he paid her a visit)

The verb can become other parts of speech:

He was *fishing* from the bridge. (verb)

Fishing is forbidden on the Hassayampa River in Arizona. (noun)

He lost his favorite *fishing* pole. (adjective)

He has become *fishing*-crazy. (adverb)

In these forms the word retains many of the qualities of the action-bearing verb, and at the same time it adopts many of the qualities of the form it assumes.

The verb can indicate states of mind (in time) of the writer and others:

. . . for it had come to be believed that the Mississippi . . .

. . . when it may be said to have become . . .

. . . whom I have been trying to describe . . .

If I had really known what I was about to require of my faculties, I should not have had the courage to begin.

The last-quoted sentence indicates another characteristic of the verb as well as the one indicated; the ability of the verb to indicate the degree of probability of the statement to other ideas.

The verb can indicate the direction of the action:

These men continued to run their keelboats . . .

The Pacific receives and carries . . .

When a circus came and went . . .

The verb can indicate the aspect from which the action is viewed:

I feel justified in enlarging upon this great science. . . . I feel sure no one has ever yet written a paragraph about it who had piloted a steamboat himself. . . . If the theme were hackneyed I should be obliged to deal gently with the reader. (Mark Twain, *Life on the Mississippi*)

I was a-stannin' heah, and de dog was a-stannin' heah; de dog he went for the shell, gwine to pick a fuss wid it: but I didn'y; I says, "Jes make youseff at home heah; lay still whah yo is, or bust up de place, jes as you's a mind to, but I's got business in the woods, I has!" (*Ibid.*)

The paragraph just quoted is a demonstration of one way in which we use verbs: as we become involved in reliving our experience, we shift our point of view from the past to the present. The tendency to do this is in all of us; ask anyone to tell you about a game he has seen and you will see this. In formal prose, the tendency should be resisted.

The amateur writer tends to present his material in disconnected paragraphs; the professional has a knack for writing sentences and paragraphs that give the impression of continuing action. The verb is very helpful in this case:

The fainter and farther away the scowmen's curses drifted, the higher Mr. Bixby lifted his voice and the weightier his adjectives grew. (*Ibid.*)

And he *was* always *talking* about "St. Looy" like an old citizen; he *would refer* casually to occasions when he "*was coming* down Fourth Street," or when he "*was passing* by the Planter's House," or when there was a fire and he *took* a turn on the brakes of "the old Big Missouri," and then he *would go on* and *lie*. . . . (*Ibid.*)

Parallelism is a way of emphasizing a point either in sentences or paragraphs; repetition of the verb or the verb form is a good way to achieve parallelism:

Huck Finn is persuaded to end the dismal suspense by *swimming* down to a huge raft which they have seen in the distance ahead of them, *creeping* aboard under cover of darkness, and *gathering* the needed information. (*Ibid.*)

. . . *if to be received by an Indian chief* who has taken off his last rag in order to appear at his level best *is to be received hospitably;* and *if to be treated abundantly* to fish, porridge, and other game, including dog, and have these things forked into one's mouth by the ungloved fingers of Indians *is to be well treated.* (*Ibid.*)

By adding modifiers to the verb we can add still more to its basic meaning:

On our trip we *fly over* Chicago.

The pilot has said we must *overfly* Chicago.

What you do badly you must *do over.*

Whatever you do, don't *overdo.*

When you have outlined in the past you may have been criticized because your outline was limited to subjects only and was not in the form of "complete sentences." The *complete sentence,* by definition, includes a verb. The past several examples ought to have given you a reason why the verb is important in the outline. There is another reason: since most paragraphs that begin with a topic sentence explicate or elaborate on the predicate of the topic sentence, and since the predicate includes the verb, it is wise to include the verb in the outline as a way of indicating the direction the paragraph will take.

Although the distinctions outlined above (and these are but a tiny sample of the range of possibilities) are complex and subtle, most of us learn how to make them at a very early age. We continue to make such distinctions all of the time, even though we can't describe them, even though we are probably unaware we use them. To a writer, however, even finer distinctions than these can be very important. Such distinctions are, as I have indicated, the hallmark of the professional writer. The more important your subject (whether or not you are a professional), the more you need to master detail in action.

Static Language

There is more to be said about the use of verbs in sentences. Despite the ease with which ideas can be organized on the basis of time sequence and continuing action, despite the astonishing variety that can be communicated by the English verb, some people seem to prefer static prose. I am not talking about mental motionlessness alone; what is almost as bad is that some people go to a great deal of work to kill a language that would live with less effort on their part.

For instance, they pad a sentence with adjectives in the notion they are thus describing the subject. But too many adjectives are either ambiguous or meaningless; they are the fatal potion that puts the language to death. If you must use modifiers, try to use the verbal modifiers, as in these examples: a little *sighing* opening of her lips; the *folding* doors into the parlor were *closed;* some of the apples had got *spoiled, lying* on the ground; he hunted over the apples that lay almost *rooted* in the *tufted* grass; *wandering* over the lawn, he stopped to look.

Secondly, one of the virtues of the English verb is often hired out to kill action. By one of two devices almost any verb can become a noun. A path where we walk becomes a walk. That is, if you use the verb as if it were a noun, it takes on some of the qualities of the noun and loses some of the qualities it had as a verb. You can reverse the trick if you wish: the Secretary of Defense talks about "Vietnamizing" the war in Southeast Asia. Purists to the contrary, businessmen continue to use language habits that they themselves deplore; they will continue to "contact" other businessmen at appointed times. Actually, the vocabulary of English is multiplied by such functional shifting, and 50 years from now even English teachers will contact their students.

The trouble is with the other device, mostly. Add a *-tion* or a *-ment* suffix to a verb and you have a noun. "Determine" becomes "determination," "measure" becomes "measurement " Add a noun-determiner (as we were calling them in 1972, *tne,* a preposition *of,* and an empty verb *accomplished,* ana you have monstrosities like:

The measurement of the head loss was accomplished.

instead of,

We measured the head loss.

True, *measurement* or *determination* sentences have a rhythm of sorts, but the idea is chained down by symbolic markers (*the, of*) and the empty verb which here is necessary to fill the grammatical hole dug by the sentence maker.

As a given root-word moves from action-form to name-form, the action becomes less and less significant:

Integrate by September 1, 1969. (basic)

To integrate by that time will present problems. (infinitive)

Integrating the schools is the biggest problem. (gerund)

Integration concerns North and South alike. (suffix-noun)

Each change raises the level of abstraction by deemphasizing the concept of change and motion. The basic verb conveys the greatest degree of motion. The infinitive form conveys a strong sense of purpose and specificity, but it limits the action. The gerund generalizes the action, and the suffix-noun—the most abstract form—creates a finite and static pattern of the whole action.

Properly used, these devices increase the range of English expression. Improperly used, they kill the language—*the, of,* and *accomplished* in the above example add no new information and get in the way of the facts.

Whenever you are tempted to use as a noun a word that is commonly used as a verb, try to revise the sentence so the verb takes its normal place. You will find that your revised sentence is probably shorter, livelier, and less subject to misinterpretation.

General Patterns

Although you should be concerned about subtle meanings of verbs and about maintaining the life of your sentences, you must also be concerned about the general patterns that are used in describing actions under varying conditions. Your choice of patterns will depend on your answers to these questions:

Are you describing an action that took place at a particular time:

On the 17th of June, 1673, the canoes of Joliet and Marquette reached the junction of the Wisconsin with the Mississippi.

Are you describing an action that took place over a period of time:

. . . the great Mississippi, the majestic, the magnificent Mississippi, rolling its mile-wide tide along, shining in the sun . . .

Are you describing an action that happened periodically:

Brown was always watching for a pretext to find fault; and if he could find no plausible pretext, he'd invent one.

. . . for we used to swim a quarter or a third of a mile . . .

Are you describing an action that took place in a short time:

When we presently got under way and went poking down the broad Ohio . . .

Are you describing an action that was completed at some time in the past:

Now when I had mastered the language of this water and had come to know every trifling feature . . . I had made a valuable acquisition.

Are you describing an action that might have taken place at some time in the past:

Then, if that sunset scene had been repeated, I should have looked upon it . . .

Are you describing some scene in the past with reference to some later moment, also in the past:

All the value any feature of it had for me now was the amount of usefulness it could furnish . . .

These are just a few of the possible patterns—and these examples were all found in just a few pages of Mark Twain's *Life on the Mississippi*. Similar patterns could be found for the present and for the future. Indeed, Charlton Laird has somewhere described 27 different ways of using the verb to indicate the future, and he adds that no one has catalogued all the possibilities of the verb.

There are other patterns, some of which are based on your purpose. For example, if you are reporting action so that someone else can evaluate and repeat it, you might write:

The salt was added to the water, and the mixture was boiled for ten minutes. (passive exposition)

If you were commanding someone to do something, you might write:

Add the salt to the water and boil the mixture for ten minutes. (command voice)

Do you want intellectual understanding:

Election day is the second Tuesday in March. (active exposition)

Or immediate action:

Register today and vote next Tuesday. (command voice)

You must decide how a particular sequence fits into the total action. Suppose, for example, you are preparing an account of the method that you used to solve a particular problem. You must describe one set of actions that occurred at a particular time in the past. The pattern you should choose is probably the simplest one imaginable; it is very much like writing a diary or simple journal:

On May 10 we injected into the popliteal vein of a dog ten drops of a liquid prepared by crushing a portion of the bulb of a dog which had died of ordinary canine madness, in three or four times its volume of sterilized broth. (Louis Pasteur)

It is logically possible and desirable to use several verb tenses in one description:

Rabies, whether in dog or man *comes* originally from the bite of an animal. It *is* never spontaneous. In fine, then, the first question *to be solved* is that of *knowing*. But in what way *shall we ascertain* the possible existence? Suppose a mad dog *were to bite* several sound dogs. . . . Into a second dog we *injected* . . .

All of these tenses of the verb are used within a few hundred words by Louis Pasteur in reporting his experiments with rabies.

If you are reporting or describing actions that take place simultaneously, you must choose one to be given intellectual precedence. The actions may take place all at once, but you can describe them only one at a time. In such cases you might proceed as in this example:

When the automobile engine is running, a number of actions are taking place at once: ignition, carburetion, compression, lubrication, and so on. . . . Ignition takes place when a mixture of air and fuel is compressed in the presence of an instantaneous spark. . . . Carburetion takes place at the same time as ignition. . . . Both carburetion and ignition depend on the rotation of the crankshaft.

If you are preparing an article about a research problem for a local newspaper, your college paper, or for a high school audience, you may decide to describe many steps that will appeal to a popular taste:

We had a lot of problems building the distillation apparatus. Neither of us had ever built anything out of glass, and so we had to learn how to heat glass, blow it, and fuse it. One day Joe was just getting ready to blow a tube into a bulb shape when . . .

If you were asked to describe the same research to a group of scientists, you might write as follows:

For our research we constructed a standard distillation process. We then placed a mixture of ethyl alcohol, water, and the experimental serum in the apparatus.

When you describe, keep these questions in mind:

• How much should I tell?

• How much does my particular audience need to know about the details of the happening?

• Does my audience need to know everything that happened? (Who lit the Bunsen burner is not important unless in the process he set fire to the building.)

• Will my audience be satisfied with just a description of the critical part of the event? Or will it want some context?

• How should steps in the description be grouped so that emphasis is maintained on the main action?

• Are there any dramatic possibilities in my description? If so, how should I take advantage of them? Will I run the risk of long-windedness or of boring my audience, or will I truly hold their attention with details that give point to my description and that keep the action moving toward its logical end?

When you are reporting an event, be sure that you report all pertinent information. For instance, if you are reporting an experiment, you must present the constants that cannot be varied without danger to the experiment: temperatures, quantities, terminologies, formulas, weights, kinds of equipment, times, and so on.

Some aspects of an event are significant; some are not:

John Smith was killed at precisely sixteen minutes and thirty-two seconds past eight P.M. last evening when his 1971 Hippo Eight overturned. (Are the time and kind of car that important?)

A Connecticut visitor to Arizona was killed last night when his sports car dropped into a wash at the corner of East McDollard and Rincon and overturned. (On some Arizona highways and city streets there are road hazards that visitors to the state ought to know about.)

Who

A particular problem facing the reporter of events is the degree to which he should use the active or the passive voice. When you write about happenings, you find circumstances in which it is necessary to make a choice between sentences such as these:

Alexandre Gustave Eiffel designed and built the Eiffel Tower. (active voice)
The Eiffel Tower was designed and built by Alexandre Gustave Eiffel. (passive voice)

The New York Mets won the 1969 World Series title.
The 1969 World Series title was won by the New York Mets.

In general you should avoid the use of the passive voice; yet there are occasions when its use is desirable or even imperative. Use the passive voice (1) when the agent is not known or cannot be described, (2) when the "agent" is not a person, (3) when the agent has no existence.

(1) Playing in the nursery with his elder brother of whom he was fond, *his arm was broken.*

(2) Abraham Lincoln *is enshrined* in the *hearts* of his countrymen.

(3) A Connecticut visitor *was killed* in an automobile accident.

Use the passive voice when that which is acted upon is more important than the actor or the agent:

Jesus *was crucified* by a mob of his countrymen and Roman soldiers.

Use the passive voice to emphasize the action:

If ever a youth *was* cordially *admired* and *hated* by his comrades, this one was. (Mark Twain)

That boy had been notoriously worldly and I just the reverse; yet he *was exalted* to this eminence, and I *was left* in obscurity. (Mark Twain)

Like the main-travelled road of life, it *is traversed* by many classes of people. (Hamlin Garland)

Sometimes the writer judiciously mixes the passive and the active to avoid the monotonous repetition of the subject (1) or to provide variety in a paragraph (2):

(1) The water was brought to a boil. In the meantime, Smith was trying to remember: was it safe to add sulphuric acid to boiling water?

(2) You have all heard it repeated . . . that men of science work by means of induction and deduction, and that by the help of these operations, they . . . wring from Nature certain other things, which *are called* natural laws . . . and that out of these . . . they build up hypotheses and theories. And it *is imagined* by many that the operations of the common mind *can be* by no means *compared* with these processes, and that they *have to be acquired* by a sort of special apprecenticeship to the craft. (Thomas Henry Huxley)

If you are a significant person in the action, use "I":

> Who killed Cock Robin?
> I, said the sparrow,
> With my bow and arrow.

If the report of what took place implies *why* something happened as well as *what*, emphasize the *actor* rather than the action:

The experiment had been attempted by others, but it was Count Rumford who designed the equipment which made it possible to demonstrate that friction produced heat.

It may be grammatically convenient to have a personal subject and the active voice:

> We suppose that ordinarily it doesn't rain in the desert.

rather than the impersonal subject and the passive voice:

> It is supposed that ordinarily it doesn't rain in the desert.

A combination of active and passive voice may be used to maintain emphasis on the subject:

> Pasteur discovered the cause of rabies in animals. His discoveries were verified by the research of others.

Use a personal pronoun if your state of mind is important:

> I think the President is wrong when he says that . . .

Use a personal reference if it is significant that a person acted. Not:

> It was decided to expand the war in Vietnam.

but,

> The President decided to expand the war in Vietnam.

Use a personal reference with a verbal modifier:

> Climbing the stairs, I slipped.

Incidentally, on the subject of verbal modifiers as used in the last sentence—unless you know what you are doing, don't begin sentences with verbal modifiers. Even Presidents of the United States get into trouble with them. One President (who had

never been a member of the United States Senate) sent this
telegram to a friend who was a Senator:

> Having been a long time member of the Senate, I congratu-
> late your state . . .

Another bit of advice—never begin a sentence with *being*.
You may find yourself in the same verbal predicament as the
President—but even if you don't, the use of the word leads to
bad style.

Use a personal reference if you are dealing with a specific
occurrence or giving directions:

> Open the door.

Under such circumstances, the existence of the person is factual, a part of the situation.

Do not use personal reference when dealing with theory.

Don't use "It is interesting that . . . it is obvious that . . .
it is important that . . . it is thought that. . . ." Either use
the imperative (Think!), a personal pronoun (I, you, we), a
simple adverb (interestingly, importantly), or (perhaps the best
choice) nothing at all.

If you want to kill your style, if you want to be tedious, ver-
bose, or exasperating, use the passive voice on every occasion.
On the other hand, if you want your style to be lively, if you are
concerned about your reader, if you are willing to stand up and
be counted, use the active voice.

Questions for Discussion

How many times has the author of this text violated any of
the precepts listed above? What other "errors" have you caught
him making?

Bring in examples of good and bad style. How many cases
can you find of errors in usage, grammar, and the like? (This
is not a contest; it's simply for your own enlightenment.) What
do you do about a case where an example of bad usage (Cigarettes taste good *like* cigarettes should) eventually becomes a
case of acceptable usage? Do you fight it at the beginning, then
gradually acquiesce? Or do you continue to man the barricades?

7

Patterns
of Persuasion

In 1900 the average factory worker worked 55.9 hours a week; his agricultural peer worked 67. When they had finished their day's work, they went home and read the evening paper. For recreation there was the corner saloon, an occasional vaudeville show, perhaps a magazine. A few families owned a player piano or a phonograph. The automobile was practically nonexistent, and there were not many telephones in workers' homes.

In the 1970's there is a strong tendency toward the 35-hour factory week, and the agricultural employee is disappearing from the scene. Where he exists, he relies on machines to do a great deal of his work, and his average work week is not much over 40 hours. For recreation for both there is the tavern, the motion picture, television, radio, the stereo, the telephone, the power boat, the camper, the family swimming pool, the pool table, all kinds of magazines, paperback books. And so on.

Here is one of the problems the writer faces—competition for the reader's time.

In 1900 commercial and industrial records were kept by hand. The typewriter was coming into use, but many letters were still being handwritten, and carbon copies were made by means of a press and damp tissues. There was a minimum of record-keeping as a result.

Today commerce and industry are threatened with drowning in a deluge of paper. The computer, spewing out information at a hundred lines a minute or better every 24 hours of the day, consumes paper by the ton. The mimeograph, ditto, offset press, printing press, and the office copier stack up printed copies of information at the rate of millions of sheets per hour. IBM cards are purchased by the truckload, and there are companies whose only business is to dispose of the used cards. Forests can hardly grow fast enough to supply the mountains of woodpulp our society consumes daily, weekly, monthly, annually.

Now to the consumption of paper has been added the consumption of electronic tape for the tape recorder, dictaphone, and the computer. And film—microfilm, microfiche film, motion picture film, color film, repro film, video film, and video tape.

Paper, tape, and film—all store words that writers have written.

American business and industry are pyramidal in structure. The output of words on paper, cards, tape, and film begins at the bottom of the pyramid and, through a process of digestion, condensation, abstraction, and judgment-making, moves up to the top, to the place "where the buck-passing stops," in the words of former President Harry S Truman.

Here is the other problem the writer faces—competition for the time of the busy businessman.

Competition. It sets up a need for you to identify your reader and his problems. It forces you to give him what he wants—what he will pay attention to. It demands that you conserve everybody's time—including your own.

Be brief when you write, is the advice. But not too brief, is my comment. $E = MC_2$ may be enough for an Einstein. The high school physics student needs a textbook, but at the same time, he cannot use the complex theoretical formulations on which the text is based. Brevity, conciseness must be set off against the particular audience's need for completeness.

There is another aspect to the problem of brevity as these quotations show:

In large bodies the circulation of power must be less vigorous at the extremities. Nature has said it. The Turk cannot govern Egypt and Arabia and Kurdistan as he governs Thrace; nor has he the same dominion in Crimea and Algiers which he has in Brusa and Smyrna. Despotism itself is obliged to truck and huckster. The Sultan gets such obedience as he can. He governs with a loose rein, that he may govern at all; and the whole of the force and vigor of his authority in his centre is derived from a prudent relaxation in all his borders. (Edmund Burke, *On Conciliation With America*)

In all the despotism of the East, it has been observed that the further any part of the empire is removed from the capital, the more do its inhabitants enjoy some sort of rights and privileges: the more inefficacious is the power of the monarch; and the more feeble and easily decayed is the organization of the government. (Henry Peter Lord Brougham, *Inquiry Into the Policy of European Powers*)

Burke's statement operates at a low level of abstraction; Lord Brougham's statement (based on Burke's) operates at a higher level of abstraction and is, therefore, more concise because it is less particularized. On many occasions and for many readers it would be the more desirable passage. The differences between the two have been commented on by E. J. Payne, a British critic:

[Burke's] particularising style is the essence of poetry; and in prose it is impossible not to be struck with the energy it produces. Brougham's passage is excellent in its way; but it pales before the flashing lights of Burke's sentences.

Sir Arthur Quiller-Couch (through whose energies I learned of the above materials) has this to say anent these passages:

. . . men who have written learnedly on the art agree in treating our maxim—to prefer the concrete term to the abstract, the particular to the general, the definite to the vague—as a canon of rhetoric.[1]

So conciseness and brevity should not be obtained at the risk of ambiguity or by the use of jargon or a highly abstract style.

[1] Sir Arthur Quiller-Couch, *On the Art of Writing*, G. P. Putnam's Sons, 1961.

And if one has developed an effective writing style, one should maintain that.

To be concise, complete, and intelligible at the same time calls for careful selection of detail, close attention to manner of presentation, and accurate gauging of the audience. One must ask, "For whom is this concise and complete?"

Persuasive Writing Patterns

In nonfictional prose writing (the kind we are considering) there are two basic patterns—the organic, which derives from the subject, and the classical, which derives from the application of an external form to the subject.

In either case the composition will have a beginning, a middle, and an end or, in another set of terms, an introduction, a body, and a conclusion. But in the organic pattern the three parts will derive from the subject, while in the classical form they will derive from the application of some external pattern to the subject.

Ring Lardner's "How to Write Short Stories" is included in this text as an example of the organic composition. Randolph Bourne's "A Philosophy of Handicap" is an example of the classic composition. Sometimes the term "structure" is used rather than pattern. Bourne's composition would be identified as an example of a formal structure, and Lardner's would be termed informal. You should be cautioned, however, that pure examples of either type probably do not exist. Often, patterns of writing are controlled by the medium in which the written piece will appear. Books are written in chapters or sections, newspaper stories are written in short paragraphs, sometimes of one sentence each. The pattern may also be dictated by its use in an organization; internal and external considerations play a part. The internal communication tends to make use of printed forms, to be economically produced, and to rely strongly on the background of common interests and knowledge possessed by members of the organization. The external communication tends to rely less on forms, to be self-conscious of the image being produced, and to be more dependent on the whims of top management. The use of some forms, such as purchase orders, statements, invoices and checks, simply indicates that in some areas the internal organization and the external overlap a great deal. The manufacturer of steel and the consumer of steel are part of a world in which steel is basic and central.

The pattern may have a relevance to time and space. A building, for example, exists in space and over a period of time. But it is possible to think of a building apart from space (as in a blueprint) or apart from time (a building that no longer exists, or that is projected). A process takes time and probably takes space, but while its spatial aspects can be ignored, its temporal aspects probably cannot. Ideas and generalizations (and their repositories) generally are considered as being apart from time and space; they exist in a timeless present.

The choice of patterns may be determined by the writer's purpose: instructing, informing, narrating, describing, proposing, defining, reporting, deceiving, persuading, recording, showing relationships, explaining, comparing, contrasting, analyzing, classifying, evaluating, judging, entertaining, presenting personal opinions, and so on.

The major external patterns (external in the sense they exist apart from any body of information or knowledge) that writing may take are as follows:

• Chronological: First, second, and third. Yesterday, today, and tomorrow. But we may begin at the beginning and work to the end, begin in the middle, go back to the beginning and then to the end, or begin at the end, then go back to the beginning.

• Spatial: We begin with the whole, then work through its parts. Or we begin with a part, work toward the whole. In either case there must be some sort of logical progression, and this progression must be clear to the reader. In both this case and the one above transitions and shifts must be clearly indicated.

• Chronological and spatial: A number of related circumstances changing more or less simultaneously in time. The process is complicated. Usually we take one circumstance at a time, carry it forward a certain amount of time, then go back and pick up a second circumstance. Or, it is possible to complete the sequence of each circumstance. In any case both spatial and temporal relationships must be made clear: While the carburetion process has been taking place in the carburetor, the ignition process is also underway in the battery, timer, and spark plugs.

• We can analyze an object or process in terms of its functions. We may begin with the function of the whole, then show how the function of each part contributes to the total function. The reverse procedure is possible.

• We can use a technique in which we begin with a generalization and move to the specifics. Or we can begin with the specifics and conclude with the generalization. A third variation permits us to begin with a set of specifics, create a generalization from them, then move on to a new set of specifics. Randolph Bourne's "A Philosophy of Handicap" is a good example of this pattern.

• If our subject contains a lot of "dry" fact, otherwise difficult to understand, the facts can be illuminated by anecdotes and ex-amples, interspersed between pairs of facts in a sandwich or layer-cake technique. The interpolated materials not only help explain, they also help relieve the dryness. But whatever is inter-spersed must be relevant to the subject and not offered, like a politician's jokes, merely to keep an audience awake.

• The cause-and-effect pattern: If this happens, then what logically comes next? The pattern may be reversed: These are the effects, what are the causes? In either case a third step might be to discuss remedies or to offer solutions.

• The *in media res* or "cliff-hanger" pattern: Begin with the most intriguing paragraph in your article, begin with the climax, begin with some highlight of the subject. You catch your read-er's attention, and you get him to ask, "How did this come about?" So you go back and show him—then go on to your conclusion. The term for the description of something that happened earlier is either "cutback" or "flashback."

• A pattern in which you assume that your reader is intelligent or emotional and will raise certain objections: You answer these objections. One device that is used is the "straw man." You pre-tend that you know what your reader's objections will be—you set up a figurative man of straw as a target for your slings and arrows. Then step by step by step you demolish your straw man.

• The "disclaimer": You announce that you will not write about a certain subject, and then you do in a negative style. "I will not tell you the low tricks that my opponent has played—how he has told the voters he is a conscientious citizen when as a matter of fact he has not voted in the last three elections. No, I will not tell you that."

• Begin with something very familiar and common as Thomas Henry Huxley does in his essay, "On a Piece of Chalk." Then move step by step to something complex. This is a good pattern to fol-low where your complex concept is too difficult to be discussed at once or where it is idealogically or emotionally unacceptable.

• The elimination pattern: You consider all possibilities and demonstrate one by one that each is unacceptable—until you come to the possibility you espouse. This pattern is most familiar in the detective novel.

• If you are reporting work you have performed or conclusions you have reached, you may want to lead your reader step by step along the same path you took. If he is very busy or likely to be impatient, you can report your results or conclusions first, then begin the step-by-step pattern.

• The interview pattern: You write about a subject as if you had asked a series of intelligent questions and got a series of articulate responses (even though it didn't go that way). The effect is one of immediacy—your reader becomes a part of the action.

• The so-called "inverted pyramid" pattern: You assume that there is some chance an editor will cut your article to fit a certain space, not by editing, but by literally scissoring your manuscript so that the latter part of the article disappears into the wastebasket. So you present a summary in the first paragraph, just in case that is all that he uses. In your second paragraph you elaborate your most important fact or idea from the first paragraph. In your third paragraph you elaborate the next most important fact. In succeeding paragraphs you add other information, on a scale of descending significance. This is the pattern used by many newspaper writers.

• In some cases (such as in Chevrolet's *Friends*) the artwork for each page is laid out first. The writer is then told how much space he has to fill and is shown where each block of space is. He must then compose his copy so as to achieve the total effect desired by the editor.

No matter what pattern you follow, you must, as you write, assume that your audience is not understanding you, or is not accepting your points. Either being the case, you can fall back on:

• Testimony: Support for your thesis from a co-worker, or a person in authority, or one whose status is generally accepted. Support from an authority must be carefully used, however. Millions of mothers accepted the wisdom of Dr. Benjamin Spock, the baby specialist; many were less willing to accept his advice on what to do about the Vietnamese situation.

• Example or anecdote: Use either as a particular to support your generalization—with caution, of course. Some writers create hypothetical examples: "If Einstein were alive today, he would . . ."

• Specific instance: An example closely related to your thesis.
• Concrete illustration: To illustrate an abstract concept: "When Keats said that 'Beauty is truth, truth beauty,' he meant . . ."
• Repetition, either directly or indirectly (variations on a theme).
• Restatement: Repetition by paraphrase.
• Summary.

Patterns Determined by the Role of the Author

The role that the author assumes as he composes may determine his pattern. For instance, he may see himself as historian or recorder:

There are, or were when the last census was taken in 1920, altogether some 24,000 morticians, funeral directors and undertakers in the United States. That is three times as many as there were thirty years ago; the population is less than twice what it was thirty years ago, and the total number of deaths not much more than a third larger. In 1890, the average mortician took care of 124 funerals a year; in 1920 he had only 56.[2]

He may see himself in an historical tradition of narrating or relating:

In the little village of Thetford in the ancient county of Norfolk, in southeastern England, there appeared in the late winter of 1737 an ill-clad child whose father, an humble pious Quaker, took him early to the meetings of a score of his fellow worshippers in the little church by the doors of the jail, filled in those days by the victims of religious and governmental intolerance.[3]

He may assume that his reader has adopted an attitude which needs to be changed, or that he is in ignorance of some cause:

The second reason why they will not be represented at the peace conclave is an even more practical one. Outside the borders of Russia, there will not be enough Jews left in Europe to profit by representation were it given them.[4]

He may have taken the role of a director, an instructor, or a teacher:

[2] Elmer Davis, "The Mortician," *The American Mercury Reader*, p. 134.

[3] William E. Dodd, "Tom Paine," *The American Mercury Reader*, p. 55.

[4] Ben Hecht, "Remember Us," *The American Mercury Reader*, p. 51.

Since you are an American, write like an American. . . . Express yourself in the pungent idiom of your time, your land and your people; there is no apology necessary; that idiom may produce sound literature as well as the language of the dons. Don't be afraid of slang if it will make your point better and more forcibly than literose expression. Much that was erstwhile slang has already been accepted into the dictionaries of formal English; much more will be accepted in the near future. But, on the other hand, don't make the mistake of believing that a mere imitation of Brook, Indiana, will get you any farther than an imitation of Cambridge, England.[5]

He may be trying to create a mental picture for his reader:

A kitten is not a pretty thing at birth. For many days it is a wriggling mite of lumpy flesh and sinew, blind and unaware, making soft sucking noises with its wet, toothless mouth, and smelling of milk.[6]

He may be trying to persuade you to accept one view rather than another, or he may be trying to explain one particular in terms of another:

Ground burial, one learns, is out of date and barbarous; mausoleum entombment is modern, progressive, and humanitarian, "as sanitary as cremation and as sentimental as a churchyard." When sentiment blends with sanitation, who can resist the joint appeal? "Here your departed loved ones will rest in permanent peace in an individual white marble tomb or crypt high above the ground where neither water, damp, nor mold can enter." And again: "You have the choice of just two things: the one typifying death in darkness, looking down, always down, into the grave; the other typifying death in light, death in sunshine and brightness, death in the hope of the Resurrection." [7]

His purpose may be to provide a definition of a term or particular he thinks his reader may be unclear about:

The statesman is one who divines the long future, foresees the place of his class and nation in it, labors intelligently to prepare his countrymen for their fate, combines courage with discretion, takes

---

[5] George Jean Nathan, "Advice to a Young Critic," *The American Mercury Reader*, pp. 353–354. Reprinted by permission of Julie Hayden Nathan.

[6] Alan Devoe, "Our Enemy, The Cat," *Down to Earth: A Naturalist Looks About*, Coward-McCann.

[7] Davis, *op. cit.*, pp. 130–131.

risks, has good luck, exercises caution where it is necessary, and goes off the stage with a reasonable degree of respectability.[8]

Although every writer is persuasive to some degree or another, sometimes one finds a writer being overtly persuasive:

Remember us in Wloclawek. Here also the Germans came when we were at worship. The Germans tore the prayer shawls from our heads. Under whips and bayonets, they made us use our prayer shawls as mops to clean out German latrines. We were all dead when the sun set. *Remember us!* [9]

The above passage is emotional, and uses the literary device of having the dead seemingly speak.

Sometimes the writer can be emotional and analytical at once:

Sometimes it is nothing but a shadow passing on the sun; sometimes nothing but the torrid milky light of August, or the naked sprawling ugliness and squalid decencies of streets in Brooklyn fading in the weary vistas of that milky light and evoking the intolerable misery of countless drab and nameless lives. Sometimes it is just the barren horror of raw concrete, or the heat blazing on a million beetles of machinery darting through the torrid streets, or the cindered weariness of parking spaces, or the slamming smash of the El, or the driven manswarm of the earth, thrusting on forever in exacerbated fury, going nowhere in a hurry.[10]

The emotional writer assumes that by using emotion he can arouse emotion in others; the analytical mind assumes that by dividing a whole into its fragments that the impression of the whole can be rendered more fully.

Sometimes a writer writes to give information as in this Walt Whitman report of himself:

Mr. Whitman, at the present date, continues to occupy a third-class clerkship in the Attorney-General's office, where, since the close of the war he has been employed.

Sometimes a writer overtly takes on the role of judge or evaluator, the two roles being similar but different in degree:

I am convinced not merely that it has a chance of winning but that, given the full material backing of the United States, it has only

[8] Charles A. Beard, "What Is a Statesman?" *The American Mercury Reader*, p. 41.

[9] Hecht, *op. cit.*, p. 53.

[10] From pp. 187–188 in *The Hills Beyond* by Thomas Wolfe (Harper & Row).

a minor chance of not winning. . . . In the same sense that Germany today surrounds England, *the Empire and its allies surround Germany and the conquered area under its tutelage.*[11]

Sometimes a writer thinks that his pill of knowledge is too bitter to swallow, or else he thinks that he can make a point in a light-hearted way, and so, for the moment, he adopts the guise of the entertainer:

Nevertheless, [the term "mortician"] has lately roused the fury of that captious purist, Mr. Aldous Huxley, who wants to know by what right the embalmers of the dead class themselves with such persons as mathematicians and academicians. Mr. Huxley, whose erudition is universal but not always accurate, forgets that the functions of academicians and morticians are essentially not very different.[12]

Beginnings and Introductions

A survey of articles written by well-known writers or published in outstanding publications shows the following.

Almost half of the articles surveyed begin with a statement of fact or opinion:

It is fashionable these days, in any discussion of language, to lament the misconceptions of eighteenth-century grammarians and rhetoricians—their faith in universal grammar, their distortion of English to force it into the mold of Latin grammar, their enthusiasm for prescription which created a school tradition still stifling thought about language.[13]

When the lights of Europe were hidden under the bushel of medieval scholasticism, China was living in the glow of a golden age.[14]

One by one, the frumpy-looking four-door sedans with skinny taxicab tires and Super Econo six-cylinder engines are being slipped into low gear and pointed toward the edge of an abyss.[15]

[11] Major Alexander De Seversky, "Crusade for Air Power," *American Mercury Reader,* p. 198.

[12] Davis, *op. cit.,* p. 129.

[13] Robert M. Gorrell, "Structure in Thought," *College English,* May, 1963, p. 591.

[14] Babette Deutsch, reprinted from *The Writer's Book.* Copyright, 1950, by Authors League of America, Inc.

[15] Daniel A. Jedlicka, "Gaining Respect on Woodward Avenue," *Esquire,* September, 1969, p. 113.

Many of these introductory lines, as well as what follows, are written in the present tense as a means of gaining immediacy, of putting the article in the reader's own present. (In some cases, however, the subject matter dictates the tense: "Abraham Lincoln *was born* on February 12, 1809"; *"Gone With the Wind presents* the South's side of the Civil War.")

Approximately one-third of the surveyed articles began with a situation:

Last night I dreamed I went back to Broadway (picture Joan Fontaine loping up the driveway smothered in shawls if you must picture something).[16]

Ranger Ralph Tingey awoke to hear someone pounding on his cabin door. It was 1 A.M. on August 22, 1967, and when Tingey opened the door he found two exhausted mountain climbers.[17]

A sixth of the articles began with quotations of several types:

"The glories of our blood and state
Are shadows, not substantial things." [18]

"But *really,* now—Romeo and Juliet stark naked? I mean—how far *can* movies go these days?" [19]

Two articles began with editor's notes in italics, designed to give the articles a context. The effect is, however, to give the article a sense of urgency or importance.

A few articles began with rhetorical questions:

Have your chickens stopped laying? Has your son developed warts on his thumbs? [20]

It is obvious that the tone of this piece is humorous. Where appropriate, humor is a good attention-getting and -holding device. But to use it where it is inappropriate is to give your reader a sense he has been conned.

---

16 Wilfrid Sheed, "Theatre," *Esquire,* September, 1969, p. 40.

17 E. D. Fales, Jr., "The Impossible Rescue," *Reader's Digest,* September, 1969, p. 50.

18 Denis Brogan, "How It Looks from the Colonies," *Esquire,* October, 1969, p. 26.

19 Judith Crist, "Sex and Violence in Movies and TV: How Harmful Are They?" *Good Housekeeping Magazine,* August, 1969, p. 59.

20 J. H. Plumb, "Perspective," *Saturday Review,* September 27, 1969, p. 24.

This article uses another device—the "you" point of view. A variation of this is the apostrophe, the direct salutation:

Hi, members of the class of '73 and future leaders of America.[21]

Hesitate, reader, one moment before you plunge into the following ten-page unprecedented Joe Namath section of this magazine.[22]

As you might suspect, these articles tend to be tongue-in-cheek and mildly satirical.

The article can begin with dialogue in the present tense for immediacy, and the dialogue can be taken from a dramatic point in the action:

"Lute, I think I'm going mad." I speak through clenched teeth to Lute Jerstad, lying beside me in the two-man tent. For several hours I have been fighting a terrifying claustrophobia.[23]

The introductory sentence or paragraph is a "hook," designed to stop us at the point, to involve us in the article. But it is more than that—it is also an indication of the kind of engagement that the author wishes to enter into with us. Thus he can speak in his own voice:

It was commencement day on College Hill and I was making my way leisurely across the green as if I had not a care in the world. Actually, I had many cares, and the graduation gown's length kept me from strutting.[24]

He can adopt the plurality of the editorial "we," even though he speaks only for himself:

Lately, we've been pondering the pigeons in Bryant Park. It seemed to us that they showed a decided preference for the paving, and trod the grass gingerly and seldom.[25]

Sometimes the voice does speak for a group:

[21] "The Sour Grapes Statement," Esquire, September, 1969, p. 89.

[22] "Joe Namath as World Metaphor," Esquire, October, 1969, p. 103.

[23] Barry C. Bishop, "How We Climbed Everest," National Geographic, p. 477. Copyright National Geographic Society, Washington, D. C.

[24] Barry Beckham, "Listen to the Black Graduate, You Might Learn Something," Esquire, September, 1969, p. 98.

[25] John Updike, "No Dodo," Assorted Prose, Alfred A. Knopf, 1969, p. 53.

These proposals would never have come about if we had not been a thoroughly *un*representative group of the faculty.[26]

The writer can speak to a rhetorical *you:*

If you want to tell a lot of people something, but you don't own a newspaper or a TV or radio station, and you haven't got the money to purchase a big ad in The New York Sunday *Times,* what you want to do is put out a leaflet. Tom Paine did it.[27]

He can speak to *you* directly:

Don't worry too much about your heart, as so many healthy people seem to be doing nowadays.[28]

He can make you a partner in an event in which he has taken part, or in a dialogue he has shared:

Seiji Ozawa sat on the terrace of the country club, idly spinning an ice cube in a half-glass of Campari and soda and watching the shadows lengthen on the elegantly kept greens of the golf course he didn't have time to use. "Six days," he said.[29]

He can share an idea with you:

Who gets appointed to the FCC, by whom, and under what circumstances are matters of fateful importance to the nation.[30]

These are a few of the strategies a writer can use to involve you in his writing. All of these openings came about as a result of a writer's evaluation of his reader's intelligence, his mood, his goals and drives, and similar concerns, and as a result of a writer's decision about himself, his subject, and his purpose.

Assignment for Discussion

Bring to class examples of article openers. Look for types other than those identified here. Discuss what the openers reveal to you about the writer and his audience. Then, by examining several

[26] "Exclusive and Unauthorized: The Report of Professor X," *Esquire,* September, 1969, p. 104.

[27] James Simon Kunen, "kaPOOMcha: The Mimeograph Revolution," *Esquire,* September, 1969, p. 102.

[28] Henry Morton Robinson, "The Heart—Wondrous and Courageous Organ," *Reader's Digest,* 1948.

[29] Robert C. Marsh, "Ozawa in Transit," *Saturday Review,* September 27, 1969, p. 45.

[30] Robert Lewis Shayon, "New Boys for the FCC," *Saturday Review,* September 27, 1969, p. 45.

from one magazine, try to determine if the magazine seems to be published for more than one kind of reader.

The Body or the Middle

Any composition is infinite in its possibilities, and so are its parts. What has already been said about external patterns applies to the body of the composition. What will be said about various patterns, about sentences, paragraphs, and style also applies. Still, because of the infinite variety of possible compositions, it is not possible to cover the subject completely. Only a beginning to the topic is possible.

As you read—in this text and elsewhere—you should consider carefully the patterns you encounter—in the whole and in the parts. Examine and analyze the rhetorical strategies used—from individual sentences to entire books. The best teacher of writing is the professional writer—not in what he says he does but in what he does. Learn from his compositions.

Closings

Many writers have trouble in beginning a paper: "I know what I want to say, but I don't know how to begin." Just as many have equal trouble in closing, and so the paper fades off into nothingness as if the writer had fallen asleep while telling his tale.

The *summary* is one type of closing:

Nuclear war, with or without anti-missiles or elaborate shelters, is no longer "thinkable" due to a fatal flaw in the assumptions of all our military war-gamers, namely the unexpectedly severe biological sensitivity of the mammalian reproductive system to genetically important by-products of nuclear weapons, which now must be regarded not merely as vastly destructive explosive and incendiary devices, but as the most powerful biological poison weapons that man has yet invented.[31]

An event that brings to an incontrovertible end the sequence of events being reported:

When the ten seconds were over Sullivan failed to respond, and Corbett was declared the winner. Then Sullivan asked in a weak voice: "Say, am I licked? Did that young fellow do it?"
His seconds sorrowfully admitted that that was the case.[32]

[31] Ernest J. Sternglas, "The Death of All Children," *Esquire*, September, 1969, p. 1d.

[32] "The Death of King John," *Collier's*, September 10, 1892.

A call for action, or a solution to a problem that has been presented:

Take a look at yourself as the man in the white jacket shakes his head over you, tells the boys with the stretcher not to bother and turns away to somebody else who isn't quite dead yet. And then take it easy.[33]

A non-summary statement that anticipates a point not implied in the article:

"We went six miles," said Coffyn [speaking of an early airplane flight].
But we had gone farther than that. And how much farther we will go no man can tell.

A similar statement inculcating a moral:

And as long as man lives the tale will be told to the uplifting of men, for showing them the divinity which is man's and his kinship to God.

A paradoxical statement that teases the mind:

Yet in that manner it is worthy of note that it took a decided brunette to write the story ["Gentlemen Prefer Blondes," by Anita Loos] and that, after vainly trying at least thirty golden-haired actresses in the leading role [in the dramatic version], the manager of the production on Broadway was driven to buy a wig the color of canned corn and place it on June Walker, who, in her own right, is about as blonde as a ton of coal.[34]

A key word or phrase, perhaps the title of the piece:

. . . So he stayed, saying nothing; only, with the sense of her own sustained, renewed and wonderful action, knowing that an arm had passed round him and that he was held. She was beside him on the bench of desolation. (Henry James, "The Bench of Desolation")

An aphorism, perhaps one that is familiar:

> Verily, it takes all sorts to make a world.
> The Coast Guard is neither wet nor dry; it's
> just the Coast Guard.

[33] J. C. Furnas, "—And Sudden Death," *Reader's Digest*, 1935.

[34] A. Woollcott, "She Didn't Mean to Do It," *Collier's*, December 11, 1926.

An answer to a question that has presumably been raised in the reader's mind by the paper (in this example the answer is ironic):

Figuring hurriedly with a blunt pencil and a blunter arithmetic, this twenty bucks a week for eighteen hours a day works out to what? Too much for the pleasure given the public; too little for the pain given the patient.[35]

There are probably as many kinds of closings as there are trees in the forest; here are just a few. But each indicates an attitude on the part of the writer, an attitude deriving from his viewpoint toward himself, his audience, his subject, and perhaps his medium.

One External Pattern—The Report

The pyramidal structure of American industry and commerce, whatever its function—manufacturing, processing, transporting, selling, repairing, advertising, publishing, mining, growing— thrives on information. It cannot, in its present state at least, live without information. If you take employment in industry or commerce, whatever your primary job you will also be a link in the organization's information process.

That process is one-way—from the bottom of the pyramid to the top—most of the time, but communiques do come down. It also flows from within the pyramid to without—to customers, suppliers, government agencies, the mass media.

A cardinal rule: As information moves to the top of the pyramid, it must be compressed. In a plant having a thousand persons on the production line, a lot of information is developed at that level. If the company is managed by one man, the amount of information that reaches him must diminish—say in the proportion of one one-thousandth of what the quantity is at the bottom. The ratio is not important. But the information that reaches top management must be abstracted from all the relevant information that is generated at the bottom. At the bottom, for instance, each of the one thousand production employees works an average of eight hours a day and earns so many dollars for the day's work. You have one thousand people walking out of the plant at the end of the day, each concerned about his gross pay and his take-home pay. Top management is concerned with the total

[35] John B. Kennedy, "Good Night, Lady," *Collier's,* July 23, 1932.

number of dollars it must have available for the inevitable pay day, the total number of dollars to be set aside for payment into social security. On that same day ten people have written several hundred purchase orders. Top management must know how much operating income has been obligated by those purchase orders and when the money will have to be ready.

The flow of information upward is through reports. Reports consist of printed forms, formal and informal memorandums, telephone conversations, face-to-face meetings, letters. Printed forms—the IBM payroll card, the purchase order, the paycheck —are designed to simplify repetitious reporting and to standardize the reporting of information. Formal memorandums are designed to make sure that information flows—and that it is recognized as a certain type of information when it is received.

As information flows upward it is compressed. Accounting receives all information about expenditures and receipts of monies and forwards a Daily Statement of Receipts and Disbursements —perhaps a one-page form. Sales receives hundreds of orders and sends to management a Report of Daily Sales. Similarly, Personnel, Receiving and Shipping, Production, Purchasing send along similar reports. With these reports in hand, management then makes the necessary short-range and long-range decisions about capital, operating funds, manpower, materials, plant.

These reports must present management with all of the information needed to make decisions in such a way as to save management the maximum possible amount of time. Reports must be presented, in other words, so as to enable management to make a "Yes" or "No" decision.

The Memorandum Report

This usually takes up some aspect of the company operation that cannot be handled by the printed forms available. For instance:

October 17, 1972

To: James McDougall, Executive Vice-President

From: Henry James, Plant Superintendent

Sales has accepted an order for 1,000 deluxe Widgets to be delivered not later than November 15. Inventory is depleted on this item at present, and production lines in operation have been committed to production of the standard Widget until December 1. Please authorize opening of the production line in Building M for 20 working days, and the employment of 10 additional machine operators.

Such memorandums must state the problem, the pertinent factors, and the solution desired. Even though a matter such as this has been already decided in a meeting or in a telephone conversation, the written paper work is required. All necessary facts must be presented, all authorities cited. It is not only a matter of making management's decision one of "Yes" or "No"; it is also a matter of delegation of authority and responsibility.

Assignment for Writing

Write a memorandum to a member of the college administration citing some action that you or a group including you think is necessary. Outline the "chain of command" through which the memorandum must pass. (In class you might discuss why the "chain of command" concept exists—as it does in colleges, industry, commerce, government, the military—and what are the consequences of by-passing some links in it.) Be sure that the memorandum states all relevant or pertinent facts and outlines the desired action in such a way that the appropriate administrator may answer "Yes" or "No."

A Second External Pattern—The Proposal

Proposals propose action of some specific kind. Within an organization, they move from lower echelons to higher echelons. External proposals move from one organization to another.

Proposals may be initiated by the proposer, or they may be initiated in response to an overt or implied invitation. Within an organization, an engineer may propose a new model design or a new production technique. A state highway commission may advertise for bids for a highway development. The federal government may set up a bureau to consider means of attacking some social problem. The mere existence of a foundation, such as the Ford Foundation, implies that the foundation will look at proposals.

The proposer may construct his own proposal, creating both problem and solution. He may work within broad guidelines laid

down by another and designed to allow him to innovate programs. Or he may work within very tight restrictions as in bid-
ding on a project for which designs have already been made.

The proposal:

• Must specify in precise terms just what the proposer intends
to perform or do. The language of a proposal is usually formal
or legalistic for the proposal, when approved or accepted, becomes a contract. Internal proposals are the least formal; proposals to governments or foundations are formal; bid proposals
tend to be couched in legalese. In the latter cases, a lawyer's advice is often useful.

• Must specify the benefits to be gained from the proposed action. Where the proposal is in response to some sort of need, the
need must be described and documented. Such documentation
often requires considerable research.

• Must support the proposer's statement that he is able to do
what he proposes. Usually this includes references to past experience with similar or analogous activities. The more substantial the background of the proposer, the less need be said about
reliability or the willingness or ability to carry a project through
to a conclusion.

• Must specify the time of performance as exactly as possible.
Most proposals specify exact opening and closing dates. In some
cases failure to perform within the time promised results in financial punishments or other kinds of punishment (civil of
course).

• Must specify the cost as exactly as possible. In some cases
it is possible to estimate and then negotiate for additional funds
as the work progresses. In other cases a fixed cost may be sup-
plemented. In most cases, however, the proposed cost may not
be changed once it has been approved. The proposed cost must
take into consideration direct and indirect labor costs, overhead
and burden charges, interest, insurance and taxes, rents and
storage charges, expendable and nonexpendable supplies and
equipment, transportation, office expense, depreciation and am-
ortization charges—any expense that is relevant and applicable.

• Must specify all sources of funds. If a proposal for a joint
university-government project is being made, the financial responsibility of each party must be stated.

• Must specify personnel available or necessary. Such specifications may be specific (Professor X will research one-third time

the spring quarter), or somewhat less specific (Three draftsmen will be assigned to the project).

• Must specify buildings, space, equipment, and the like to be made available or that will be required. In the latter case provision for disposal or future use (after the proposed project is completed) must be described. Where any unusual problems may arise (such as the disposal of atomic wastes, for instance), these must be clearly outlined. In case the proposed project would require alterations, remodeling, or changes of any kind, before and after the project, these must be described, and the financial responsibility stipulated.

• Must stipulate the assignment of any patents, profits, or other benefits or rewards that may derive from the project.

• Must match the terms laid down by any guidelines or granting organization. In addition, proposals must, by stipulation or implication, conform to all applicable ordinances, rules, laws, and regulations.

The style of the proposal is in the conditional mood. "Would" and "should" replace "will" and "shall." Later, if the proposal is accepted, it is sometimes rewritten as a "Plan of Operation." In such cases, "should" and "would" are replaced by "shall" and "will."

Assignment for Discussion

Try to locate guidelines such as those prepared by the United States Office of Education, the Department of Health, Education and Welfare, and the like. Discover what you can about such organizations as the Rockefeller Foundation and the Ford Foundation. Inquire as to the techniques for innovations on your own campus. How, for instance, do new courses, departments, and programs come into existence? What is the machinery for hiring *additional* teachers? How do you get approval for a new student program such as a fraternity, a magazine, a dance, an entertainment?

Assignment for Writing

Prepare a proposal (for presentation to the appropriate parties) for some useful innovation on campus, in your neighborhood, or in your town. Be sure that you know the routing of such proposals (in a city with a city manager, is your proposal addressed to the city clerk, the council, the manager, or a department head?).

Problem-Solving

The approval of a proposed project often leads to the writing of periodic, progress, and final reports. Sometimes a number of copies are made and distributed to interested parties.

The form of such reports usually is based on an outline for problem-solving established by John Dewey some years ago. Because this outline is also utilized in establishing research and development procedures and small group operations, it is well worth knowing.

I. Recognition of the problem. It may be personal, social, civic, governmental, institutional, organizational, industrial, legal, moral, religious, academic.

Problems may be categorized as:

Cases of determining fact.

Cases of determining the value of something.

Cases of determining a process, a system, a method, a technique.

Cases of determining the feasibility or usefulness of a system, a process, a method, or a technique.

Cases of comparing, contrasting and evaluating two or more systems, objects, methods, techniques, processes, designs, proposals and the like.

Cases of determining a design or model.

Categories are not necessarily limited to these.

II. Verbal definition of the problem. Definitions must be as precise as possible; language must be clear. The definition is often made in the form of a statement. Not: We must do something about the water supply. Rather: The hardness of the water must be reduced from 19 points to 15 points. Or: Based on predictions of population growth, the City of Phoenix will require 1 million more gallons of potable water in 1973 than it did in 1969.

III. History of the problem. Last year we didn't have this problem; why this year. Or: Professor X, in his analysis of air pollution in California, failed to consider the increasing reliance of the scheduled airlines on the jet plane. The history answers the questions: How, when, and where did the problem begin? Who recognized it and defined it? Who or what is affected by it, and to what extent or degree?

IV. Benefits to derive from a solution to the problem, or harms to derive if the problem is not solved, or both.
V. Hypothetical solutions to the problem. In one way the "proposal" discussed above is an extended form of the hypothetical solution. In general, the considerations outlined there apply here.

Small Group Operations (Committees)

Committees are usually formed for determining fact, defining problems, solving problems, or implementing solutions. When a committee is formed, its purpose should be defined and the members informed. Its activities should be limited to its purpose.

Committees are of two types. The first is the permanent or standing committee, which usually is subject-oriented: committee on finances, committee on committees, and the like. Such committees may work in any of the areas noted above. The second type of committee is the *ad hoc* committee, which is formed to deal with a specific problem; when its work is completed it ceases to exist.

Committees usually file reports of their work with the authority that created them. The reports may be informal, in letter form, in which case they are much like minutes; or they may be formal, in which case they will follow the form outlined below, or some variation of it.

The Formal Report

The formal report necessarily derives from Dewey's outline. It may be short, medium, or long. Its form is based not only on the Dewey outline, but also on the work done and a consideration for the audience for the report.

The elements of the formal report are:

I. Statement of the Problem.
   A. Definition of the Problem
   B. History of the Problem
II. Hypothetical solutions to the Problem
III. Work done to verify the hypotheses
IV. Conclusions, evaluations, and judgments
V. Recommendations and proposal for future work where necessary

All elements of the report except "work done" are described elsewhere in this text. Work done consists of: designs; models; tests; experiments; calculations; committee meetings; telephone calls; letters, authorizations, or approvals of modifications in the original proposal; executive decisions; financial statements and related papers; legal papers; photographs, drawings, sketches, figures, tables and graphs; any other form of pertinent information.

Most of the "work done" will come to the report writer in the form of paper work, the nature of which is indicated by the above list. He may wish to supplement this with interviews with project workers.

There are two basic patterns for the report form. The first pattern begins with a brief summary of the problem, followed immediately by the conclusions and recommendations. The balance of the report consists of:

> Detailed statement of the problem
> Hypothetical solutions
> Report of work done
> Detailed conclusions
> Evaluations
> Proposal for future work

Philosophically, this pattern begins with the skeletal syllogisms, or, in other words, the important generalizations. These permit the reader to understand the framework of the report before he is obliged to examine it in detail.

In this pattern, the balance of the information is provided as a record. In case there is some doubt about the conclusions or recommendations, now or later, the record is there.

The second pattern is one which is preferred by most scientists, the editors of most scientific journals, and by many report writers. This pattern is based on the assumption that the reader wishes to follow the original mental and physical situations as they originated and developed. The pattern of the report is:

> Statement of the problem
> History of the problem
> Hypothetical solutions
> Report of work done
> Conclusions, evaluations, judgments, recommendations
> Proposal for future work

Proponents of the second pattern often recommend a brief abstract of the report at the beginning. In any case, your reader will want to know, before he begins to read the report, the answer to this question: What's in it for me? One way to answer that question is in the title.

Let it be said that a good deal of figurative blood flows whenever and wherever the more enthusiastic supporters of the two patterns come together.

Assignment for Discussion

Examine reports of work in publications such as *Science* or *Scientific American,* in some of the scholarly journals you find in your library, or in one of your professor's offices. Identify the various sections of the report according to the terms outlined here. If you can find examples of both types of reports discussed here, compare them and discuss the merits of each form as you see them.

Assignment for Writing

Write a report of the work of some committee on which you have served; of some research you have done; of some experiment you have performed; of some problem you have solved. Follow one of the forms outlined.

Topics for Discussion and Writing

1. Ask a local businessman, industrialist, or educator to speak to your class on the problems he sees in communications. He could include in his remarks something about the decision-making process, the quantity of paper work, and the relationships within his organization and with the several audiences with which his organization is concerned.
2. Bring to class articles that interest you. Good hunting grounds are the pages of *Reader's Digest, Harper's, Atlantic, Esquire, Playboy,* and often *Time, Newsweek, Life.* You may find collections of articles in the library. Examine the structure of the articles—their introductions, the pattern of development, the closings. What can you deduce about the voice that is speaking in each one? To what extent does each article represent personal experience? research? reading? What seems to be the philosophy of each writer?
3. Write an article on some subject that interests you. Perhaps a place, or a person, or a way of doing things—something that

you personally know about. You may want to implement your personal knowledge with some reading. Try to give your article point—something that will make it meaningful to your classmates.

Further Reading

Technical Report Writing, James W. Souther, Wiley, 1957.
Writer's Market, Writer's Digest, Cincinnati. Annually.
English Prose Style, Herbert Read, Beacon Press, 1952.
Writing and Selling Non-Fiction, Hayes B. Jacobs, Writer's Digest, 1969.
Writing and Selling Feature Articles Third Edition, Helen M. Patterson, Prentice-Hall, 1956.

8

Definition, Description, Narration

We are constantly responding to the question, "What do you mean by that?" Either it is asked directly or it is implied. When we write we must anticipate the fact that our reader will be asking this question as he reads. He will be asking for definitions because we are taking him into areas where he has no awareness or knowledge. There is no point in taking him very far into areas he already knows about. In one sense everything we write is definition; still, specific definitions must be based on our estimate of our readers' ignorance.

There are a number of ways to define, and it is important that you know what they are; you ought to know what is being done for and to you and what is not. It is also important that you know how to define. Not every method will work in every case, so you ought to be able to make a choice.

The definition ought to be simpler than the term you are defining, if at all possible. Most of the time you are trying to explain the unknown in terms of the known; you must find some
way to latch your mind onto your readers'. So you proceed from
simple concepts to complex ones. If the terms of the definition
are less well known than the word to be defined, the reader will
learn nothing. There is no point in telling him that a "codger is
a senile valetudinarian."

Yet some dictionaries do this all of the time. How many times
have you looked up a word to find that you have to look further
to find definitions of the words in the original definition? There
have undoubtedly been times when you have come full circle
back to the original word, as ignorant as you were at the beginning. Sometimes such a definition is supertechnical from carelessness or perversity; sometimes from the dictionary maker's
need to be brief; sometimes from his concern for delicate social
matters. But occasionally the problem results from the need of
giving exact limits to a generally used and carelessly limited
common idea. Try, for instance, to make an adequate simple
definition of "red"—or, for that matter, "definition."

You should not define a term in terms of itself. Statements such
as "a radish is a plant in the radish family" or "pressure is the
result of pressing" are not very useful—they add no new information to the reader's stock of knowledge. If your reader doesn't
know the word being defined, he won't know it any better as a
different part of speech. On the other hand some compound
terms may be partially repeated: "An atomic bomb is a bomb in
which the explosive power is released by fission of the atom."
Here the genus (bomb) is part of the term, but we presume that
our readers already know what a bomb is. We are distinguishing
a very special type of bomb.

Still, one must leave the famous "A rose is a rose is a rose" to
imaginative writing. Although the statement implies that all
definition is merely approximation and therefore unsatisfactory,
yet for a writer's purposes the definition is useful and necessary.

Finally, from a logical viewpoint, most dictionary definitions
are redundant: "An aardvark is a large burrowing nocturnal
mammal with extensile tongue, powerful claws, large ears, and
heavy tail that feeds largely on termites" is simply an equation,
both sides of which are equal. Sooner or later, if we want to
know what an aardvark is, we have to visit the zoo.

Uses of Definition

The uses for the definition are many. Primarily, you define either to specify in your paper what the term means in that paper (as in a legal contract or at the beginning of a statute, or even in a mathematical statement such as "let X equal . . ."), or to set limits on an idea that you wish to explore only in part. Most common terms are defined just for convenience, or for recalling the half-forgotten. In research the definition that genuinely explores a concept is important. Although the form of logical definition may not reflect these differences of purpose, for the writer framing the definition, purpose determines the degree to which the definition is elaborated.

Definitions may be partial, logical, operational, or extended. Perhaps the most common form of definition that we all use when we speak or write is the circumlocution (although our reasons for using circumlocutions may be haste or ignorance). When we say "a huge shaggy-haired brown and white dog with a large head" instead of "St. Bernard," we are being circumlocutious, but we are also defining.

Partial definitions are used when you are merely identifying an idea and a whole definition is not required. Perhaps the genus (class) alone will do:

A halogen, a non-oxygenated radical, can be used.

Here the parenthetical phrase is less a definition than it is an implied statement of the reason that a halogen can be used. However, the genus also serves to identify a particular aspect that is important.

Here are some partial definitions:

He . . . had contented himself with becoming not a full-fledged doctor, but an *officier de sante*—an inferior category of medical man then in existence. (*Madame Bovary*)

. . . to take the place of *Saint Antoine*, that dramatization of the thought of the entire world . . . (*Madame Bovary*) (Appositive used to define partially)

Writing—and from here on I speak of novels, short stories and articles, including essays and non-fiction . . . (James Michener)

A short story must have a single theme—Edgar Allan Poe's element of "artistic piquancy" . . . (Richard Summers)

. . . liberation of the "world countryside" (Asia, Africa, Latin America) in order to encircle and destroy the "world cities" (Europe and North America) . . . (*The Arizona Republic*)

. . . rapid advances in hydroponics (growing crops in chemically buffered troughs of water) . . . (*The Arizona Republic*)

Another form of the partial definition is essentially demonstrative. One might call it a *definition by pointing* as opposed to a definition by logic. "The top scale on your rule" and "the red-haired boy over there" are examples of pointing out. So is the picture of the aardvark in your dictionary. The statements or picture identify the particular subject, but they do not explain it. The demonstrative definition must be used with caution.

Defining by analogy provides only a partial definition. "A torus is a geometrical figure that is shaped like a doughnut." "The Van Allen rings are banana-shaped."

Specific instance is another kind of partial definition. For example, under the term *abandon* in one dictionary we find:

> She danced with abandon.
> We will have to abandon the drought area.
> She abandoned her child.

In this case, specific instance is used to establish nuances (shades) of meanings.

The negative definition is a definition that attempts to pinpoint a notion by saying what it is not: "Work consists of whatever a body is *obliged* to do," says the narrator of *The Adventures of Tom Sawyer*, "and Play consists of whatever a body is not obliged to do."

F. Scott Fitzgerald once defined the ideal housewife in this way:

> Did she work for a while in her husband's office and learn how his business was run, so that she could talk to him about it in the evenings? . . . Did she buy a football guide and master the rules so that she could discuss the game understandingly with her sons? . . . Nor did she organize a family orchestra in which Clarence played the drum, Maisee the harp and Vivian the oboe. She knew nothing about football nor did she ever intend to. . . .

No; she was not one of those appalling women who know more about the business of everybody in the house than anyone knows about his own. She never bored her boys by instructing them in football. . . . And she never dragged the paper industry onto the domestic hearth. She couldn't even solve her own daughter's algebra problems. . . . In fact she was not at all the model mother, as mapped out by Miss Emily Hope Dempster. . . .[1]

Definition by etymology is another form of partial definition. If we look up the word *abacus* we will find that it is derived from the Greek word meaning "counting board." Definition by etymology is sometimes a useful way of defining; it helps, perhaps, when we confront *teleology* for the first time, if we know that *tele-* derives from the Greek word for "end," and *-logy* derives from the Greek for "word." Sometimes though the etymology of a word is simply a means for getting us off our point and into a historical discussion. Here is an excellent example of the etymology technique:

A *toomuller* is a peculiar American-Jewish phenomenon, yet one that is easily recognized as a manifestation of the ancient and universal zany or buffoon. The name derives from the Yiddish *toomul*—translating roughly, "tumult"—and originated in the famous "Borscht Circuit" of summer resorts in the Catskill Mountains northwest of New York City. There, as in resorts everywhere, a rainy day can portend calamity. . . . Hotel and vacation-camp managers learn to sniff boredom before it begins, and are ready to call their *toomullers* at the first fall of silence. These young men . . . are prepared to leap into action, to make a *toomul* to disrupt the creeping *ennui;* improvising mock mayhem, chasing each other in gymnastic abandon, toppling into swimming pools, punctuating their frenetic excursions with prat-falls and other assorted slapstick. *Toomullers* must learn to make people laugh. . . .[2]

Another form is *definition by synonym.* For instance, under the several definitions of *abdicate* in *Webster's New Collegiate Dictionary,* we will see the abbreviation **Syn.** in bold black letters. Following the abbreviation, the dictionary makers differentiate

[1] F. Scott Fitzgerald, "Imagination—And a Few Mothers," *The Ladies' Home Journal,* June, 1923. Reprinted by permission of Harold Ober Associates Incorporated. Copyright 1923 by Frances Scott Fitzgerald Lanahan. Copyright renewed.

[2] Martin Dworkin, "The Clowning of Danny Kaye." Reprinted from the March, 1956, issue of *The Progressive* magazine. Copyright © 1956 by The Progressive, Inc.

among *abdicate, renounce,* and *resign.* A variation of the form is
the equation: "A spinster is an old maid."

The opposite of definition by synonym is *definition by antonym.* In the case of *abdicate,* we see the abbreviation **Ant.,** followed by the directions to look up *assume.* We must be cautious
about definition by antonym. In the phrase, "he has a black
heart," *black* is not the antonym of *white.*

Logical Definition

Although the proper study of language includes many problems, most people limit their interest to the essential meaning
of words. Lawyers, for instance, may spend weeks trying to find
out just what was meant by certain words. The time spent by
the ordinary reader is not easily noted, but it is undoubtedly
great.

Words stand for concepts (for even objects and actions come
to us as concepts); the examination of concepts is basic to any
serious study. Before you attempt general explanation, you must
assign meanings to words, or you must find the commonly assigned meaning.

If you deal in something more than routine ideas, sooner or
later you must imitate the dictionary makers. Even an unabridged dictionary does not cover most technical, industrial, or
commercial fields; it is primarily literary, historical, and classical. No dictionary can hope to keep up with your daily usage of
language, or with invention or creation.

Various books of synonyms may help you to distinguish fine
points. Special technical and scientific glossaries may help. But
in the end only the context will tell. How is the word used elsewhere? What words are in the same general area? What figures
of rhetoric are close by? What could the writer have meant? You
must deduce the meanings of the words of others by the way others use them; your readers must do the same with your words.
This remark is not intended to encourage sloppiness; you must
give clear indications of what new or special words mean by formal definition, by suggestion, or by use in context. Even after
you have the basic meaning, you still must make the fine intellectual and emotional distinctions.

A definition is that explanation of a concept which distin-
guishes it from all other concepts. In a *logical definition,* the principle is to place the term (word) into an appropriate genus

(class) and then explain the differences between the term and the class. A handy formula of definition is:

A _____ is a member of a _____ that is _____.
(word)   (class)   (how different)

A *lamp* is a *vessel* with a *wick for burning oil.*

An *electric lamp* is a *globe* (a type of vessel) with *filaments.*

Sometimes the logical definition is seen as an equation— everything to the left of *is* should equal everything to the right of *is.*

Sometimes the logical definition is seen as a technique that sets limits about a term. A variation of this notion is the notion that we "nibble" away at the class until only the word is left. Let me illustrate both notions by an example. The word *dog* stands for a class of mammals, and includes all sizes from Chihuahua to St. Bernard, wild and tame specimens, specimens with various hair lengths, and so on. When I define *St. Bernard* I must eliminate all sizes except *large,* all hair lengths and types except *long and shaggy,* and so on.

The procedure for the logical definition is as follows:

1. Assign the word or concept to a class, that is, a group of things having similar qualities. For example, the term *chair* can identify any one of a class of furniture, some of which are quite dissimilar in appearance, but all of which have one characteristic —they can be sat in or on. Sometimes the class itself must be arbitrarily defined—Christian, conservative. Sometimes the class is not at all easy to establish. For many years chemists tended to identify certain residues as "inert matter." (Breakfast foods still do.) But the discovery of radium came about when the Curies became curious about a certain residue which resulted from their experiments and which they had labeled as "inert matter."

2. Enumerate the pertinent special qualities of the thing being defined that differentiate it from other members of the class. Proceed from the general to the particular, remembering that what is "general" and what is "particular" may depend upon your audience and other circumstances.

When we extend the partial technique of defining by synonym or antonym, we begin to define by comparison (in which the two concepts are similar in most respects) or by contrast (in which the two concepts are dissimilar in most respects).

Here is an example that combines some aspects of both methods:

An undertaker is a man who waits for someone to die and then tries to grab him. A mortician is a trained professional worker who realizes that a certain number of people are bound to die within a given period, by the law of averages, and prepares himself to give the Service that is required and give it as well as possible.[3]

The Operational Definition

The operational definition depends on the process of classification; the operational definition depends on the process of analysis:

An operational definition *tells what to do* to experience the thing defined. Asked to define the co-efficient of friction, the physicist says something like this: "If a block of some material is dragged horizontally over a surface, the necessary force to drag it will, within limits, be proportional to the weight of the block. Thus the ratio of the dragging force to the weight is a constant quantity. This quantity is the co-efficient of friction between the two surfaces." The physicist defines the term by telling how to proceed and what to observe. The operational definition of a particular dish, for example, is the recipe.[4]

The operational definition offers one solution to the philosophical dilemma posed by the so-called *conceptual, contextual,* or *constitutive* definitions we have been discussing. That dilemma is the one described here:

The essence . . . which every definition tries to state is simply the point which it is for the time being important to elucidate. It follows that the essences and definitions of things are necessarily plural, variable, relative, and never absolute. . . . A single, unmistakable and absolute definition of a thing, true without reference to any context, would have to be one that would serve for any purpose for which it is possible or convenient to use the term. Such a definition is barely conceivable, but quite incredible, and assuredly not extant. (F.C.S. Schiller, *Formal Logic.*)

In the operational definition we are concerned with (a) the property of something at a moment of time, or (b) the change or rate of change in a property under changing conditions or constant conditions.

In making an operational definition we should include:

[3] Elmer Davis, "The Mortician," *The American Mercury Reader,* p. 129.

[4] Anatol Rapoport, "What Is Semantics?" *American Scientist,* January, 1952.

1. The object or class of objects to be observed.
2. The conditions of environment under which the observations should be made.
3. The operations, if any, that should be performed under those conditions or in that environment.
4. The tools or instruments, if any, that are required to perform the specific operations.
5. The observations that should be made.
6. The treatment of the data obtained.

In the case of the situation described in (b) above, we also consider the changes or rate of changes in terms of time and the stimulus for the change.

Here is an operational definition of "cutting in":

First . . . the enormous cutting tackles, among other ponderous things comprising a cluster of blocks generally painted green, and which no single man can possibly lift—this vast bunch of grapes was swayed up to the main-top and firmly lashed to the lower masthead, the strongest point anywhere above a ship's deck. The end of the hawser-like rope winding through these intricacies, was then conducted to the windlass, and the huge lower block of the tackles was swung over the whale; to this block the great blubber hook, weighing some one hundred pounds, was attached. And now suspended in stages over the side . . . the mates, armed with their long spades, began cutting a hole in the body for the insertion of the hook just above the nearest of the side fins. This done, a broad semicircular line is cut round the hole, and the main body of the crew, striking up a wild chorus, now commence heaving in one dense crowd at the windlass . . . at last, a swift startling snap is heard . . . and the triumphant tackle rises into sight dragging after it the disengaged semicircular end of the first strip of blubber. Now as the blubber envelopes the whale precisely as the rind does an orange, so it is stripped by spiralizing it . . . (Moby Dick)

The Extended Definition

For the most important use of definition, the exploration of new concepts, the logical definition and the operational definition are essential but are rarely enough in themselves. Any concept new to the reader is difficult enough for him at best. Any strange idea must be related to knowledge he already has. The list of differences between the term and the general class may not be clear to the reader. Strange terms arise in operational definitions. Each separate difference, each new concept, each strange idea may require an explanation. In other words the definition itself must be explicated. When you read, for example, that

gemmation is a form of asexual reproduction in which a new organism develops from a protuberance of some body of the parent

you may want to know about several of the words used in the definition. The extended definition is the generalization that the writer explicates or develops at greater length.

Most extended definitions follow the deductive pattern; they begin with a logical definition or with a generalization and then follow with a discussion that is limited to the matters in the initial statement. Within the extended definition we may find details, illustrations, comparisons, contrasts—but on a larger scale than in the partial or simple definition. We may find analogy, definitions of terms, etymology, analysis, negation (the identification of a concept by describing what it is not). We may in an extended definition find any combination of these techniques.

A classic example of the extended definition is the *Poetics* of Aristotle. If you recall the *Poetics*, you will remember that several kinds of definitions are used in the essay. But the whole essay is also a definition.

One final note—definitions never include value judgments.

Assignment for Discussion

Bring to class examples of techniques for defining that you have found in your reading, television viewing, movie watching —anywhere. Discuss the types and effectiveness of the various definitions. In what ways do the types of definitions used influence or help develop a writer's style; do you find a writer using one type of definition to the exclusion of others? Do some writers use definitions more than others? Do some subjects seem to require more definitions?

Assignments for Writing

Write an extended definition of some concept, object, or action, either as a means of understanding or as a means of explaining it to your classmates. The subject might be scientific (hydroponics), social (a new dance), cultural (Chicano), or avocational (a 1931 Franklin Merrimac Sport Phaeton).

Write a brief essay explaining the following four lines of verse:

> I play it cool and dig all jive
> That's the reason I stay alive
> My motto, as I live and learn
> Is: Dig and be dug in return [5]

Description

I have already said that description and definition are often so alike as to be indistinguishable. Now I will add that *description* and *explanation* are very similar. But don't be overly concerned about such terms; don't get caught up in jargonistic arguments. The terms are useful for brevity, but clarity may require paraphrase: "When I'm explaining, I'm telling it like it is."

It is important that you know how to convey information to others, though. And that is what I'm trying to get you to understand. In John Ruskin's words:

> The greatest thing a human soul ever does in this world is to *see* something, and tell what it *saw* in a plain way. . . . To see clearly is poetry, prophecy, and religion, all in one.

Ruskin uses the word *see* here as we often use it—meaning both to receive images through the sense of seeing and to understand what has been received. But he adds another shade of meaning—the ability to place something in a context, to give it point. Good description does all three.

Our everyday language reflects Ruskin's philosophy. When we say, "Do you see the point?" we mean, "Do you understand?" When we say, "He has eyes but sees not," we mean, he's looking around, but he doesn't understand what is going on. When an irate politician told a group of Iowa farmers that they were "too damned dumb to see" what he was talking about, he was not referring to their sense of seeing at all—he was talking about their understanding.

We talk about the man who can "visualize" his problems, about others who have "far-seeing visions." We think that if we can bring a man face to face with an aardvark he will understand it. Many a student has been abused with the notion that the scientific method is used to examine only physical appear-

---

[5] Langston Hughes, "Motto," *The Panther and the Lash*, Alfred A. Knopf, 1967, p. 11.

ances that can be measured and analyzed with physical procedures. Any reputable scientist will straighten you out on this
point in a hurry.

My first point, then: Seeing is not only confronting an object,
an action, or a concept, but it is also understanding what you
see—in terms of itself and in terms of its function in our universe.

Relationships

Samuel Taylor Coleridge in *The Friend* begins a discussion on
this subject with a quotation from Shakespeare's *Henry IV*, Part
One:

FALSTAFF. What is the gross sum that I owe thee?

MRS. QUICKLEY. Marry, if thou wert an honest man, thyself and the
money too. Thou didst swear to me upon a parcel-gilt goblet, sitting
in my dolphin chamber, at the round table by a sea-coal fire, on
Wednesday in Whitsun week, when the prince broke thy head for
likening his father to a singing-man in Windsor—thou didst swear
to me then, as I was washing thy wound, to marry me and make me
thy lady, thy wife. Canst thou deny it? Did not goodwife Keech, the
butcher's wife, come in then and call me gossip Quickley?—coming
in to borrow a mess of vinegar: telling us she had a good dish of
prawns—whereby thou didst desire to eat some—whereby I told thee
they were ill for a green wound. . . .

Coleridge's point is that Mrs. Quickley has a fantastic memory for details and a compulsion for repeating them, whether
they are relevant or not. (All of us know at least one Mrs.
Quickley.) He notes that we should "contemplate not *things*
only, or for their own sake alone, but we should also contemplate the *relations* of things, either their relations to each other,
or the observer, or to the state and apprehension of the hearers."

"To enumerate and analyze these relations, with the conditions under which they alone are discoverable," says Coleridge,
is to use "the science of Method." Method is "the due mean or
balance between our passive impressions and the mind's own
reaction on the same."

The Word Is Not the Thing

When you attempt to recreate physical existence or abstract
notions, you find out how inadequate, how inefficient our lan-

guage is. Poets, who probably understand our universe better than others, have known this for centuries. Would-be poets think they can put a few words on paper and tell all.

Baffled, we long for other techniques—the drawing, the photograph, the diagram. "A picture tells a thousand words," we glibly reassure ourselves, ignoring the fact that *Life* must use at least ten times a thousand words in every issue. An *Esquire* cover pictures a young man face to face with a pig. The picture is a visual pun, of course; *Esquire's* editors, not too sure that we will get the point, add the title "The Kids vs. The Pigs." Even then we have to make a translation in order to understand the picture. Another *Esquire* cover has a drawing of a barefoot football player in a green-and-white costume and a fur coat open at the front so that the number "12" on the costume shows. The figure is standing, giant-sized, on a much smaller Empire State Building. His right arm is cocked to throw the ball he holds; in his left hand he grasps the miniature figure of a girl. Tiny planes buzz round him. Slowly we realize the illustration is a parody on *King Kong*. But if we think we understand what the cartoon is about, why do the editors furnish 20 pages of copy and additional illustrations inside? Would we get their point, "Joe Namath, World Metaphor," from looking at the cartoon? The cartoon conveys a message of sorts, but if we are to learn the "higher truth of Joe Namath," we must read. The cartoon's function is not only to convey a message but also to attract our attention, to get us inside where the words are.

Seeing, therefore, is not necessarily understanding. The problem the writer faces may be either recreating the image of the object or presenting the significance of the object in terms of its physical attributes—or both.

Assignments for Discussion

Bring to class pictures of an object and a building. Discuss what the pictures help us to see or understand, what questions they raise, what they do not tell us.

Also bring pictures that have been presented with no words, not even the artist's title. Discuss how we arrive at an understanding of these pictures.

Patterns of Description

When it is necessary to describe something that has no physical existence (like a job, a building, or an object yet to be built or made), we can sometimes fall back on drawings, but more often than not we require words. Even models or schematic tables of organization or responsibility need explanation. And, whether we are explaining a job, an object, or an abstraction, subjects that may offhand seem to be quite unrelated, they represent different forms of the same kind of intellectual perceptions. Each is concerned with some form of existence as a static concept, abstracted from whatever form of physical reality it may have.

All good description is based upon patterns, and the patterns ought to be apparent to our readers. The patterns may be spatial, temporal, or logical. Whatever the pattern, don't forget: your reader is more likely to be interested in the relationship between the object and some larger intellectual questions. It's one thing to know Joe Namath stands 6'1" and weighs 200 pounds. But why did *Esquire* choose Namath as subject rather than some other professional football player of equal physical stature?

You must understand your subject. That means a structural analysis; you decide what are assemblies, subassemblies, components, connections. Then decide upon the order of description. Generally, it is best to take a look at the whole. Then as each unit is described it can be related to the whole or to other units or both. Remember: keep your reader in mind; you know what you are describing, but your reader doesn't. Use illustrations as necessary, but key them to your copy. If your subject is technical, use precise terminology; define your terms as necessary.

Patterns can be spatial; you describe the United States, moving from the northeast down along the Atlantic Coast. As this example illustrates, you make arbitrary choices; you might just as well have begun with California and moved eastward. In such cases you also have to make arbitrary decisions about parts: what is the northeast? To a resident of Iowa, Ohio is in the east; to a resident of New York, Ohio is the midwest. If you organize along spatial lines, you choose a base, a chassis, a frame as your departing point. You use transitional phrases or words to indicate movement from one space to another: "Moving on to the midwest, we find. . . ."

Even in dealing with static objects, you may proceed along

temporal lines. An electrical system may be described as if you were describing a string of beads: First, second, third, next. You analyze a magazine article or a book beginning with the first paragraph or the first chapter. You analyze a job beginning with the first matter: "On this job safety glasses and steel-tipped boots are required."

Spatial and temporal may be mixed: "The second electrical component in the circuit is a transistor, located one-half inch above transistor number one."

Here is an example of a description based on spatial organization:

The driver reduces his speed appropriately as he approaches and crosses an intersection or railway grade crossing, hill crest, or as he travels upon any narrow or winding roadway, or when special hazards exist with respect to pedestrians or other traffic, or by reason of highway or traffic conditions.

Here is an example based on temporal and spatial considerations:

The driver, in preparing to leave a place where he has parked parallel to the curb, looks over his left shoulder if he is parked on the right side of the street or over his right shoulder if he is parked on the left side. While continuing to make sure that the lane next to his car is clear, he signals his intention to move away from the curb. He enters traffic in the nearest lane and remains in that lane until the adjacent lane is clear.

The preliminary intellectual examination of the work is but half the job. Even after you understand your subject, you must still ask: Why should my reader be interested? Who is he? What does he need to know? Is he going to teach others how to drive a car, or is he going to rewrite the ordinance? For instance, the above paragraphs are simple descriptions of what a driver ought to do in one situation. If the paragraphs were designed for a lawyer, a judge, or a police officer, they might be worded much differently. In what ways?

The above paragraphs are general statements. If we were teaching a student how to behave when he came to drive a 1972 Impala from the curb, our copy would have to be more detailed. Consider, for instance, the paragraphs that would have to be written in the following cases: a description of tools in general, a description of wrenches in general, a description of a screw type valve lifter for late model L-head engines. Your consideration of course will be based on the need for the paragraphs: Will they be intended as specificatory for a catalog, promotional for a sales brochure, or instructional for the mechanic who will read them? And—at what level of generalization?

Let's consider the description of several homely objects.

A Simple Mechanism

The simplest form of monkey wrench has three parts: a long handle with a jaw extending at right angles from one end, a movable jaw sliding on the handle, and an adjusting screw to hold the movable jaw in place on the handle.

Such a statement is the structural analysis of a mechanism into its component parts. The description that follows will be in three parts, each a detailed description of one component, and each detailed description in the order listed above. You have prepared your reader for that order; now follow it. If you cannot, go back and rewrite the introduction.

You can show the relationships among the components either by an attached drawing or by a sentence in each paragraph: "The U-shaped movable jaw slides on the handle between the fixed jaw and the wooden hand-grip."

In a final summary paragraph you might describe how the wrench is operated. "The wrench is held in one hand while the adjusting screw is turned by the apposed thumb and forefinger of the other." NOTE: If you are writing description, *do not write:* "HOLD the wrench in one hand, and at the same time grasp the adjusting screw between the thumb and forefinger of the other." The style of this last sentence is the style of INSTRUCTIONS. Description, explanation is always written in the *third person, past, present, or future tense.*

If your description included the principle of operation of the wrench, you might want to compare or contrast the monkey wrench with a pipe wrench or a Stillson wrench. A separate description of either of these two wrenches would be more demanding than a description of a single monkey wrench, because each one has certain important features that are not found on a monkey wrench. Even then each might be analyzed in terms of three parts or functions; one subsection would have to include details about the serrations on the jaws, for example.

Apparatus

Any description of apparatus will have to take into consideration the unique qualities of the apparatus or the unique purposes of the description. Here also you begin with a description of the whole:

Volta's *couronne de tasses* was constructed of a row of cups half filled with various liquids and linked with metallic arcs.

The whole apparatus must then be analyzed in terms of its parts so that it can be adequately described. However, the subsections may differ greatly, because the design of any piece of experimental equipment depends on certain crucial properties, dimensions, materials, shapes, and these may vary considerably, causing variations in the amounts of description required. In any description precise details about these crucial qualities must be expressed:

Volta found that cups made of glass or wood or earth or anything but metal worked for his voltaic pile. The cups were filled to the halfway mark with pure water, salt water, or lye. One extremity of each arc was coated with copper and the other extremity with zinc.

Incidental qualities can be glossed over. We may not care how the base support of experimental tubing is constructed, but we may be very much interested in the angle of that tubing with respect to the horizontal:

A long tube was therefore furnished with a cap and stop-cock, then exhausted of air and filled with chlorine, and *being held vertically with the syringe upwards,* air was forced in, which thrust the chlorine to the bottom of the tube. (Michael Faraday)

It may be irrelevant that the company laboratory is in Room 1232 of the R & D building, but it may be extremely relevant that the room is exactly 1232 feet above sea level. The relevance of the property described depends upon two factors: its uniqueness or originality and its ultimate uses in the apparatus. However, it would be unwise to omit from the description of the apparatus any of its major segments, no matter how conventional they might be. Even if you do nothing more than indicate that the part or function exists, you ought to remind the reader that it is there.

Layouts

Although any layout, office, plant, or school, may ultimately have a physical reality, it always has an existence as a system of organization. The pattern is likely, moreover, to be more significant than any of the individual parts. The principle is doubly apparent if you consider, for example, the layout of an expressway cloverleaf:

The most common type of modern interchange (intersection) is the cloverleaf. AT A CLOVERLEAF ALL TURNS ARE RIGHT TURNS.

The fact that the term "layout" is used is enough to suggest that our interest is in the relationships more than the components.

Yet our understanding of the layout comes from more than merely seeing it. The furniture mover will use the layout to place a desk three feet from the drafting table; the executive will ask why the desk was located there. Industrial engineers and efficiency experts owe their livelihood to the need to answer why. The former will respond in terms of the lighting, ventilation, heating, acoustical control, space per person, and general storage; the other will respond in terms of the activities carried out: billing, typing, information supply, supervision.

The layout described in terms of functions is viewed as a report of separate observations classified by a meaningful system. In short, such descriptions tend to become highly analytical and verge on evaluation.

Departments

A department exists not as a physical entity, but as an abstraction; therefore its parts are not objects in the usual sense, but rather functions. Functions are only incidentally related in any physical way. Rather, they have a common property that is determined by means of classification. The introduction to a description of a department is therefore a list of classes:

The shipping department receives, opens, and distributes incoming shipments, and packs and ships outgoing merchandise.

Each paragraph in the description becomes a detailing of the various responsibilities included in the classes:

Opening a shipment implies not only careful unpacking but also careful checking of the material received against a bill of lading, making claim for any damaged items, and notifying the proper department of the condition of goods.

The order in which classes are described is variable; it may be chronological, it may be spatial, it may be in terms of descending importance ("first things first"), or cause-and-effect. In any event, the order must be predicted in the introduction.

One-piece Objects

Suppose that we are describing a physical mass as, for instance, a piece of steel. Although here the object is concrete rather than abstract, our interest in it is probably in terms of its component properties (percentages of iron, carbon, and other elements) or its physical properties (Rockwell hardness, tensile strength) rather than its spatial properties alone (a one-inch cylinder six-inches long, weighing ten pounds). Hence, we are likely first to make a chemical or physical analysis. Although this may be described in tabular form, nonetheless we are still describing.

In all these descriptions we are interested not only in having the reader see what we are describing but also in having him understand *why* we are describing. Therefore, we apply a rule of *relevance* to detail; we will include that which not only helps us *see* but also helps us *understand*. We use a drawing or photograph for that which is best described by those means. Where figurative language is helpful, we use that:

. . . several different varieties of bacteria are found as chains of small granules, rods, and long oscillating threads . . . (Robert Koch)

Assignment for Discussion

Discuss the merits and faults of this description of a piece of apparatus by Sir Benjamin Thompson, Count Rumford, who contributed to our early knowledge of the nature of heat:

Let A be the vertical section of a brass rod which is an inch in diameter and is fastened in an upright position on a stout block, B; it is provided at its upper end with a massive hemisphere of the same metal, three and a half inches in diameter. C is a similar rod, likewise vertical, to the lower end of which is fastened a similar hemisphere. Both hemispheres must fit each other in such a way that both the rods stand in a perfectly straight vertical line.

D is the vertical section of a globular metallic vessel twelve inches in diameter, which is provided with a cylindrical neck three inches long and three and three-quarters inches in diameter. The rod A goes through a hole in the bottom of the vessel, is soldered into the vessel, and serves as a support to keep it in its proper position.

The center of the ball, made up of the two hemispheres which lie the one upon the other, is in the center of the globular vessel, so that if the vessel is filled with water, the water covers the ball as well as a part of each of the brass rods.

Some questions: What does "massive" tell us about the hemispheres? Where is the cylindrical neck attached to the vessel and what is its use? What would a sketch of this apparatus show? A clue: Rumford's apparatus was designed to demonstrate that friction produces heat.

Assignments for Writing

Rewrite Count Rumford's description of his apparatus, following the prescriptions given in this chapter. Compare your description with your classmates'. How does yours compare or contrast with theirs?

Write a description of a complex tool (a sewing machine, a power mixer, a wheel aligner, a power mower), a place (your home, a section of your school plant, a small industry), or an apparatus with which you are familiar, provided that the apparatus is something more than a cooking pan. Keep in mind the *why* as well as the *what*.

Motion

Movement is crucial in America. "Don't just stand there, do something," the football coach implores. "Do something about the terrible situation we're in," we command our politicians. "Get a little hustle in it," the sales manager tells his salesmen.

Even though we are goods-conscious in our society, processes are as important as products. Long lines of tourists queue up outside Ford's River Rouge plant, Goodyear's Akron tire plant, Budweiser's St. Louis brewery. Budweiser may offer a glass of beer at the end of its tour; the others offer only a glimpse of motion, but their crowds are just as large. Our society is always on the go; constantly it asks, "What's happening?"

Our dependence on motion produces several paradoxes for the

writer. On the one hand description of motion through chronological organization is the simplest of all writing patterns. Many school teachers begin writing courses by assigning exercises in "the order of time." The TV sheriff tells the hysterical victim of violence, "Just start at the beginning, Ma'am." "Tell it like it is," we command our peers. The method desired by such demands is the method used by the laboratory worker in recreating his research on a step-by-step basis.

But on the other hand actions are not always so simple. While the heroine of the TV drama is undergoing violent assault, what is the hero doing? And the sheriff? Where is the villain now that the dastardly deed is about to be proclaimed? Where is the hero? As the old silent film subtitle would say, "Meanwhile, back at the ranch. . . ."

There's also the matter of emphasis. We may have to know what the murderer's victim died of before we can reconstruct the crime. Or our reader may be impatient for other kinds of information—he has his own problems.

The Basic Patterns

We apply the same basic patterns of organization to all descriptions of sequence—past, present, or future, specific or general. The patterns are best illustrated in the generalized descriptions of the textbook writer or of the man who describes standard procedures. The purpose of such descriptions is generalized understanding—as differentiated from narration which is more concerned with the situation of the individual.

Whenever the reader must understand the principles of the process, he must be made to see the patterns; therefore, your first step is to think of the process in terms of its *organizing principle* and major components:

Four times within the first half of the twentieth century gloomy observers shook their heads. . . . The first time was after World War I when . . . The second time was in the mid-twenties when . . . The third time was in 1927 when . . . The fourth time was after World War II when . . .[6]

There are four classes of idols which beset men's minds. . . . To these, for distinction's sake, I have assigned names—calling the first class, *Idols of the Tribe;* the second, *Idols of the Cave;* the third,

---

[6] Theodore Peterson, *Magazines in the Twentieth Century,* University of Illinois Press, 1964, p. 40.

Idols of the Market-Place; the fourth, *Idols of the Theatre.* (Francis Bacon)

We had not got well settled into our harbor duties which, as they are a good deal different from those at sea, it may be well enough to describe. In the first place, all hands are called at daylight. . . . The great difference between sea and harbor duty is the division of time. (*Two Years Before the Mast*)

I began to feel the first discomforts of a sailor's life. The steerage . . . was filled with old junk. . . . Moreover, there had been no berths put up. . . . The sea, too, had risen. . . . To crown it all, we were allowed no light. (*Two Years Before the Mast*)

If you are explaining the unknown, you work in terms of fairly well-known concepts (comparison and contrast):

Death is at all times solemn, but never so much as at sea. A man dies on shore; his body remains with his friends, and "the mourners go through the streets"; but when a man falls overboard at sea, and is lost, there is a suddenness in the event, and a difficulty in realizing it, which gives it an air of awful mystery. A man dies on the shore—you follow his body to the grave and a stone marks the spot. You are often prepared for the event. . . . A man is shot down by your side in battle, and the mangled body remains an object and a real evidence; but, at sea, the man is near you—at your side—you hear his voice, and in an instant he is gone and nothing but a vacancy shows his loss. (*Two Years Before the Mast*)

You analyze the process into three to six individual major operations. There is nothing magical about the numbers; three to six steps are what your reader can ordinarily comprehend and remember. Your reader cannot master an unknown process in its entirety in a single glance; neither can he conveniently picture a process described only in terms of several dozen minor and unarticulated operations. Ask a man what he has done this day, and he is likely to say: "Before breakfast, I . . . , After the coffee break . . . , When the noon whistle blew. . . ." We organize our days (and lives, for that matter) around such divisions: "When I was in high school . . . , Last summer . . . , In my sophomore year. . . ." I can ask you to list 20 automobiles—or I can ask: What cars, respectively, do Buick, Chevy, Ford, and Chrysler make? Which is easier to respond to?

Moreover, main steps in an unknown process are likely to be analogous to steps in a process that your reader already knows.

Most processes start with a preparation stage. Therefore, a general heading, "Preparing thus-and-so," immediately suggests familiar operations.

But the main operations must be more than just familiar and easily remembered. They ought also to be relatively parallel in intellectual importance. For instance, if I asked you what your three main college activities were, you might respond: (1) attending class, (2) studying, (3) socializing. You would not include checking books out of the library as one of the three steps, nor would you include looking up phone numbers of members of the opposite sex, although it might seem to you that you spent an inordinate amount of time in these activities.

Determining what operations are relatively parallel in intellectual importance is a matter of classifying, and determining levels of abstraction. If you were to outline them, the main steps would all be represented by Roman numerals or capital letters. If you were making a flow chart, each of the main steps would have its own box and each box would be similar in size.

There are complications even in this simple operation. For example, you might list the main steps in painting a wall as gathering the material, cleaning the wall, mixing the paint, applying the paint, and cleaning up. Your friend might argue that the first three are essentially preparatory and should be listed under that heading; another friend might argue that you begin with the process itself. And your teacher might say that the cleanup is self-evident, not essential to the understanding. Yet for beginners nothing is self-evident; surely we don't know what painting is until we have experienced the joy of scraping paint from a window and thoroughly cleaning the brush.

One more caution. In my example above, I listed "attending class, studying, and socializing" as intellectual equals. You might argue for "social life." If we take the first two as verbs of action, then you are wrong; if we take them as noun-equivalents, then you are right. It is best, however, to stick to similar patterns. Your reader will appreciate these little signals that the patterns represent. In the example, the gerund form of the verb (attend*ing*, study*ing*, socializ*ing*) create the pattern.

When you are describing a process, it ought to be named in the title, the first sentence, or at least in the first paragraph:

The Kodak Flexichrome Process fills a place in the field of color photography that has been somewhat overlooked.

The analysis into main steps ought to be stated in the introduction; it is fundamental to the understanding of the whole process.

If the *subject* of the first sentence is the name of the process (as in the Kodak example), the *predicate* may be a definition (perhaps partial) or a list of steps:

Firing clay is the process that converts the plastic into a vitreous process.

Firing clay requires careful and thorough drying, gradual heating, sustained roasting, and gradual cooling.

The definition may be made a parenthetical part of the subject:

Firing clay, a process that converts the plastic into a vitreous substance, requires careful and thorough drying, gradual heating . . .

A list of steps not only gives your reader an excellent opportunity to examine the steps of the process; it also provides you, the writer, with a guide to your writing. In this case successive paragraphs or parts of your paper (even headings) might read as follows:

Careful and thorough drying of the clay is best done slowly . . .

Gradual heating begins as soon as the clay is in the furnace .

Sustained roasting at a temperature of 700° is . . .

Gradual cooling is as important as gradual heating and is . . .

Such repetition provides useful transitions, adds coherence, and provides review steps for your reader.

Finally, you can refocus your reader's attention upon what he has learned by repeating the steps as a conclusion:

If the potmaker has begun with a good design and has followed the steps in the process—careful drying, gradual heating, sustained roasting, and gradual cooling—he is bound to have a pot which he can proudly show to his friends.

The timeworn advice of "telling them what you are going to say, saying it, and then telling them what you have said" is ideally worked out in this system of description or explanation.

There are other patterns that can be used. Here is an example of the chronological pattern taken from an account of the building of the Verrazano Narrows Bridge:

Before the spinning could begin, however, the men would have to build a sky platform on which to stand. This platform would be the two catwalks, each made of wire mesh, each twenty feet wide, each resembling a long thin road of spider web, or a mile long hammock. The catwalks would be held up by twelve horizontal pieces of wire rope, each rope a little more than two inches thick, each more than a mile long. The difficult trick, of course, would be in getting the first of these ropes across the sky over the towers of the bridge—a feat, that, on smaller bridges, was accomplished by shooting the rope across the bridge with a bow and arrow, or, in the case of Charles Ellet's pedestrian bridge, by paying a boy $5 to fly a rope across Niagara on the end of a kite.

But with the Verrazano, the first rope would be dragged across the water by barge; then as the Coast Guard temporarily stopped all ship movements, the two ends of the rope would be hoisted out of the water by the derricks on top of the two towers [600 feet above the water], more than four thousand feet apart. The other ropes would be hoisted up the same way. Then all would be fastened between the towers, and from the towers back to the anchorages on the extremities of the bridge, following the same "say" lines that the cables would follow; when this was done the catwalk sections would be hauled up. Each catwalk section, as it was lifted, would be folded up like an accordion; but once it had arrived high up on the tower, the bridgemen standing on the platforms clamped to the sides of the towers would hook the horizontal ropes, and then shove or kick the catwalk sections forward down the sloping ropes. The catwalks would glide on under the impetus of their own weight and unfurl— like a rolled-up rug might unfurl if pushed down the steep aisle of a movie theater.[7]

Here the writer has begun with a sentence that prepares us for the balance of the description. His time sequence is developed through phrases: before the spinning, this platform, the two catwalks, the difficult trick, the first rope, then as the Coast Guard, the other ropes.

Beyond this, *what* has the writer gained using the subjunctive for something already done when he wrote his description? What is served by the reference to the use of a bow and arrow or a kite to get a rope into place? How about the $5 paid to the boy? Does the imagery of "a road of spider web" or the rolled-up rug unfurling down the theater aisle produce a clearer image? Is the whole description clearer because you have seen the Verrazano Narrows Bridge or another one like it? How has the author built up suspense in his description?

[7] From pp. 62–63 in *The Bridge* by Gay Talese (Harper & Row).

Detail and Tone in General Description

The kinds of detail that are used in explaining the principle of a process or procedure are somewhat different from those used in a report of work accomplished. All details that are incidental or appropriate for only one place or one operation of the process should be eliminated. For instance, if we were making a generalized description out of the bridge paragraphs, we could delete the references to the necessity of the Coast Guard policing the bay, and to the other ways in which a rope was gotten across the towers on other bridges.

Likewise, operations that must be performed to carry on the process but that nonetheless are not crucial to the understanding of the process may well be eliminated.

Although purists would argue that the use of analogies or similarities as a means of explanation leads to distortions of the truth, as of now such analogies and similarities are the only means that the layman has for gaining some idea of the unfamiliar. As a matter of fact the use of parallel explanations or analogies, definitions, or similarities may be more important than naming secondary steps in a difficult-to-understand process.

As description becomes more generalized, the language used can become less technical or more technical—are you moving toward a popular audience or away from it? The tone changes too. The more technical the language, the more formal the tone. For instance, in a more technical description of the bridge operation, the subjunctive (used to increase suspense) would be replaced by the simple past tense.

Assignment for Discussion

Bring to class examples of motion description that seem to you to illustrate patterns discussed here or other kinds of patterns. Discuss the relative merits of each example.

Assignment for Writing

Write a description of a research, repair, sales, or manufacturing procedure with which you are familiar. You might write about the making of an article of clothing, the preparation of a meal item, alterations made in the conversion of an automobile. Be sure that you describe the process as a general operation and not as an account of a specific activity that you engaged in. Select a specific audience. These requirements will mean some care for the language and tone of your paper.

Narration

In logical definition we deal with concepts in the abstract, removed from daily life. In operational and extended definitions we are still concerned with concepts, but often we are defining specific examples and we move much closer to daily life. In description and narration we move as close to reality as the word can take us. Although definition may exist in the pure state, we demand that description and narration have an immediate purpose for us.

Description and narration are very much alike. Description usually is concentrated on the general; narrative concentrates on the specific. Although narrative can be organized along spatial lines, it is much more likely to follow chronological organization. Therefore, it is likely to begin at the beginning:

I was born a slave on a plantation in Franklin County, Virginia. I am not quite sure of the exact place or exact date of my birth, but at any rate I suspect I must have been born somewhere and at some time. (Booker T. Washington, *Up From Slavery*)

When I was a boy, there was but one permanent ambition among my comrades in our village on the west bank of the Mississippi River. That was to be a steamboatman. We had transient ambitions of other sorts, but they were only transient. (Mark Twain, *Life on the Mississippi*)

But it may begin with a description of a character:

Toby was a rube in the grand tradition. His hair had a sheared-on-the-farm look. He usually wore overalls and these likely as not were held up by one gallus. He spoke a barnyard brand of English and many of the more cultivated customs of society were beyond his ken. Yet underneath Toby's country appearance and unsophisticated manner there ran deep currents of native wit, of cunning and resourcefulness. Unlike many of the rubes before him, Toby was True Blue. Sometimes he actually rose to the heroic, though invariably he made it appear accidental.[8]

[8] Neil E. Shaffner with Vance Johnson, *The Fabulous Toby and Me*, Prentice-Hall, p. 2.

It may begin with a description of a place:

If you had traveled in eastern Iowa in 1917, the year of my birth, you might have found yourself in a quaint-looking village suggestive of the old country. Hearing the older people speak you might have imagined yourself in an out-of-the-way German *Dorf*. The *Dorf* would have been an Amana village and the language an Amana dialect.[9]

It may begin with an incident that occurs chronologically in the middle of the narrative—the device the Romans knew as *in media res*:

On Palm Sunday, my father was preaching a particularly resounding sermon. The church was packed, and father warmed to a responsive house like an old trouper playing Hamlet's gravedigger.[10]

It may begin with a summary or a conclusion:

Everyone knows the popular conception of Florence Nightingale. The saintly, self-sacrificing woman, the delicate maiden of high degree who threw aside the pleasures of a life of ease to succour the afflicted, the Lady with the Lamp, gliding through the horrors of the hospital at Scutari.[11]

Once underway, the narrative may move sideways through space, back and forth in time as it works to hold together its several possible strands. But those shifts in time and space must be made clear to the reader:

From within came strange noises. Through the open auditorium windows sounded the organ, desecrating a gospel hymn. . . . From the ugly administrative wing seethed another sound: the strident notes of two pianos, neither in tune, playing separate marches, one for the juniors, the other for the intermediates.
Sunday School had started in full voice.
Back home, I knew, father was dressing carefully.[12]

[9] Yambura, Barbara S. and Eunice Bodine, *A Change and a Parting*, 1st edition, © 1960, Iowa State University Press, Ames, Iowa, p. 17.

[10] From *One Foot in Heaven* by Hartzell Spence. Copyright 1940 by Hartzell Spence. Used with permission of McGraw-Hill Book Company.

[11] Lytton Strachey, *Eminent Victorians*, Capricorn Books, 1963, p. 129.

[12] Spence, *op. cit.*

The narrative may end in any number of ways as long as all the loose strands have been brought together and any curiosity or anxiety roused in the reader has been resolved:

The Cardinal's memory is a dim thing to-day. And he who descends into the crypt of that Cathedral which Manning never lived to see, will observe, in the quiet niche with the sepulchral monument, that the dust lies thick on the strange, the incongruous, the almost impossible object which, with its elaborations of independent tassels, hangs down from the dim vault like some forlorn and forgotten trophy—the Hat.[13]

It is pleasant to speculate about what Max would have thought had he heard that this was to be the ultimate destiny of his mortal remains. He might well have been amused; as he had been amused to hear that an official memorial service had been held in the same place for George Robey. Was it not equally incongruous that he, the impish ironist, should lie with Nelson and the Iron Duke beneath the grave and monumental arches of the national pantheon? But he was also a patriot, with a romantic taste for the historical and the ceremonious. And he would have been gratified too.[14]

Note that both of these narratives end on a note of irony. Such literary devices as irony, a hint of poetic justice, a faint touch of humor, and the like are favorite choices of authors when they bring their narratives to an end.

Assignment for Discussion

Bring to class a nonfiction narrative that has pleased you. Discuss with your classmates the techniques used by the writer— style, the use of anecdotes, suspense, humor, wit, detail, dialogue —that you find particularly interesting.

Assignment for Writing

Write a narrative account of some experience of your own or one that you know about. Try to use some of the techniques used by the author of the piece discussed just above.

---

[13] Strachey, *op. cit.*, p. 128.

[14] David Cecil, *Max*, Houghton Mifflin Company, 1965, p. 498.

9

Evaluating, Judging, and Directing

The two outstanding features of our way of life are our system of free enterprise and our attitudes toward the integrity and rights of man. The one provides us with jobs, money, health and comfort, and more material goods than any other society has ever known; the other makes us a hyperactive political entity. Often the conflicts between the two force us to make choices.

Between the two features and their demands on us, a stupendous amount of information is generated. Some idea of the amount of that information may be gained from one statistic: 3,427 tons of paper was thrown from office buildings in the course of a parade in New York City. Most of that paper undoubtedly contained information. Most of that information was undoubtedly current.

Both politics and the consumption of goods require that we make decisions and direct people. We are required to choose among willing (if sometimes inept) politicians at all levels from dogcatcher to president; we are forced to make consumer decisions at all levels from lead pencils to palatial yachts.

Few of us realize how much our lives are directed. From the columns of "Dear Abby" to the instructions on a can of tomato soup; from the tag on a mattress to the pages of a slick consumer magazine; from the command to "Open This End" to the bales of manuals required to operate an electronic fortress; a barrage of directions is constantly being fired at us. Don't protest. Without them you would be lost in the jungle of consumer goods. Ask any father who has tried to help his son put together a plastic model of the Apollo 12.

As a member of this society, you are very likely to have something to do with this flow of information. Either you will originate it, or you will be on the receiving end. In either case you ought to know what is going on.

Comparisons and Contrasts

The decisions that we are required to make may be divided into two kinds: the *absolute judgment* and the *relative judgment*. The differences between the two are relative, and you needn't worry about them, but it is important that you learn how to make judgments. You will make many of them.

When we make a judgment we usually do so in one of these situations: from a set of standards or *criteria* (the absolute judgment); from a choice of two or more options (the relative or *comparative* judgment). In the latter case a set of standards *may* be used. Sometimes the standards are not stated but implied. For instance, given a choice between hard-bound and paperback editions of the same text, we take the paperback. Why?

Although we often rely on our "common sense," as often as not we take what is available or what some eager salesman cons us into buying. The judgment of someone else controls such instances.

The patterns for expressing the results of relative judgments are more complicated than those for expressing absolute judgments; nevertheless, the former pattern is more commonly used. Even when the grounds upon which the judgment can be made are expressed, the relationships among the grounds are by no means fixed. Often it is impossible to set a precise value on each ground. As a result the pattern for the expression of comparison is extremely flexible. As often as not the pattern is persuasive in type and uses some of the techniques of persuasive rhetoric.

The form of a comparative judgment can be epitomized simply: Item A is better than item B (for me), because A excels in qualities W, Y, and Z, even though B is better in terms of quality X. But that simple statement conceals many difficult concepts, as we shall see.

Comparison is so fundamental to explanation that it is automatic for most of us. Comparison is responsible for semantic growth in our language. We see abstract similarities among a tree, a watershed, and a commercial institution, and so we speak of the tree *branch,* the *branch* of a stream, and a *branch* bank. Such comparisons often aid our ability to understand very difficult concepts:

From the foregoing facts it appears that a *current* of electricity is produced. (Joseph Henry)

. . . some physicist, turning over the numerical data, much as a resting pedestrian might idly turn over a stone . . . (James Clerk Maxwell)

Such varieties work in several ways that we use in making judgments. *Analogy* (the Henry example) depends on a series of identities. *Simile* (the Maxwell example) depends on one. *Synonymy,* a third kind, is the naming of each nuance of a class of meanings—*evaluation, estimate, appraisal.* All these devices have one purpose—to make an unknown quality meaningful by relating it to a known quality.

The two items to be compared may be obviously similar, like a Jonathan apple and a Delicious apple. Or they may be much different, like a woman and a ship:

> But who is this, what thing of sea or land,—
> Female of sex it seems—
> That so bedeck'd, ornate, and gay,
> Comes this way sailing
> Like a stately ship
> Of Tarsus, bound for th' isles
> Of Javan or Gadire,
> With all her bravery on, and tackle trim,
> Sails fill'd, and streamers waving,

> Courted by all the winds that hold them play,
> An amber scent of odorous perfume
> Her harbinger?
> (John Milton, *Samson Agonistes*)

In this analogy, incidentally, the unknown quantity is Delilah's purpose in dressing as she has. Milton makes that clear by comparing her action to the purpose of a ship which voyages to a distant land for goods.

If one is going to compare apples, he assumes that his reader is familiar with one variety of apple. But if the reader knows nothing at all about apples, he may know something about pears, potatoes, or pomegranates; he can be guided to an understanding by means of a discussion of other edible things.

As the degree of difference increases, the problem of explaining the contrast increases. When the difference is as great as between a ship and a woman, the point of comparison is likely to be only one or two qualities. Such a limited amount of similarity, however, may be all you have when you come to make a judgment: do you buy your wife a fur coat or a dishwasher?

Intellectually, comparison is at the root of *scientific method*. Our attempt in experiments to control all variables but one is merely a way of indicating that we wish to compare a certain quality under varying conditions. The process of scientific classification depends on our awareness of similarities and differences in the quality of objects being classified. Does the object have a mammary system? Does it have a backbone? Does it have gills?

Assignment for Writing

Earlier I asked you to make a list of words having common terms (coffee break, circuit break) and discuss the differences in meanings in the common terms that occur when the common term is combined with other words. Now take some of those couplets or similar couplets (ball bearing, ball park, wingspan, wingspread, worm gear, worm fence, for examples) and write comparisons of the two concepts in a given couplet. Next, try to create explanatory analogies or similes for such familiar objects as a pencil sharpener, an egg beater, the air you breathe, common salt, a rose.

If the unlike qualities of items being compared outweigh the like qualities in significance, we speak of contrast rather than comparison. For example, the technical definition of *work* is contrasted with the common idea of *work* and *labor*. Contrast is a special form of comparison; the patterns of expression remain the same.

The first question that you must ask before making any comparison is whether the items are really comparable. Can you compare apples with appellate judges? Can you compare caddies with Caddies? The question must be answered in terms of the purpose for which the comparison is made. Professional golfers employ caddies on the golf course, drive Caddies off the course.

Most technical choices are made between quite similar items. The comparison is not always designed to reveal a choice, however. Sometimes our purpose is arousing an emotional reaction rather than gaining intellectual understanding:

> Lawyer Brown is as honest as any lawyer.

Although many scientists and engineers object to limited literary comparisons they can serve a purpose:

> And though the example which I shall here choose, namely, that of a water-mill with iron hammer appears to be tolerably romantic, still, alas, I must leave the dark forest valley, the spark-emitting anvil, and the black Cyclops out of sight, and beg a moment's attention to the . . . machinery. (Hermann Von Helmholtz, *Uber die Erhaltung der Kraft*)

> An aerodyne is like a powerful fan in a bottomless garbage can.

> The fuselage of the F3Y-4 is shaped like a coke bottle.

Many papers would be livelier and more easily understood if simile and metaphor returned to the technical and scientific writer's rhetoric.

Assignment for Discussion

Bring to class comparisons found in *Life*, *Time*, and *Reader's Digest*. Look also for instances of the clarification of difficult concepts. Discuss these in terms of the qualities being compared (sensory, emotional, logical). Evaluate their effectiveness for you, making sure you establish your criteria.

The good evaluative *specifications* are absolute. An object to be tested either meets or does not meet the standards. In comparison, however, judgments are made in *comparative* or *superlative* terms:

> Ford is a *better* car than Chevy.
> Not for me. Chevy is the *best* car on the road.

An idea is better or best, a concrete mixture is stronger or strongest, a slide rule is more versatile or most versatile.

All of these statements are based upon a quality represented by an adjective or an adverb; all contain an expression of *degree*. The grammatical and rhetorical function of degree is to express decisions or judgments.

Rating an object on the basis of any one quality is fairly simple —just a matter of elementary ranking:

> John is tall.

Most people can observe even very minor differences between two items:

> Bobby is taller than John.

As the number of items increases, the possibility for error increases:

> John is a better football player and does better in math.
> But Bobby is our best pitcher and gets B's in English.

As this last example demonstrates, very few judgments are based on single qualities. Most judgments are based on a complex combination of qualities. If you were making a choice of automobiles between Ford and Plymouth, you would undoubtedly consider such matters as oil consumption, gasoline consumption, price, brake horsepower, body style, and certain special features possessed by one or the other. You would probably also consider the reputation of the dealer who was trying to sell you the car.

When, as in the case of the cars, you have examined all of the variables, you will find that you cannot make just one ranking; you must make several. As you do so, suppose you find that Ford excels here and here and here; Plymouth is better there and there and there; but the Chevy dealer is the one who truly stands behind the cars he sells. What do you do now?

What you do in complex cases is decide which of your comparative qualities are most important to you or, perhaps, *is* most important to you. You rank the qualities accordingly. Then you may have to make some compromises. You may have decided that Ford has more muscle power, and that appeals to you most, but Plymouth is offering $500 more for your trade-in. And that bright red fastback in the Chevy lot is available for immediate delivery. Now what do you do?

Such complex interpretations of the same situation should explain why judgments are not easy to make, and why our society places so much value on the people who can make good judgments. Faced with such difficult choices, many people make snap judgments; they react impulsively and trust that the law of averages will carry them through. Others stutter and stammer and then withdraw; unable or fearing to make a choice among this year's models, they keep driving the old ones. The people chosen for management in industry, commerce, education, the military are ordinarily the persons who demonstrate the best judgment-making ability.

The difficult part of making judgments almost always has to do with the weighting of our standards. We are all anxious for peace—but what price are we willing to pay for it? In dollars or the blood of our young men? In the risk of being overrun by an unfriendly power?

The degree of importance of standards depends upon many background problems that are most often expressed in the *report* of the comparison—you don't buy a Mongoose V-8 because you can't afford to buy one, but you tell your friends you have heard rumors that the Mongoose people are going out of business—and then where would you get parts? For the comparison to be convincing and sound (and if you want to be able to live with yourself) you had better look to the problem itself, however; for the problem led to the choosing of the standards. From this examination you must present convincing reasons for the weighting you give any particular standard.

Once you have weighted the standards, you must decide on the degree of significance any one quality will have. The problem of weighting must take into consideration this factor as well as the factor of ranking. An anecdote illustrates this point very well. At a dinner party some years ago, George Bernard Shaw asked an attractive young lady next to him: "Would you sell your body for a million dollars?" "Yes," she said. "How about three dollars?" he asked. Eyes flashing, she turned on him. "What do you think I am?" GBS smiled. "We've already established that," he said. "Now we're merely haggling over the price!"

Writing the Report of the Comparison

Because the comparison itself implies such a complex judgment, there are many forms that the report of comparison may take. The two most common are:

Discuss Object A first in terms of all its merits and faults: Merit 1, Merit 2, Merit 3, Fault 1, Fault 2, and so on. Then turn to Object B and discuss it in terms of its merits and faults. If similar merits and faults are being compared, it is a good idea to use the same order in each case.

In more complex cases of comparison, the list of faults and merits may not fall so neatly into the patterns described here. In such cases this first plan is very good:

The bay of Monterey is wide at the entrance . . . but narrows gradually as you approach the town, which is situated in a bend, or large cove, at the south-eastern extremity. . . . The shores are extremely well-wooded (the pine abounding upon them), and . . . everything was as green as nature could make it—the grass, the leaves, and all; the birds were singing in the woods and great numbers of wild fowl were flying over our heads . . . the town lay directly before us, making a very pretty appearance, its houses being of white-washed adobe. . . . The red tiles, too, on the roofs contrasted well with the white sides and with the extreme greenness of the lawn. . . .

San Juan is the only romantic spot on the coast. The country here for several miles is high table-land, running boldly to the shore, and breaking off in a steep cliff, at the foot of which the waters of the Pacific are constantly dashing. For several miles the water washes the very base of the hill, or breaks upon ledges and fragments of rocks which run out into the sea. Just where we landed was a small cove, or bight, which gave us at high-tide, a few square feet of sandbeach between the sea and the bottom of the hill. . . . Directly before us rose the perpendicular height of four or five hundred feet. (*Two Years Before the Mast*)

In the second plan, we take Merit 1 of Object A, and Merit 1 of Object B. Then ve go on to Merit 2 of Object A and Object B. And so on. If the blocks of information for Objects A, B, C, etc. are large, this plan is the better one. Here is an example of the second plan:

examination, or that you have made your choice on the basis of a rather insignificant criterion. For example, a lady in choosing a dress from a ready-to-wear rack often will find several in the same design and style, but each one of a different color. If she comes home with a red dress and explains her choice in those terms, she may be asked: "But why that red one?" In other words, the important criteria in her choice may well have been the style, the fabric, the price, or the uses for which the dress is intended.

Often your paper will *imply* the set of standards:

> You can always tell the landlubber from the true seaman. An [experienced] sailor has a peculiar cut to his clothes, and a way of wearing them. . . . The trousers, tight around his hips, and thence hanging long and loose around the feet, a superabundance of checked shirt, a low-crowned, well varnished black hat, worn on the back of the head, with a half-fathom of black ribbon over the left eye, and a slip-tie to the black silk neckerchief, with sundry other minutiae, are signs . . . a sunburnt cheek, wide step, and rolling gait . . . bronzed and toughened hands. . . . (*Two Years Before the Mast*)

If the objects of your comparison are exceedingly complicated, they should be described in your introduction so that your reader will be able to follow your copy. If you are comparing several complicated and similar objects, a description of the one ultimately chosen will probably be sufficient; minor differences for each of the others can be described in a subsequent paragraph.

Charts and tables are especially valuable for summarizing statistics on which choices are based. The objects are listed horizontally, the qualities down the left side. Use a rule for vertical columns, but not for horizontal listings unless there are a great many vertical columns and a great many qualities. In that case, a horizontal rule every fourth or fifth line should be sufficient. (It never hurts to base your chart or table on a good one you have seen in a text or catalogue.)

Such a table can be referred to in the text, thus eliminating much detail from the prose comment. Place the table strategically in the text so that your reader can refer to it while reading the copy. If you use more than one table, number them, and then refer to the specific table by its number.

You must keep in mind, however, that mere tabulation is not the expression of a judgment; it is only a summary of facts and figures. Therefore, some text is still necessary.

Some judgments are syllogistic (inductive) in style of reasoning; others (such as the Dana paragraph just above) are hypothetical (deductive).

Your Dependence on Others

A great part of the time you depend on others to make your judgments for you. (Likewise, others will depend on you to make their judgments for them.) When you watch football in person, you still depend on the newspaper writer or the television commentator to tell you what you saw; when you attend a film or play, you look for the critic's judgment, and perhaps use it as your own; the Eric Sevareids among our news broadcasters exist to tell us what the significance of the day's news is. I never saw Babe Ruth, Lou Gehrig, Mickey Mantle, or any of a hundred other baseball players (except for snippets of action in a newsreel); yet I am convinced that Ruth was the greatest baseball player who ever lived, thanks to writers like Grantland Rice and Paul Gallico who did see those players and who made up my mind for me.

As a result we are often more interested in who makes a statement than in what was said. We take a stand on political matters because the politician of our choice offers an opinion. Furthermore, we tend to do this even though we are aware that the logicians have fancy Latin names to categorize these fallacies.

Still, if the President of the United States can rely on a host of advisors, if the local school board can retain an out-of-town consultant, your dependence upon the judgment of others is not a bad thing. You are perhaps better off to accept the opinions of those who have carefully studied a subject; your doctor and your plumber are subject to human error just as you are, but it's usually best to accept their judgments. Ours is a society of specialists whose interdependence and interaction make things go. Even our wisest men don't have time to think everything through. In many matters you must be content with accepting whatever is the generally accepted judgment or, perhaps, whatever is the judgment recommended by those in whom you have confidence. You may for a time accept the dubious notion that the world is flat or some other strange idea, but at least you get on with the business at hand.

At this point I must digress to make my position clear. I am not conducting a philosophical argument, but merely offering advice on the ways in which we get our daily work done. If, for any reason, you are unwilling to accept the judgments of others, that is another matter. I support, in general, your freedom to accept or reject. The right to dissent is an implied right in our society. Presidents do not agree with their predecessors in office; Supreme Court justices dissent with each other. One bit of advice: If you want to secure followers on any but emotional grounds, you had better be prepared to demonstrate your expertise—even if that means calling in advisers!

End of digression.

If you accept the fact that not all of the judgments you espouse are really your own (we're all plagiarists!), you ought also to be willing to accept the fact that people are going to call upon you to help make up *their* minds. The ordinary administrator cannot possibly hope to be in direct touch with everything going on in his own company or school or political agency. Even if his organization is so remarkably managed that computers can give him daily tabulations of important business indicators, he will still find innumerable situations—major and minor—for which he must depend upon the opinions of his subordinates. And, of course, consultants. Consultants spend their lives giving opinions to those who hire them.

Occasionally, some naive executive thinks that if he insists his employees give him only facts, he can reserve for himself the right of judgment. He overlooks the fact that anyone who furnishes facts has gone through a process of selection and organization that will tend to control the ultimate judgment. The power of the writer is the power to select facts and organize them into an intellectual discourse—a discourse that explicitly or implicitly will express a judgment. In order to organize, you must first analyze. And analysis depends upon a point of view.

You will see this if you re-examine the passage beginning "death is at all times solemn" a few pages back. Dana wrote that passage to present the sense of loss he felt when a fellow seaman was swept overboard. But he is not only describing his sense of loss—he is also trying to persuade you to agree with him. That is his point of view as he writes. Therefore, he has selected certain facts and organized them in such a way as to make his case. As a matter of fact, you can take his materials and rewrite them in such a way as to make the point that unexpected death anywhere is shocking. I challenge you to demonstrate this statement to yourself.

In a very real sense, therefore, the writer who is assigned the task of preparing a report, of publicizing a technical analysis, or of summarizing a discussion—that is the man given the *de facto* power of decision. Ghost writers are very powerful spirits indeed. One example—in a current newspaper, a man who wrote the speeches for a major presidential candidate in the 1968 elections shows that most people did not read the speeches (out of 200,000,000 Americans, very few heard them, for that matter), but they read the speechwriter's summaries instead; by the speechwriter's own admission, one of the most attention-getting summaries misrepresented very badly the speech that was given.

Patterns of Judgments

There are numerous ways of presenting judgments. Fundamentally, all of the patterns of argument and logic are the patterns of judgment: definition, description, comparison, the syllogism, and so on.

However, a few of the forms are especially common in technical situations—the situations we often find in business, industry, government, and education. Technical men tend to evaluate objects against a set of established standards or specifications: there are standards for measuring the hardness of metal, the tensile strength of steel, the smoothness of a finished metal piece, the tint and shade of color to be applied, the grade of lumber, and so on. Such standards are more precise than those in other areas—today's newspapers report a local school board meeting in which proponents and opponents of a school textbook argued over the morality, patriotism, and similar qualities of the book. Because such terms as morality and patriotism are hard to define—at least to the satisfaction of one's opponents—such meetings tend to be futile and wrought with emotion.

Established standards or specifications represent judgments in themselves; they are established because they have been demonstrated in tests and experiments and because arbitrary agreements have been reached as to the significance of the tests and experiments; or they have been established because of judgments made by experts; or they have been established by consensus.

Let's take one case. The residents of a town ten miles from an expressway are unhappy because no direct route to the expressway has been provided by the engineers. The residents enlist the support of local farmers and politicians and appeal to the engineers. Eventually the engineers reverse their own initial judgment and agree to the building of a new interchange and a connecting route. There is one judgment.

Next, based on their experience in building highways, the engineers lay out a route. The proposed route is publicized (a job for a writer), and now the farmers are unhappy—the proposed route cuts diagonally through some producing farm land. Again negotiations, again a judgment as to the route.

Time now to build the road. Here, for once, the expertise of the engineers will be accepted. They lay out the specifications for the road; the specifications represent the first judgment that a road will be built, the second judgment as to the route of the road, and a third judgment (made by the engineers) as to the precise nature of the road. Here is a sample of the language in which the third judgment is expressed:

Continuing southeasterly for approximately ¾ of a mile, thence northeasterly on a north 87° east bearing, crossing the west line of section 33 approximately 267 feet south of the northwest corner section 33, T6N–R1W. Continuing on a bearing north 56° east, crossing west line section 27 just south of west ¼ corner.

Incidentally, one could quarrel with some of the language of this specification (which was one actually released by a state highway department). Three-quarters of a mile is 3960 feet; what is "approximately" ¾ of a mile—3961 feet? 3965? 3970? It could make a difference to a farmer who had a well in the area. However, the road has already been staked out, and the prospective contractor, standing at a point "approximately ¾ of a mile" from another could probably see the stakes with the naked eye.

Specifications are fundamentally legal. That fact in itself is largely irrelevant in terms of the intellectual judgment implied. On the other hand it is exceedingly relevant to the writer; his expressed statements must be so sufficiently accurate, complete, and precise that they have to be accepted by people who might willfully misunderstand them. The statements should be subject to only one interpretation each. Specifications must be drawn so that later, someone—perhaps someone who had no part in drawing up the specifications—can say: "This object, article, method, or what-have-you *is* or *is not* acceptable according to the specifications."

A second pattern for expressing judgments is similar to one described elsewhere:

- A description of the need for a change.
- A proposal to alleviate that need.
- An explicit statement as to how the proposal will work to accomplish what is claimed for it.

In such a pattern, the most desirable location for the expressed judgment is at the beginning. The judgment is ordinarily expressed as an answer to an implied question: What shall I think? What shall I buy? Shall I accept it at all?

For many readers the simple answer (think this, buy that one, yes, it is a good product) is enough. If they have confidence in you, in your ability to make judgments, and, if they are in a hurry, that will be quite sufficient. If they are in doubt or want to know how you arrived at your judgment, they can continue reading.

However, I must warn you again that you must follow the local ground rules. Many do not agree with the judgments just presented, and not all of those who disagree are cranks or crackpots. When in Rome, do as the Romans do. Work for the better way, but in the meanwhile accept the judgments of those who have employed you.

The Intellectual Basis for Specifications

Writers may write specifications, but if they are primarily writers (rather than engineers or scientists or manufacturers) they do not create them. They work with the people who do.

Specifications are created in response to needs. Needs almost always exist in terms of time, manpower, materials, equipment, space, and money. Questions that lead to specifications are like these:

What is needed by this rocket as it passes through a given density at a given speed for a given time?

How long must this highway last? What kinds and amounts of traffic will use the highway during that time? Therefore, what should be the nature and durability of the highway?

How long will Widget X be expected to serve a given consumer? Shall the components last the same time, or would it be better for the consumer if we produced a less expensive unit which could be repaired from time to time?

The choice of language used in expressing judgments will reflect the degree of care used in making the judgment. "The metal should withstand high temperatures" is the judgment of a weasel. What if it doesn't? What does "withstand" mean? What are "high" temperatures—the metal that would withstand the temperatures produced by a burner on an electric range might become fluid under the temperatures experienced by a spaceship during re-entry. "The metal should be capable of undergoing a temperature of 750°F for one hour without any resulting changes in Rockwell hardness, tensile strength, or in its percentages of elements." Such a statement is not only precise—it also indicates that the mind which produced it knows what it is about.

However, such statements have to be made in terms of all of the pertinent factors. For example, a scientist might respond in answer to the above specification: "Well, that metal will cost you $10,000 a pound, and probably take two years to manufacture, given our current knowledge of metallurgy. Are you willing to pay the price and wait that long?" If you suggest that the process might be speeded up, he might respond, "Then it will cost you $20,000 per pound."

Judgments are made in terms of variables such as these. Good standards are written to be followed—not to be ignored nor cast aside.

The points on which an absolute judgment may be challenged suggest the places that must be carefully defended:
1. You forgot this standard. (You forgot to ask what it cost!)
2. You gave an improper value to that standard. (You forgot, we have to buy oil and gas too.)
3. You included an irrelevant standard. (Who cares whether it has a mirror behind the sun visor.)
4. You did not make an adequate test. (You might have tried it on the highway.)

Assignments for Discussion

Discuss the bases on which you have made certain judgments —your choice of college, your choice of major, your choice of courses. What were the criteria that guided you in making each decision? How carefully did you set up criteria and follow them? What were the standards on which you based your criteria?

Think of some activity in which you have engaged that you have regretted. If you had an opportunity to relive the experience, what would you do differently? What standards entered into your first decision? What standards would you apply now? Why have your standards changed?

Assignment for Writing

Assume you are thinking of buying an automobile. Describe the steps leading to your decision, following the "Comparison" formula outlined above if two or more cars are involved, or following the "specification-judgment" pattern if your decision is based on your criteria for one automobile. Be honest with yourself and outline all of the factors that influence you. Then evaluate your judgment. If you deviated from any standard, why?

Directions and Instructions

Directions and instructions are written for many purposes:

- How to assemble something;
- How to operate something;
- How to sell something;
- How to manufacture something;
- How to work at a job;
- How to behave in public;
- How to use proper language;
- How to take care of ourselves;
- How to make money or increase our accumulation of capital;
- How to spend money; and so on.

Directions and instructions range from the very simple to the very complex. I have written instructions so simple they were printed on a card, and so complex they ran to 1600 pages and cost the taxpayers $100,000. Sometimes we ignore instructions at great peril to our lives; in one case a man purchased a flame thrower to eliminate some weeds, failed to read the instruction sheet, and eliminated himself instead.

Directions are always printed in the imperative mood (the *command* voice—the one that says, "Do this"). Here, for example are two paragraphs about the same subject matter:

DESCRIPTION

A vertical section of a brass rod was fastened in an upright position on a block. It was provided at its upper end with a massive hemisphere of brass, three and one half inches in diameter. A similar brass rod was attached to a duplicate hemisphere and the unit was set upon the first unit so that the flat surface of one hemisphere rested upon the flat surface of the other.

DIRECTIONS

Obtain two brass rods each one inch in diameter, and two hemispheres of brass, three and one half inches in diameter.

Attach one of the brass rods to one of the two hemispheres on its curved side, at a point corresponding to its pole, assuming that the face of the hemisphere is its equator. Make sure that the brass rod is perpendicular to the face of the hemisphere. Weld firmly in place.

Do the same with the second rod and hemisphere.

Drill a one inch hole vertically in the face of a substantial metal block or work table. The hole must be three inches deep. Set the free end of one of the rods in this hole and weld firmly in place.

Before you can begin to write directions, you must make an analysis of your subject. The analysis must be made in terms of the uses to be made of the directions.

Your analysis will probably be affected by the audience for your directions. You will have to evaluate your audience, according to your subject. For instance, if you are going to instruct someone in maintenance and repair, you will have to decide the degree of maintenance with which you are concerned and the abilities and training of the repairman.

Take as an example your automobile. It is assumed that occasionally you will have a flat tire, and so the manufacturer provides you with a spare tire mounted on a wheel, a jack, a wheel cap removal tool, and a wrench. He also provides you with instructions on the use of this equipment in removing the flat tire and replacing it with the inflated one.

The average service station is capable of mending the tire and replacing it on its wheel. It also has facilities for tune-ups and minor engine adjustments, including replacement of some assemblies—the air filter, the battery, and so on.

If more extensive service is required, the car is taken to the garage, where service work up to the level of a major overhaul of engine, transmission, and so on can be accomplished.

Thus a broad range of experience can be brought to bear on maintenance and repair of the car—from the layman's to the experienced engine and transmission mechanic's. Each of these people works with tools related to his education and training— from the simple tools furnished with the car to very complex equipment. Each requires a different level of directions.

Once you have decided on your subject and your audience and have made an analysis of your subject, make a list of materials your reader will need. If you are instructing an amateur in house painting, tell him to get ladders, horses, planks, scrapers, ground cloths, and paint thinner as well as brush and paint.

Make a list of ways in which your reader may evaluate his progress. How will he know that a coat of paint is the right thickness? What if the second stage in his son's Model 12 Apollo doesn't ignite?

Your analysis should take into account dangers or hazards that might be encountered or useful advice you can offer. "Never carry a full bucket of paint up a ladder—only a half-filled bucket." "Be sure the ladder you intend to use will support your weight." "Don't fly the model aerodyne with a copper wire in the presence of high-voltage lines."

Decide whether illustrations, photographs, and sketches will be helpful. (It would have been easier to explain the "hemisphere" subject on pages 214–215 with a simple sketch.) If you use any of these aids, be sure they are of good quality. If you are going to reproduce them, take your aids to a print shop and let the printer pass on them. If you use illustrations be sure that all parts are clearly and consistently labeled—it might help if your reader knew which lever you were referring to.

Writing Instructions

Always begin your instructions with a WARNING if the reader is likely to be exposed to any risk of life or limb or similar hazard. Such warnings should be printed in bold letters in bold inks (red is useful because of its symbolic values, but nothing is bolder than black on white) and set off in boxes. Repeat such warnings as often as necessary. Law courts tend to be sympathetic toward the heirs of poor farmers who have set themselves aflame with a flame thrower, unless it can be shown that the hazards were very plainly stated.

Write a statement that explains the purpose of the instructions. On very simple objects this may be nothing more than a descriptive title: Unpacking the Lawnmower. In a long instruction manual the statement may run to several paragraphs; however, it should be held to an acceptable minimum.

List the expendable supplies, and the tools and various forms of equipment needed, separating the list of supplies from the list of tools. Be precise in your listings: 40 $\frac{1}{4}$ inch wire brads, a $\frac{3}{32}$

inch alloy steel hollow head set screw wrench. If he will need gasoline, specify the octane (service station operators never know what octane gas works in a power mower). If materials and tools are somewhat out of the ordinary, tell him where he can get them. "The brads may usually be purchased at a place that frames pictures." Give him names of standard brands: "one-half pint of oil, the equivalent of Standard Oil Company's FINOL." Put yourself in your reader's place—try to anticipate the problems he will face. At one place where I wrote instructions, we had an employee who was kept around to sweep up broken glass, wipe up spilled fluids, and the like. He was, to say the best, not very bright. But he served one very useful purpose for us. Every time we had a new set of instructions we gave him a sample set and a piece of the relevant equipment, and then left him alone. When we came back, if the equipment was operating smoothly, the instructions were approved. If it wasn't operating smoothly, it was back to the typewriter.

Next make a layout for the instructions themselves, keeping in mind that illustrations should be adjacent to the relevant text. The complexity of the layout will vary according to the complexity of the object or process being explained. For very simple processes, list the steps in numerical order. Do not omit any step; secondary steps may be implied if the general heading covers a well-known procedure. For example, "Start the Car" implies several substeps which usually need not be listed, except for students and new car owners—"You will find the starter switch conveniently located under the back seat."

The remarks made elsewhere about confining main divisions to four or five applies equally well to instructions. If 45 different operations are required to assemble the Jet-Tiger bicycle, divide them into main divisions: Unpacking, Front End Assembly, Rear End Assembly, and the like. Furthermore, it is wise to subdivide major divisions so that no one division has more than four or five parts. Number these: I, II, III, IV, V; subdivisions A, B, C, D, E; sub-subdivisions 1, 2, 3, 4, 5. Then you can refer your reader to any part of the instructions; "in Step II, C, 3, you assembled . . ." Notice that the main headings can be in the indicative mood.

Implied in this advice about numbering is the advice to keep grammatical units short. Five paragraphs on a page looks better than one long one; and you don't want to discourage your reader. (As a matter of fact, one of your major problems is getting your reader to read any instructions, no matter how well prepared they are.) Furthermore, such devices help your reader measure his progress—can he really get done in time to keep that golf date? And they give him an occasional opportunity to take a break.

Keep your subheadings in the imperative mood, except for occasional explanatory statements: "About six inches from the door is a friction brake."

Your reader may from time to time be exposed to hazards that *do not* threaten life and limb. These should *not* be marked out with the word WARNING; that term should be reserved for situations indicated earlier. Use terms such as: "Danger—this fluid will flame at temperatures above 100°F"; "Caution: Lid must be tightly fastened when fluid is not being used." Differentiate among such matters as hazards to people and hazards to equipment.

State warnings positively if at all possible. "Don't stand near the safety valve" may be misread; it is better to say: "Stand back from the safety valve."

When it is necessary to put warnings in the negative, emphasize the *negative elements:* "Do NOT touch the BARE wires with the NAKED hands."

Give him check points and techniques as necessary or useful: "Be sure the crank spins freely before going on to the next step."

Tell him when he is through: "When the liquid in the test tube turns green, the process is complete."

Assignments for Discussion

In a class session, take turns in *ad lib* fashion giving the instructions you would give to a stranger on campus, directing him to the student union, the fieldhouse, the stadium, the president's home, the maintenance shop. Let your classmates decide how well you have done.

Bring to class instructions that have seemed to you to be somewhat less than adequate. Try them out on your classmates.

Assignments for Writing

Rewrite a set of instructions that have not seemed adequate to you.

Some seemingly simple matters pose considerable problems for instruction writers. Write a set of instructions for lacing a pair of climbing boots, ski boots, or gym shoes; for changing the ribbon on your portable typewriter; for opening the door of a locked automobile when the keys are not available.

10

The Organization
of Language

I begin this chapter with a disclaimer. I intend to write about the ways in which language is used in phrases, sentences, and paragraphs, and about the styles of language that result. But I must warn you that our language can be described as Cleopatra once was:

> Age cannot wither [it], nor custom stale
> [Its] infinite variety

How can I describe completely a language whose grammar has yet to be defined and perhaps never will be; whose range of expression is as infinite in possibilities as the stars and planets and nebulae and galaxies may be in number; whose recognizable forms and patterns are as "restless, shifting, fugacious, as time itself" (in O. Henry's words)? Finally, how can I write about a language that is not made by scholars, pedants, and teachers (although as people they help make it), but is made by people themselves? The answer is: I can't. If you truly want to learn all about our language, you must go to the people who use and who have used it. You can begin by going to our literary people, our poets and dramatists; weary of literature, you can walk along our streets and listen; tired of walking and listening, you can fall back on our journalists, our scientists, our politicians, our historians. And on and on.

But I don't intend to abandon you altogether, leaving you floating like an errant chip on the heaving sea of life. I may not be able to describe language to you as it ought to be described—there is neither world enough nor time for that—but I can give you some clues.

Many books about composition approach language prescriptively; that is, they say, here's a simple sentence, there's a complex one, here's a subordinate clause, there's a coordinate one, here's an inductive paragraph, there's a deductive one—and so on. The notion, apparently, is that you will follow these models—that when you come to write, you will say: "This time I will use this type of paragraph or sentence, next time that one." But I honestly don't believe that is the way it works at all. I believe that when a writer is writing, he is concentrating on making his point—for that is his chief business, and the one he had better be about. It's all right to write pretty, provided you answer your reader's question: "So what, Mac?"

There no doubt are literary-minded persons who take the time to revise and rewrite, working for sentence and paragraph variety as they do. But even those persons are aware that revision and rewriting must be for the primary purpose of making their point and making it more effectively.

Now don't misunderstand. I am not about to support bad or mediocre style simply because it makes a point—although I can cite you book and chapter of cases where a worthwhile point has been made rather badly. To write badly or in a mediocre fashion is to ignore or to insult our audience—or worse, to lose it altogether. On the other hand good style will not only hold an audience—its reputation will attract new readers.

I believe that when a writer is at work, he is not only concentrating on his point—I also believe that the way he makes that point is going to be determined by the kind of person he is. If his mind operates syllogistically, you are likely to find his style is syllogistic—as the style of many parts of this text is. If his mind sees parallels, he is likely to rely on parallel constructions—as in this particular paragraph. If he sees the world figuratively, you are likely to find a great many figures of speech in his writing. If he likes to support his generalizations by examples, you will find that many of his paragraphs are developed in that way. If he tends to see one subject in its relationship to another, he is likely to develop subjects through comparison and contrast.

Most of the time we don't have an opportunity to see the writer at work; what we get to see are the results of his work. So we must begin there, with the finished product, and analyze it, hoping to learn from the analysis how he worked. But, actually, all we can know is the substance and style of his work at the point when he decided to turn it over to the public.

There are three characteristics we can put our fingers on—the subject of a paper, the voice that seems to be speaking in the paper, and the "style" of the paper itself. By "style" here, I mean the selection and organization of words and symbols into sentences and parts of sentences, the figurative and symbolic patterns that are used, the levels of generalization. I also mean the organization of these units into paragraphs and the organization of the paragraphs into the whole. Style must of necessity include the characteristics of the voice, but for pedantic purposes I am differentiating between the two.

For instance, the voice that speaks below is educated, conversational, and pessimistic:

Well, and what of it? They asked me that, and that I did not answer. I was stunned by the discovery that it was philosophically true, in a most literal sense, that nothing is known; that it is precisely the foundation that is lacking for science; that all we call knowledge rested upon assumptions which the scientists did not all accept; and that likewise, there is no scientific reason for saying, for example, that stealing is wrong. In brief: there was no scientific basis for an ethics. No wonder men said one thing and did another; no wonder they could settle nothing either in life or in the academies.[1]

The organization of the paragraph is inductive. It begins with a rhetorical sentence that leads to a realization which explodes in a series of parallel clauses. From this explosion there is derived a brief summary, and from that the topic sentence.

[1] *The Autobiography of Lincoln Steffens*, Harcourt Brace Jovanovich, 1968, p. 127.

The effect of the organization is to let us experience the discovery made by the voice in the same syllogistic fashion in which the voice made its discovery. The paragraph is developed, in microcosm, along the same lines that scientists usually use in writing a lengthy report.

The subject of the paragraph is the world of knowledge and of ideas; in keeping with that subject, the language is largely abstract. The verbs nearly all relate to mental activities; of the other words, they are nearly all either relational or nouns. There are only four adjectives and one adverb. There is no symbolic or figurative language. The negative idea is expressed seven times, in the words "no," "not," and "nothing." Ten of the nouns relate to the subject of knowing.

The importance of the paragraph is that it shows us briefly and concisely a very important discovery, a discovery that when achieved marks the arrival of the discoverer upon the threshold of maturity.

The Sentence

There have been many attempts to define what the English sentence is, and while all are partially successful, anyone who reads very much can find exceptions to the definitions. Aside from the sentence fragments (oh!, stop!, where are you? here, what did he . . .) the easiest way to identify a sentence is by the signals that the writer or speaker gives; the intonations in speech, or the blank spaces, uses of capitals, and punctuation marks in writing. Even then problems arise. (See the final statement in the *Saturday Review* paragraph on page 250.)

I'm going out on a limb at this point and say that (with exceptions) the sentence is not important in itself; it is actually one unit in the development of a paragraph (as the word is one unit in the development of a sentence). I'm going to argue that the writer (again with exceptions) is not concentrating on sentences as he writes; he is concentrating on ideas (as I am now), and ideas are developed through paragraphs. The sentence is not an end but a means, and its form is not the result of concentration on the sentence but the result of concentration on the subject, the purpose, the audience, and the voice.

The exceptions are: dialogue, as in fiction or drama; ordinary give-and-take speech; and some styles of journalism which I have described elsewhere.

I am not saying that we can overlook the sentence. We must be sure it fits into our overall scheme as we intend; we must be sure that it is clear, that it is not redundant, that it puts emphasis where emphasis is needed, that it is relatively consistent with the overall pattern. And, certainly, either in the original writing or in revision, we can concentrate on each sentence.

I argue for this position for two reasons: (1) my impression of what I do as I write, and I write a great deal; (2) the impression I get as I examine the work of a great many writers. I admit that in this latter statement I perhaps overlook the raw amateur whose degree of literacy has not yet reached the point where he can see beyond the one specific sentence over which he labors. But my advice to this somewhat special case would be: take your eye off your sapling and put it on the forest. In other words go to your subject, analyze it into its main sections, then its subsections, then its sub-subsections. If your sections, subsections and sub-subsections are each written in sentence form, this procedure ought to make the writing of the paper almost automatic.

Or, I would tell him, think of your paper as being analogous to a deck of playing cards—52 in number, 13 in each of four suits, each suit running sequentially from ace through ten and followed by the jack-queen-king. Write each of the facts you can think of or that seem pertinent on a separate slip of paper, and let's assume that you end up with 52 slips (the number is not important —just be sure that each fact is written in a form that includes subject and predicate). Now sort out the 52 slips into four piles, so that the facts in each pile are related to one central idea. Next, arrange your facts sequentially, according to some logical basis. Then decide which pile of facts is your leadoff pile and the sequence of the other three piles. Now start copying your facts onto a sheet of paper, supplying whatever transitions are needed. The analogy may strike you as crude, but the technique is used by many writers. But I digress.

Ezra Pound, in one of his essays, describes the reaction of a European who is asked to define "red." His response: "It is a color." If you ask him what "color" is, he responds that "it is a vibration or refraction of light, or a division of the spectrum." If you persist and ask him what "vibration" is, he responds that "it is a mode of energy" (*The ABC of Reading*, New Directions, Ch. 1). Pound's point is that the European becomes less and less specific. Pound prefers the Chinese who would probably define "red" by assembling the symbols for "rose, iron red, cherry, flamingo"; the Chinese would move toward concrete terms.

Francis Christensen has quoted John Erskine's "A Note on the Writer's Craft," to much the same point:

When you write, you make a point, not by subtracting as though you sharpened a pencil, but by adding. When you put one word after another, your statement should be more precise the more you add. If the result is otherwise, you have added the wrong thing, or you have added more than was needed.

What you wish to say is found not in the noun but in what you add to qualify the noun. The noun is only a grappling iron to hitch your mind to the reader's. The noun by itself adds nothing to the reader's information; it is the name of something he knows already, and if he does not know it you cannot do business with him. The noun, the verb, and the main clause serve merely as a base on which the meaning will rise.

The modifier is the essential part of any sentence.[2]

Professor Christensen has made a strong case for Erskine's advice in his *Notes Toward a New Rhetoric—Six Essays for Teachers,* a very useful book for any learning writer. To a certain extent I agree. Although it seems to me that often sentences spring full-blown from my head (like those warriors of old who sprang ready to fight from the dragon's teeth which Jason sowed), that may not be the case—it may be true that I begin with nouns and go on adding and sharpening. I do agree to this extent, however; the advice is very good when one comes to revise his work.

Erskine's paragraph says nothing about similar additions to the verb, but they are equally important as we shall presently see.

The kinds of additions we can make to the noun and the verb are:

• To the NOUN: modifiers that are attached to the noun and fixed in place and that may not be removed without serious damage to the sense: *a green morocco* chair, *the metal reading*-lamp, *some autumn* sunshine, *one large, white bony* hand. Some modifiers can, of course, be moved to an *appositive* position: a large hand, *white and bony,* came into view.

• To the VERB: the same kind of attached modifier: squeaked *softly,* passed *rapidly.* These modifiers almost always immediately follow the verb.

[2] John Erskine, "A Note on the Writer's Craft," *Twentieth Century English,* Philosophical Library, Inc.

• To the NOUN: the unattached modifier (other than the appositive) which may be inserted into a sentence at various points, depending on the emphasis:

Holding their hooded cameras ungainlily, the photographers clustered.

The photographers, *holding their hooded cameras ungainlily,* clustered.

The photographers clustered, *holding their hooded cameras ungainlily.*

• To the VERB: the same kind of unattached modifier:

Slowly and benignly he bowed to the managers.

He bowed, *slowly and benignly,* to the managers.

He bowed to the managers *slowly and benignly.*

Noisily and hurriedly the photographers clustered.

The photographers clustered *noisily and hurriedly.*

• To the NOUN: the attached prepositional modifier:

The King *of Siam;* Maid *of the Mist;* outlines *of Shakespeare's plays.*

• To the NOUN: the unattached prepositional modifier:

Of making books, there is no end.

There is no end *of making books.*

• To the VERB: the prepositional modifier, attached or unattached:

The two typists were sleeping *in the saloon.* (unattached)

In the saloon, the two typists were sleeping. (unattached)

The station-master gazed *toward the barrier.* (attached)

His back was *toward me.* (attached)

The sentence, when it contains noun and verb modifiers, may be compared in its principle of organization to the table of "levels of abstraction" and to the principles of classification discussed earlier:

Majestically, and as if he were carrying his own howdah, Lord Curzon proceeded up the platform accompanied by the police, paused for a moment while the cameras clicked, smiled graciously at the stationmaster and entered the Pullman. (Harold Nicolson, "Arketall")

The highest level of abstraction in this sentence is the statement: "Lord Curzon proceeded . . . paused . . . smiled . . . entered." Each of the verbs is modified by words or phrases that operate at lower levels of abstraction: "Majestically . . . as if he were carrying his own howdah . . . up the platform . . . accompanied . . . for a moment . . . while the cameras clicked . . . graciously . . . at the stationmaster." The phrase "by the police" operates at a still lower level of abstraction for it modifies the second-level abstraction "accompanied." (Keep in mind that when I talk about "levels of abstraction," I am speaking in relative terms.)

If we were to classify the sentence, our classifying terms would be:

mankind, magistrates, characteristics, behavior, in public places, specific places, specific types of behavior.

I am not attempting to persuade you that a writer consciously thinks in these ways when he writes, but I would argue that the mind does use classification procedures although perhaps at too high a rate of speed for us to notice. In any case, when we write we can analyze what we are doing in these terms; we can ask: Is this work too abstract? Does it need details at lower levels of abstraction, and if so, what *class* of details will be of most use? If we block at this point, we can consciously push the classification procedure further as in the above example. You may quarrel with me at this point and say: Why not report what I see? My reply: Did you see everything you might have? Of all that you saw, what will you use, what will you discard?

Suppose I were to add: The *pattern* of the Nicolson sentence could have been filled by other words; look around you and report what you see, using the identical sentence pattern. You would be obligated to observe a certain number of facts and these facts would have to have a certain relationship—they would have to belong to the same general class. Therefore, you might write:

Wearily, and as if he were begrudging every effort, my neighbor lumbered across the garden accompanied by his wife, paused for a moment while she said something, grimaced crazily in my direction and entered the garage.

You will have observed that not only did I *parody* Nicolson's sentence, but I also used the same scheme of classification as Nicolson did, substituting "ordinary men, neighbor" for "magistrates."

I will come back to this subject of levels of abstraction and classification when I discuss paragraphs.

Assignment for Writing

Write parodies of these sentences (if necessary see *parody* in the index), maintaining the same level of abstractions and approximately the same system of classifications while reporting something you have observed:

We caught two bass, hauling them in briskly as though they were mackerel, pulling them over the side of the boat in a businesslike manner without any landing net, and stunning them with a blow on the back of the head.[3]

A breeze blew through the room, [blowing] curtains in at one end and out the other like pale flags, twisting them up toward the frosted wedding cake of the ceiling, and then rippled over the wine-colored rug, making a shadow on it as wind does on the sea.[4]

Making his progress up and down the Main Street of little Dayton, surrounded by gaping primates from the upland valleys of the Cumberland Range, his coat laid aside, his bare arms and hairy chest shining damply, his bald head sprinkled with dust—so accoutred and on display he was happy.[5]

Most commonly we come to books with blurred and divided minds, asking of fiction that it shall be true, of poetry that it shall be false, of biography that it shall be flattering, of history that it shall enforce our own prejudices.[6]

[3] E. B. White, "Once More to the Lake," *One Man's Meat*, Harper & Row.

[4] F. Scott Fitzgerald, *Three Novels of F. Scott Fitzgerald*, Charles Scribner's Sons, p. 8.

[5] H. L. Mencken, "In Memoriam: William Jennings Bryan," *The American Mercury Reader*.

[6] Virginia Woolf, "How Should One Read a Book?" *The Second Common Reader*, Harcourt Brace Jovanovich.

Here are some other types of free modifiers:

Every literature, *as it grows old,* has its rubbish-heap, *its record of vanished moments and forgotten lives. . . .*[7]	(adverbial modifier of time) (appositive phrase, used here as a synonymous definition)
When I first encountered him . . . the trial was yet to begin. . . .	(adverbial modifier, used as a sentence opener)
that I was destined to see . . . who had laughed at him so long . . .	(relative clauses—*that* is often omitted in such clauses)
of any merely religious frenzy, *however inordinate* . . . *Not to be outdone,* I admired . . .	(negative modifiers that reduce, reject, or expand the preceding statement)
Upon that hook . . . Bryan committed suicide, *as a legend as well as in the body.*	(prepositional modifier)
He was, *in fact,* a charlatan. This talk, *I confess,* tires me. Upon that hook, *in truth* . . .	(phrases used to emphasize, particularize, or relate)
If the village barber saved any of his hair . . .	(conditional clause, here used as a sentence opener)
. . . to discharge his Message . . . . . . to shove the Prohibitionists . . .	(infinitive phrases)

The Paragraph—Voice, Organization, and Style

It was a crisp and spicy morning in early October. The lilacs and laburnums, lit with the glory fires of autumn, hung burning and flashing in the upper air, a fairy bridge provided by kind Nature for the wingless wild things that have their home in the tree tops and would visit together; the larch and the pomegranate flung their purple and yellow flames in brilliant broad splashes along the slanting sweep of the woodland; the sensuous fragrance of innumer-

[7] *Ibid.*

able deciduous flowers rose upon the swooning atmosphere; far in the empty sky a solitary oesophagus slept upon motionless wing; everywhere brooded stillness, serenity, and the peace of God. (Samuel Langhorne Clemens, "A Country Scene")

There are two sentences in this paragraph; there might have been six, but our author used semicolons to combine his last five sentences into one, perhaps because those five sentences all operate at the same level of abstraction to particularize the first sentence. The highest level of abstraction is the statement: "It was . . . morning." "Morning" is modified by "crisp and spicy" and by the prepositional phrase "in early October." This combination of attached and unattached modifiers is fairly standard practice in writing.

The five sentences that make up the second sentence all operate at a lower level of abstraction than the first sentence, but each in turn contains several layers of abstraction as a study of the following sentence will show:

The lilacs and laburnums . . . hung . . . (highest level in sentence)

. . . lit with the glory fires	(these three operate at the next
. . . burning and flashing	highest level—one modifies the
. . . a fairy bridge . . .	verb, the others the noun)

The other phrases—"of autumn," "provided by kind nature," and so on—operate at yet lower levels. Notice the steps down in "provided by kind Nature," "for the wingless wild things," "that have their homes," "in the tree tops"; with each of the phrases modifying the preceding one.

Now, what *voice* is speaking here? You know that "Samuel Langhorne Clemens" is the name of the man who wrote under the pen name of *Mark Twain,* and you also know that as Mark Twain, Clemens gained the reputation of being a great humorist. Is this humor, or is it what it purports to be, a description of "A Country Scene"?

When I first saw this passage, I was puzzled by several words: laburnums, larch, pomegranate, deciduous, oesophagus. (Lest you think I am not very bright, let me add that I have tried these words on college students; some of *them* weren't very sure of the words either.) So I turned to my dictionary and found:

laburnum: a *Eurasian* poisonous shrub or tree.

larch: a member of the pine family with short fascicled *deciduous* leaves (there's that word *deciduous* again); *fascicled,* I learned, means *clustered.* The tree grows in Europe and North America.

deciduous: meaning *falling off* at some seasons.

oesophagus: the tube that leads from the pharynx to the stomach!

About this time I realized that Twain was putting me on. What is happening, of course, is that Twain (for it is the *humorist* at work) is ridiculing what elsewhere has been called "purple prose." His ridicule is expressed in the form of parody. Twain is parodying those writers who think that writing "pretty," no matter how pointless, meaningless or nonsensical, is the goal.

In his story, "A Dog's Life," Twain described the kind of person he was parodying in this passage:

My father was a St. Bernard, my mother was a collie, but I am a Presbyterian. This is what my mother told me; I do not know these nice distinctions myself. To me they are only fine words meaning nothing. My mother had a fondness for such; she liked to say them, and see other dogs look surprised and envious, as wondering how she got so much education. But, indeed, it was not real education; it was only show.

A form of this misuse of words, one practiced usually by less educated persons, is the *malapropism,* so named for one of its better named practitioners, a Mrs. Malaprop in Richard Sheridan's play, *The Rivals:*

If I reprehend anything in this world, it is the use of my oracular tongue, and a nice derangement of epitaphs!

As headstrong as an allegory on the banks of the Nile.

A progeny of learning.

Twain is not only parodying the "purple prose" of the writer who is over-concerned with words; he is also parodying a human trait, the trait which John Ruskin identified as "the sentimental fallacy." The fallacy is shown in the reference to "kind Nature" (contrast Stephen Crane's "The Open Boat") and the attribution of human instincts to the "wingless wild things."

Here is an advertising passage that displays some of the same characteristics as Twain's passage:

Shucks—there's nothin' nicer on a winter evenin' than these big, snappy Crisp Mountain Apples, a ¾ pound hunk of aged mellow Cheddar cheese and a cozy fire. Guess that's why folks are so complimentary and downright smitten with this gift. Redder'n Russian raspberries. Crisp Mountain Apples are so crunchy and rambunctious they snap back at you (friendly-like of course). Raised way up North in the cold country, where they get firm and juicy—over 7 pounds of really regal elegant eating. Everything's bountifully bedecked—brighter than a Red Winged Blackbird and twice as noisy!

A special form of purple prose is often found in magazines concerned with ladies' fashions. There the idea of progress, the notion that automatically the styles for next year must be newer and therefore better than last year, leads to a concern for language—a search for ways of saying things that are as new and different as the styles:

. . . the leg will come through. It will come through all sorts of slits and slots and slashes. . . . It will come through as you unzip, unsnap, or unbutton your midi to the thigh. . . . So let's not get ourselves all trauchled about legs anymore. . . . The suit is back like thunder! Sharp, small, patch-pocketed jackets and pocketed midi skirts . . . lots of width and blow and go at the hem . . . a slit . . . and the leg comes through in a wrinkly boot . . . and the next day you're swinging down the street in tweeds and brolly and wrinkly suede boots. . . . (*Vogue*)

Such writing is produced, according to Donald Kaul, by "women who wear hats indoors and hold their breath while they write." There is a great deal of emphasis on the current and future tense and on words that are strange, coined, or exotic; blousons, trauchled, brolly; there are puns and assonances and consonances and alliterations, and various other forms of word-play. The aim is persuasion; the voice cajoles and threatens; if you get yourself all trauchled about things, you are out of it. And yet, for all this concern with words and sounds, a lot of information is furnished.

In other cases, however, such concern for words leads to the point where almost no information is furnished in the attempt to persuade:

Lordly New Bottle especially created for BARON CORVO—one of the world's three great gins.

The inspiration for Baron Corvo's new bottle came from a seventeenth-century bottlemaker.

Grand. Opulent. Aristocratic. Its beauty also has a practical perfection. The slim contour fits your hand as snugly as a book.

Any bottle is finally judged by what goes *inside*. Baron Corvo Gin is a rare luxury. If every man in America were rationed to *one* Baron Corvo martini *a year* there still wouldn't be enough to go round.

Serve the American gin of distinction tonight. It is now a grander gesture than ever.

The primary business of the writer is to answer the questions who, which, what, what to, where, when, how, why—and if necessary, to what effect or to what purpose or point. It is the answer to these questions, for instance, that gives the English sentence its basic form, as in this example:

Fourscore and seven years ago (when), our fathers (who) brought forth (what) on this continent (where) a new nation (answers the question of what was brought forth) conceived in liberty (why) . . .

In this example, the answer to "how" is implied in the words "conceived in," and "brought forth"; this is the language ordinarily used in describing the process of birth.

Here is a longer example as a means of making part of my point:

The Kodak Flexichrome Process fills a place in the field of color photography which has been somewhat overlooked. Most of the serious thought that has gone into the development of the various color processes has been devoted to the problem of photographing color, and much less attention has been given to the problem of coloring the photograph. On the other hand, the real objective of all photographic color processes is to produce pictures in color, and the acceptability of the finished result, however obtained, is the important consideration.

It is one thing to make a color reproduction of a subject, and it may be quite another thing to make the reproduction acceptable to the customer. To satisfy the customer, it may be necessary to modify, change, or correct the reproduction in an attempt to make the subject appear as the customer wants it to appear, whether it actually looked that way or not. But the moment a photographer tries to do something more than simply photograph the subject, he becomes involved in special treatment at some point in the process, usually handwork.

Since the human hand and the human element are so much a part of the craftsmanship of making color pictures, a process which responds to the personal direction at the point of a brush can render many valuable services in the battle for color control. The Kodak Flexichrome Process, designed especially to assist rather than resist handwork, is particularly valuable when a flexibility of treatment beyond the latitude of purely mechanical methods is desired.[8]

The writer of this brief essay is trying to persuade people who know something about photography to use a process. His approach, therefore, is primarily persuasive in a friendly way, yet he maintains a somewhat serious tone—he is not peddling a toy or a hobby.

The "when" of this writer's topic is the present, and so he sticks to the present tense. The "who" is the "Kodak Flexichrome Process," introduced as his subject in his first four words. Note that he doesn't define the process—his purpose is persuasion, not education.

The "what" is *fills*. What is filled is "a place in the field of color photography" (a limitation: if you are not concerned about color photography, please put the book back). Why should it be filled? Because it has "been somewhat overlooked." Notice that this writer is not going to anger anyone—he says "somewhat" overlooked. He leaves the weasel hole open as an escape device. Furthermore, he continues, "Most of the serious thought"—again, the weasel word, this time "most," but there is an implied compliment for his reader and others in "serious thought." His next phrase, "that has . . . color processes," is designed to classify the kind of serious thought he is talking about; his is an orderly mind as well as a persuasive one. And notice "processes"—he uses the plural because he wants to introduce his own and he doesn't want to give anyone the impression there is only one.

The subject of his second sentence has taken 16 words; his subject is a major one, not easily defined in a word or two. He seems not to be so concerned about his verbs—"fills," "overlooked," "has gone," "has been devoted," "has been given," "is to produce," and so on. These are not verbs that will attract attention; moreover they are not very specific. This writer is concentrating on a subject—color processing. Verbs suggest work—and he wants to avoid the subject of work for the present.

He likes to play with words and phrases. In his second sentence he plays off "the problem of photographing color" against "coloring the photograph." Later he plays off "assist" against "resist." In both cases he uses antithesis. He is introducing an idea that is,

---

[8] Reproduced from a copyrighted Eastman Kodak Company publication.

after all, antithetical to another, and he uses language subtly to make that point.

You will note too that the idea at the end of one sentence becomes the subject of the next one; step by step he takes you along the way. By and by, he introduces the subject of pleasing the customer—a notion that will surely intrigue the reader. He also introduces words and phrases intended to flatter the reader—"craftsmanship," "personal direction," "battle for color control." But behind the Madison Avenue touches, there is a mind that knows how to use syllogisms. In fact, he uses them so cleverly that he is able to bring his essay around to his beginning point, to repeat his subject in one final sentence designed as the "clincher" in his sales pitch.

If we were to try to identify the voice that is speaking here, we would have to conclude that it is the highly polished corporation voice with which we have become so familiar.

A different voice speaks in these *Newsweek* paragraphs:

There had never been a phenomenon quite like it in the U. S. before, and for this reason alone the Vietnam Moratorium was scarcely over before its significance was under debate the length and breadth of the land. To its organizers, of course, the protest was a whooping success, a major victory in the crusade against the war. To legions of others it was something to be quietly opposed, by flying U. S. flags at full staff or by keeping automobile headlights on throughout the day. And to the great silent majority it was a provocative spectacle which, if it did nothing else, served dramatically and often movingly to underscore the extent and poignancy of the desire of Americans to end the war in Vietnam—and their division over how to do it.

Certainly no one—friend, foe or neutral—could deny that the demonstrations reached into every nook and cranny of the land, or that the youthful liberal activists who organized the moratorium had demonstrated a high degree of organizing skill. They had taken their campaign into the streets and had done so almost without violence; the most dramatic was an attempt . . . by a small band of black militants to storm the gates of the White House itself. . . .[9]

We could explore the voice grammatically; the first sentence is a coordinated one, the first paragraph is developed by a pattern of repetition (parallelism). We could examine the development of the topic sentences in both paragraphs, the balanced comment, the use of familiar words and phrases (clichés) from vari-

[9] Copyright Newsweek, Inc., October 27, 1969, p. 30.

ous sources—"nook and cranny" smells of the lamp of poetry, "hard-nosed" is from the sportswriter's jargon, "storm the gates" is the rhetoric of oratory.

Or we could explore the voice in the words of a critic of *Newsweek:*

A kind of Armageddon-like quality pervades much of the prose: there is a surfeit of burning issues, crying needs, pent-up desires, heated debates, dim views, solid footholds, glimmers of hope. Guns are stuck to, needs are underscored, ties are buttressed, battle lines are drawn, influence is knuckled under to, sympathetic chords are struck. Sometimes images are confusingly mixed.

Newsweek is much more anxious to make broad pronouncements about the significance of a week's events, to practice the art of the "hype" [hyperbole] by which the routine is blown up into the incredible and the sensational. It is filled with "crises," "turning points," and "watersheds." . . .[10]

Or we could compare *Newsweek*'s style with the style of *Time*'s report of the same event:

The impact of M-day was more than the sum of its disparate parts. Hundreds of thousands of Americans found, face to face, that they had a common cause. Those who participated actively may be only the visibly restive; many sympathizers and many others merely interested watched the day's events unfold on television. . . . It was a calm, measured and heavily middle class statement of weariness with the war that brought the generations together in a kind of sedate Woodstock Festival of peace. . . .[11]

The voice that speaks here is dispassionate, remote, flat, almost monotonous. It is abstract until the comparison to the "Woodstock Festival." The three groups that are described in the *Newsweek* paragraph become, in *Time*, simply the "sum of its disparate parts." There is no suggestion of warmth of any kind, of any personality behind the words.

Both voices depend somewhat on parenthetical expressions ("friend, foe or neutral," "face to face"), both fall back once on the periodic syllogistic sentence: the last sentence of the *Newsweek* quotation, the third sentence of the *Time* quotation. The *Newsweek* statements are argumentative and persuasive; the *Time* sentences are basically reportage.

[10] Chris Wells, *"Newsweek . . . ," Esquire,* November, 1969, p. 153.

[11] *Time,* October 24, 1969, p. 16. Reprinted by permission from *Time,* The Weekly Newsmagazine; Copyright Time Inc.

Assignment for Discussion

Bring to class several examples of descriptions of one event which you may find in magazines, newspapers, or books. Try to find the voice that is speaking in each case, and see if you can determine how the reader's impression of an event might be shaped by the voice. *Note:* the difference in the selection of details might be one indication of voice, but it is not the only one.

The *tone* of a passage will be determined by the voice used by the writer. Tone is the subjective mood in operation, whether or not a person is enthusiastic, compassionate, dispassionate, formal, colloquial at the time he is writing. Good writers determine their tone in advance and try to maintain it—if they shift, they do it deliberately.

In scientific prose the voice is even less distinguishable than it is in the *Time* passage:

Amperometric titrations constitute a class of electrometric titrations based on the measurement of the diffusion current of the substance being titrated, and/or that of the reagent during the titrations. The current which passes through the titration cell between an indicator electrode at a suitable applied voltage is measured as a function of the volume of the titrating solution (the titrant). The end point of an amperometric titration is found at the point of intersection of two lines giving the change of current before and after the equivalent.

This paragraph has one purpose—to inform. It cannot in any sense be construed as persuasive. We can take it or leave it as it is—whether we do or don't is of no concern to the author. He is not emotionally involved in the facts of "amperometric titrations" and neither are we. His tone is neutral.

Yet this paragraph, like the ones examined earlier, has a pattern that can be ascertained; as a matter of fact the pattern may help us to the meaning of a decidedly abstract paragraph.

The paragraph is an operational definition that uses two other forms of definition—a logical definition in which a part of the term being defined is repeated (ll. 1–3), and a definition by synonymy (l. 6). The paragraph begins with a high level abstraction; it develops through a series of clauses and phrases (nine or ten of which are prepositional) of varying lower levels of abstraction.

The highest level of abstraction is: electrometric titrations. The next level is: amperometric titrations (just as an *ampere* is a lower level of *electric*). The next lower level has to do with two measurements: of the diffusion current and of the reagent. "Diffusion current" is in turn modified by one of the next lower level of abstractions: "the substance being titrated"; the "reagent" is modified by a time clause operating as a lower level of abstraction: "during the titrations." The second sentence modifies the phrase "measurement of the diffusion current"; the term "passes" is modified by three phrases parallel to each other in their levels of abstraction: (a) through the titration cell; (b) between an indicator electrode (is this grammatically accurate?); and (c) at a suitable applied voltage. The verb "is measured" of the second sentence is followed by three phrases, the first of which modifies the verb, and the next two of which modify their preceding phrases. (Are you with me?) The verb and the phrases thus represent four levels of abstraction. Question: what does the third sentence modify?

Following is a paragraph written by a student who was challenged to explain a difficult scientific concept in a paragraph that was developed through a pattern of succeedingly lower levels of abstraction. To save space, the paragraph is outlined; only the complete sentences are marked according to their levels of abstraction. Can you identify the lower levels in each sentence?

All elements consist of a positively charged nucleus surrounded by a variable number of concentric shells, each containing a fixed number of negatively charged electrons. (1)

In some elements, the outermost shell contains the whole number of electrons needed to fill or complete the shell. (2)

These are the inert or nonreactive elements, including xenon, helium, argon, krypton, and radon. (3)

The other elements contain an incomplete outermost electron shell. (2)

This makes them chemically reactive because they can gain or lose a few electrons by combining with other elements which also have elements to share. (3)

Two or more elements are said to be chemically bonded to each other when they share some electrons with each other. (2)

For example, if fluorine is missing one electron in its outer shell, it can become more comfortable or stable by combining

with an element like hydrogen, which has an extra electron to
lose or share with fluorine. (Mrs. Aimee Bakken)   (3)

The voice here is certain of itself and of its knowledge from
which it speaks—the certainty of "all elements," for instance. Yet
it is unsure of itself as far as its control over the language is
concerned; one sees this in the careful, perhaps overdone, repetition of "shells," "elements," and "electron."

The paragraph is organized along the line of a comparison; this
organization accounts for the movement back and forth between
the two levels of generality.

Here is a scientific paragraph with a recognizable voice:

What, then, is the chemical law? It is this: In the very hottest stars
we deal with the gases hydrogen, helium and doubtless others still unknown, almost exclusively. At the next lowest temperatures we find
these gases being replaced by metals in the state in which they are
observed in our laboratories when the most powerful jar-spark is employed. At a lower temperature still the gases disappear almost entirely, and the metals exist in the state produced by the electric arc.
(Sir Norman Lockyer)

This voice begins by asking a rhetorical question, one it feels
has been aroused in the minds of its readers by an earlier reference. Then, instead of responding with an answer couched in
scientific jargon, the voice defines the law with an example. In
the use of the "we" the voice implies that its audience has undergone the described experience also and is therefore capable of
following the explanation. The audience is, the voice assumes, a
scientifically informed audience, but it is not an audience that
can relate to an esoteric definition. The tone is deliberate; the
explanation careful. The writer is a man sure of his knowledge,
aware of his standing, and considerate of his audience's intellectual concerns. The rhetorical pattern that he has used is a
simple one.

Lockyer's paragraph was written some 70 years ago at a time
when many scientists still thought and wrote in a style influenced
by literary traditions. Today, scientific explanation more often
looks like this:

The method is merely to draw the utility line determined by the
assignment of utility values, and to find where this line cuts the
broken line $T_1\, T_2\, T_3\, T_4$. If R'', the point where it cuts it, is either T_2 or
T_3, the basic strategy T_2 or T_3 respectively is the prudential strategy.

If R'' lies in the part of T_3, the prudential strategy is the randomized strategy obtained by compounding the use of strategy T_2 with a probability p'' and the use of strategy T_3 with a probability $1\text{-}p''$, where p'' is the ratio of the length $R''T_3$ to the length of T_2T_3.[12]

Style in the twentieth century has to take many circumstances into consideration in a way that it did not for the nineteenth century writer. His audience lived primarily in a literary and oratorical tradition. Magazines and books, for the most part, were limited to educated readers; audiences for the spoken word were limited to the range of the speaker's ability to project his voice. There were stylistic conventions and traditions, but it was more easily possible for the writer to be his own man; it could safely be said that style was the man. In this century the impact of mass education, of mass audiences beyond the reach of ordinary speech, of science and technology, of mass media, particularly the motion pictures and television, have laid demands on the writer of a sort that tend to diminish his own personality; we are, as a recent *Time* writer wrote, a nation in which "the bland lead the bland."

Style in this century must take into account the subject, the media, the audience, the writer's purpose. Scientific subjects for popular audiences tend to look like this:

Basically, allergy is a lock-and-key affair. When the chemical key, entering or coming into contact with the body from the outside, finds its lock in the body tissues, all is well. But when lock and key don't fit, or when there is no lock for the key, or an insufficient number of locks for the number of keys, then the itching, sneezing, coughing, watery eyes, running nose and all the other unpleasant symptoms of an allergic reaction manifest themselves. (Julian DeVries, *The Arizona Republic*)

Here science has almost completely disappeared from the explanation; it has been replaced by a metaphor drawn from the homely background of the newspaper audience. The language is familiar and the situation even more so. The subject is one that the average reader can identify with. Not so the Braithwaite example.

To get back to the subject of paragraph patterns—if we examine the last several paragraphs we find:

• The pattern of the Lockyer paragraph and the first *Newsweek* paragraph are identical: 1–2–2–2 (remember 1 equals the most abstract statement in the paragraph).

[12] R. B. Braithwaite, *Scientific Explanation,* Cambridge University Press, 1953.

• The pattern of the *Esquire* paragraph is 1–2–2–1: 1–2 (I count the first full sentence as if it were two sentences, the first a higher level of abstraction than the second).
• The *Time* paragraph pattern is 1–2–2–3–1.
• If the Braithwaite paragraph is considered as having three sentences, its pattern is 1–2–2.

What does all of this mean for you besides a mumbo-jumbo of words and numbers? First of all, it means that many paragraphs begin at a high level of abstraction (for the paragraph) and proceed to a lower one, often by a series of steps in which each sentence or phrase modifies the preceding one. Some paragraphs develop in a series of steps that return us to the original high level of abstraction. Sometimes (as in the Bakken paragraph) levels of abstraction alternate in a paragraph.

Second, you can learn to write from good writers by analyzing their paragraphs for the patterns, and then using these patterns for your own paragraphs. Let me emphasize the point by analyzing the Erskine paragraph:

. . . you make a point	(1)	(the basic statement or, to put it another way, the highest level of abstraction)
when you write	(2)	(moves toward precision—a man might make a point, for example, when he speaks. This phrase is at a lower level of abstraction than the first one)
not by subtracting	(3)	(modifies "you make a point when you write" and is therefore at an even lower level of abstraction)
as though you sharpened a pencil	(4)	(modifies "subtracting" and therefore is at an even lower level of abstraction)
but by adding.	(3)	(is parallel to and on the same level of abstraction as "not by subtracting" and modifies "when you write you make a point")

If we list the numbers of the phrases in the order in which Erskine wrote them, our pattern is 2–1–3–4–3. This pattern ought to suggest ways to you of obtaining paragraph variety or emphasis by rearranging sentences and phrases in the process of revision. We shall see another example in a page or two.

Now, suppose that I want to use the Erskine paragraph as a model for a paragraph about my study. I look around for a subject at a high level of abstraction to be my number (1), and I come up with:

> I use several items as I work. (1)

I need something now for my number (2), something that will modify (1), make it more precise. So I write:

> In my work as a writer, (2)
> I use several items as I work, (1)

and now the other phrases fall into place:

> among them several dictionaries, (3)
> of which the most useful is an abridged, (4)
> and a set of the *Encyclopaedia Britannica.* (3)

This method for improving your writing ability has at least two things going for it: it gives you a professional model to follow, and it requires that you observe carefully for the details to fill in the pattern. It also requires a good deal of concentration and thought, skills that every writer needs.

Let us examine now a passage from Walter Lord's *A Night to Remember.* Although an editor commented that the book is not literature in the ordinary sense of the word, and concluded that Lord deliberately abstained from "style in the attention-getting sense of the word," nevertheless the voice which speaks in this sample is that of a professional writer. The pattern of abstractions is a complex one, designed to catch a reader's attention, set up one of the paradoxes that give the book point, and then to hold the reader's attention with specific detail that is still related to the point of the book:

High in the crow's nest of the new White Star liner *Titanic,* Lookout Frederick Fleet peered into a dazzling night. (2) It was calm, clear and bitterly cold. (3) There was no moon, (3) but the cloudless sky blazed with stars. (3) The Atlantic was like polished plate glass; (3) people later said they had never seen it so smooth. (4) This was the fifth night of the *Titanic's* maiden voyage to New York, (1) and it was already clear that she was not only the largest but also the most glamorous ship in the world. (1) Even the passengers' dogs were glamorous. (2) John Jacob Astor had along his Airedale, Kitty. (3) Henry Sleeper Harper, of the publishing family, had his prize Pekingese, Sun-Yat-Sen. (3) Robert W. Daniel, the Philadelphia banker, was bringing back a champion French bulldog, just purchased in Britain. (3) Clarence Moore, of Washington, also had been dog shopping, (3) but the fifty pairs of English foxhounds he bought for the Loudon Hunt weren't making the trip. (4) [13]

This paragraph is complex in that it has two high level abstractions (both numbered 1) and that the coordinated pair come at the center of the paragraph. The half of the paragraph preceding the center and the succeeding half are balanced in pattern and content. Lord's book focuses on the night, the crew, the ship, and the passengers, and he has adroitly included them all in his first paragraph. He begins with the night and the watchman; we are reminded of *Agamemnon*, where the introduction of the watchman starts us on the road to another tragedy. We cannot doubt that Lord had that Greek play in mind as he began his book; and whether he intended it or not, there is an irony in his initial scene. The Greek watchman in *Agamemnon* complains of the cold night and the dog's life he is forced to lead. The watchman on the deck of the *Titanic* probably would gladly have settled for the life of some of the dogs on his ship! The *Titanic* dogs serve as a symbol for the luxuriousness of the life on board the ship, and they help point out one of the book's themes: man cannot ignore nature no matter what sort of symbolic patterns he may construct between himself and his universe. The editor who said this book is not literature is dead wrong; it is literature and very good literature at that, even though it is nonfiction.

To give you an idea of the options open to Mr. Lord, here is the opening statement of Hanson W. Baldwin's "R. M. S. *Titanic*." In any narrative of a voyage (*The Odyssey, Moby Dick, Two Years Before the Mast, Life on the Mississippi, Adventures of Huckleberry Finn, A Night to Remember*) the narrator has the option of starting *in media res* (in the center of the action, as *The Odyssey* and Mr. Lord's book do), or at the beginning, as Mr. Baldwin does:

The White Star liner *Titanic*, largest ship the world had ever known, sailed from Southampton on her maiden voyage to New York on April 10, 1912. The paint on her strakes was fair and bright; she

[13] Walter Lord, *A Night to Remember*, Holt, Rinehart and Winston, 1955.

was fresh from Harland and Wolff's Belfast yards, strong in the strength of her forty-six thousand tons of steel, bent, hammered, shaped, and riveted through the three years of her slow birth.

Mr. Baldwin's essay begins with a focus on the ship and her construction; not until later will he begin to tell us about the distinguished passengers on board. His introductory paragraph, while well-written (although we certainly get a whiff of the oil of his lamp), sets up no paradoxes and points to no themes. There is no irony in the paragraph; no allusions that will suggest that the essay will deal with the tragic aspect of man's existence. Were I to choose one of the two selections on the *Titanic's* sinking to read, I would select Mr. Lord's on the basis of the evidence presented here.

Assignment for Discussion and Writing

These patterns suggest that Christensen is right when he says that explanation is often a matter of levels of generalization. For class discussion, bring in examples of paragraphs that either support his statement or that seem to you to disprove it. Analyze the paragraphs for levels of generality and also for the voice that speaks in them. In your analysis include all parts of each sentence.

Then try writing parodies of the paragraphs, including the sentences. Use as your subject matter the familiar background of your classroom, the campus, your domicile, and so on. Do you agree with me that filling out the patterns creates a need for acute observation?

Here is an even more complicated paragraph pattern from *Time:*

The heroine of *The Sterile Cuckoo* is a happy little dumpling of a college freshman called Pookie, a name that holds promises of maudlin disaster. The movie fulfills them. Pookie (Liza Minnelli) is what used to be called, back in the dim and distant fifties, a kook. She does swell things like move in with her straight-arrow boy friend while he is studying for his finals, puts tape across her mouth—'cause she's promised not to talk to him—and communicates with him by holding up signs. College is some bucolic wonderland where it is always fall,

even in the depths of winter, and the students think that S.D.S. is
some new kind of 3.2 beer. *The Sterile Cuckoo* is not only irrelevant
to today, it is irrelevant to any time at all. Liza Minnelli, who is much
too obviously the star of this project, strains to bring the whole thing
off, but the task is greater than her talents.[14]

What is the subject of this paragraph? To what is the detail
added to sharpen it? Is it "the heroine," "the movie," "Pookie,"
"college," "*The Sterile Cuckoo*," or "Liza Minnelli"? I obtain this
list by writing down the subject of each sentence on the premise
that the subject of one of the sentences must be the subject of
the paragraph. To bring the suspense quickly to an end, the one
subject that will contain all the others (in a system of classification) is "*The Sterile Cuckoo*" in sentence six. That sentence, then,
is the highest level of abstraction:

> *The Sterile Cuckoo* . . . is irrelevant to any time at all. (1)

It takes some juggling of the paragraph's prose to establish
this. The first part of the sentence is closely attached, for instance:

> *The Sterile Cuckoo* is . . . irrelevant to today . . . (2)

The balance of the paragraph sharpens the detail by explicat-
ing three parts of the subject—the heroine, the setting, and the
qualities of the actress who portrays the heroine. There are, then,
three number 3 levels:

> The heroine . . . is a happy little dumpling . . . (3)
> College is some bucolic wonderland . . . (3)
> Liza Minnelli . . . strains to bring the whole thing off . . .
> (3)

The other phrases and sentences operate at succeedingly lower
levels of abstraction:

> . . . a name that holds promise of maudlin disaster. (4)
> The movie fulfills them. (5)
> She does swell things . . . (5)
> . . where it is always fall . . . (4)
> . . even in the depths of winter . . . (5)
> . . the students think that . . . beer. (4)
> . . who is much too obviously the star . . . (4)
> . . . the task is greater than her talents. (5)

---

[14] *Time*, October 31, 1969, p. 91. Reprinted by permission from *Time*, **The**
Weekly Newsmagazine; Copyright Time Inc.

At this point you may rightfully complain that the writer did not compose his paragraph in this way—at least common sense tells us that he probably began with "the heroine" and went on. That may be the case. I make my demonstration for several reasons: This is a very professional paragraph, and you can learn quite a bit about writing from the professionals. Second, suppose we were to write the paragraph in a pattern that began with the highest level of abstraction and proceeded to the lowest:

The film is irrelevant to any time at all, and is especially irrelevant to today. The heroine is a happy little dumpling of a college freshman called Pookie, a name that holds promises of maudlin disaster. The movie fulfills them. Pookie is what used to be called, back in the dim and distant fifties, a kook. She does swell things. . .

Perhaps this is the way the writer originally wrote his paragraph, then changed his mind, rewrote the first sentence in a more effective form and reinserted it as the penultimate sentence in his paragraph. In this way he built his paragraph up to its climax, saving his best sentence for near the end. The final sentence then becomes anticlimactic, and the whole paragraph ends with a bang, not a whimper.

The writer of this paragraph is a person who is willing to make judgments, as his "happy little dumpling," "maudlin disaster," "strains to bring the whole thing off" show. He accepts the movie on its own terms—"she does swell things"—but then he shows his scorn for such activities—"college is a bucolic wonderland." Limited in space, he knows he must persuade you to accept his judgment, and so he concentrates on a chief target. The film, he suspects, was designed as a showcase for the talents of its star, and he trys to persuade his reader that neither the showcase nor the star is very good. He maintains a tone of lightheartedness until he comes to his major judgment—"the film is irrelevant."

Assignments for Discussion

Determine the levels of abstraction in the following paragraphs:

This is true of nepotism—literally *nephewism*—wherever it occurs: in business, in government or in any other organization. When a grand old man who founded a corporation forty years ago moves up to the board chairmanship and places his son in the president's office, he is doing his bit to move society back toward a system of hereditary status. The mayor of a western city was recently under political attack for having placed no less than fourteen relatives in city jobs. The fraternity which gives special consideration to "legacies" (i.e., relatives of present members), the college which gives special consideration to sons of alumni, the clubs which weigh family background in selecting new members, the mother who doesn't want her son to marry "below his station"—all are examples of the continuing vigor of the forces leading back toward hereditary tradition.

It is easy for us as Americans to see positive virtue in both equalitarianism *and* emphasis upon competitive performance. But it is not easy for us to see the disadvantages of either. The drama which still grips our national imagination is the escape from a society of hereditary privilege. And our aversion to such a society is so great as to cast any alternatives in a positive light. As a result, any bright schoolboy can write an essay on the disadvantages of hereditary stratification. Hardly any could write an essay on the disadvantages of extreme equalitarianism or of extreme emphasis upon individual performance. But such essays must be written.[15]

Discuss the voice that is speaking in this paragraph:

Due to a series of circumstances my insurance business failed about this time. Instead of accepting defeat I discovered that my hobby, the collecting of buttons of pre-Revolutionary War vintage, interested people. Soon I had a thriving little stand going on a vacant lot. Looking back on it all now, the joy in people's eyes when their eyes would fall on a sergeant's button which had been shattered by a minie ball was more important than the money we lost on the venture. My wife, Anne, remarked quietly one day after an oldster had just admired our display: "That oldster served in the same regiment as the man who wore this button." We both smiled quietly. We knew we were making history, playing a part in the American dream.[16]

What are the characteristics of the voice in this paragraph? How do you know? What is a "minie ball"? What were the dates of the "Revolutionary War"? How old was the "oldster"? Would you say that this paragraph appeared originally in *Reader's Digest* or *Saturday Review*?

---

[15] From pp. 6 and 9 in *Excellence: Can We Be Equal and Excellent Too?* by John W. Gardner (Harper & Row).

[16] Richard Mathison, "Modern Minuteman," December 3, 1949, Phoenix Nest column, edited by William Rose Benét, *Saturday Review of Literature*. Copyright 1949 The Saturday Review Associates, Inc.

At what point in the above paragraph did you realize that you were being conned by a satirist—and a special kind of satirist at that? Your satirist speaks indirectly; he seems to be saying one thing when he is actually saying another. He is a critic of social or personal mores who conceals his criticism in order to give it more sting through his cleverness and wit. The best satirists manage subtle nuances of meaning, not always possible in the direct confrontation.

The special voice in this satire is that of the parodist. At his simplest, the parodist merely ridicules; at his best, he often creates a better work than that he parodied and at the same time reveals the flaws in apparent virtues.

Whenever we read we must be on the alert for the satirist; although his primary purpose may be to attack some social or personal foible, a secondary purpose (if not an equal one) may be to con the gullible, to put us on.

The parodist or satirist works within one limitation—the work parodied, the thing satirized must be familiar to the audience or else the reader will not see the point. Sometimes, therefore, the audience of the satirist is very small; sometimes, as in the case of some television programs where the subject of the satire is widely known, the audience can be very large.

Parody can be directed at our misfortunes as well as our follies:

> Winter is icumen in,
>   Loud sing kerchoo.
> Bloweth wind and spreadeth germ,
>   Flieth hat from head askew—
>   Sing kerchoo! [17]

This particular parody points out that nature brings troubles as well as blessings, a classic theme in our literature. Its theme gets an assist from its reminder of the original:

> Sumer is icumen in,
>   Lhude sing cuccu!
> Groweth sed, and bloweth med,
>   And springeth wude nu—
>   Sing cuccu!

A cardinal rule of parody is that it must imitate the style of the original. Where the original is verse, the rhymes, meter, and verses must be closely imitated.

[17] Bradford Smith, "Winter Is Icumen In," December 20, 1958, Phoenix Nest column, edited by Martin Levin, *Saturday Review*. Copyright 1958 Saturday Review, Inc.

Assignment for Discussion and Writing

Find parodies of other works in your college library. Martin Levin's *The Phoenix Nest* (Doubleday & Company, 1960) has several. Bret Harte's *Condensed Novels* and Max Beerbohm's *A Christmas Garland* are good. Two of Lewis Carroll's poems—"How doth the little crocodile" and "You are old, Father William"—are not only parodies but better poems than their models. Bring what you find to class and discuss the aims of the parodists and their successes or failures.

Write a parody of something familiar to you—a sports column, a newspaper column, something in a magazine, a film, a book, or a TV show. Or, if you have a talent for cartooning, create a cartoon parody. You might want to look at "Little Annie Fannie" in *Playboy* or some back issues of *Mad*.

Other Models for Paragraphs

There are patterns that may be examined in the paragraph other than the ones based on voice or levels of abstraction. Take this paragraph as an example:

Because *The Constant Prince* is a fairy tale, we see the persecutors ultimately shamed and abashed by the prince as they leave him alone onstage. The lights go out for an instant. When they come on again, we see the prince's corpse lying covered with a red blanket. Is the play over? The audience doesn't seem to know, and each person leaves the theater at the moment of his own choice, for clearly part of the play is our response to this sight. Not a traditionally brave hero with super-human courage exerted for some fine political purpose, but a weak and fearful human being committed to being himself at all costs, whose resultant response to a hostile society is a tragic victory.[18]

The pattern of this paragraph is sequential through the first five sentences, with the final sentence (is it a sentence?) being used as a summary of the character who has been discussed in the essay. The paragraph has a statement at a high level of abstraction (the last one), but this statement does not serve as a topic sentence for the paragraph.

The voice that speaks here is the voice of an audience for the

[18] Henry Hewes, "The Theater," *Saturday Review*, November 1, 1969, p. 14.

play, a voice that is capable of speaking for the whole audience at one point, and that is capable of turning on itself at another: "We see . . . the audience doesn't seem to know." The voice is as indecisive and anti-heroic as the play itself seems to be. Finally, it is a perceptive voice that is able to make an evaluation of sorts, given the evidence.

Does it bother you that the final statement is not written in traditional sentence form? If you had written this sentence, how would your teacher have marked it?

Here is a paragraph that begins with a rhetorical question and continues with a series of answers to the question, constructed as parallels, both grammatically and ideologically:

If a person is old enough to perceive what is happening around him, what does he see? He sees a world divided into rigid sovereignties. . . . He sees the energies and resources of nations being diverted into ever larger ways of expunging or cheapening human life. He sees people preoccupied and swollen with meaningless satisfactions. He sees concepts of human brotherhood and social justice held up by society as its animating ideals, but he finds that his own efforts to act on behalf of these concepts will put him in conflict with that same society. He sees a world being insanely fouled by pollution. He sees the good earth being covered over with tar and cement, the lakes and streams being poisoned by detergents and chemical excrescences, the oxygen in the air being depleted. He knows that our astronauts were able to roam the heavens because no limitations were placed on human ingenuity, technological facilities or funds; and he is unsatisfied with the argument that it is impossible to mount a comparable effort to make life on earth a little less hellish. He feels that people react to youth in terms of superficials—hair or beard or clothes or, in the case of girls, absence of facial paint or fancy coiffures—and not in terms of the things that scar their vision or tear at their gizzards.[19]

There is an interesting rhetorical device here—for although it is true that people do feel as the paragraph describes, the feelings being projected here are obviously the feelings of the writer as well. The voice here is indignant, yet urbane, unhappy, yet well-educated. He is able to project ideas in series, in antitheses, in periods; and the language flows from his pen.

Sometimes the paragraph takes the form of comparison and contrast:

[19] Norman Cousins, "The Intermediate Battlefield," *Saturday Review*, November 8, 1969, p. 26.

Wit is a lean creature with a sharp inquiring nose, whereas humor has a kindly eye and uncomfortable girth. Wit, if it be necessary, uses malice to score a point—like a cat, it is quick to jump—but humor keeps the peace in an easy chair. Wit has a better voice in a solo, but humor comes into the chorus best. Wit is as sharp as a stroke of lightning, whereas humor is diffuse like sunlight. Wit keeps the season's fashions and is precise in the phrases and judgments of the day, but humor is concerned with homely eternal things. Wit wears silk, but humor in homespun endures the wind. Wit sets a snare, whereas humor goes off whistling without a victim in its mind. Wit is sharper company at table, but humor serves better in mischance and in the rain. When it tumbles, wit is sour, but humor goes uncomplainingly without its dinner. Humor laughs at another's jest and holds its sides, while wit sits wrapped in study for a lively answer.[20]

The use of analogy and simile here is carried to the point where "wit" and "humor" practically achieve the status of living beings —they become anthropomorphic. What you are being treated to is not only a comparison of the two traits, but also an operational definition.

The preceding quotation demonstrated one form of comparison —the alternation of characteristics of the subject being compared. Here is the other form in which one subject is explored first, then the second:

An examination of these two reports reveals some basic differences and implies that different weightings and interpretations must have been given to the evidence. The grand jury said that participants in a May 4 assembly on the campus failed to obey repeated orders to disperse. "If the order to disperse had been heeded, there would not have been the consequences of that fateful day," it added. The grand jury report also noted that commanding officers of the National Guard agreed that M1 rifles and other high-powered weapons are not suited for campus duty. The jury recommended that non-lethal weapons be made available to the guard but added that "guardsmen should be furnished weapons which will afford them necessary protection." Nevertheless, in the Kent State case the jury held that National Guardsmen acted in self-defense in their fatal confrontation with students. "Members of the National Guard," the jury said, "fired their weapons in the sincere and honest belief . . . that they would suffer serious bodily injury had they not done so." The report of the President's Commission on Campus Unrest differs greatly on these subjects. The guard's presence appears to have been the greatest attraction, it said, for most students who came to the May 4 rally,

[20] Charles S. Brooks, *Chimney-Pot Papers,* Yale University Press, pp. 129–130.

which began as a peaceful assembly on the commons. On the subject of weapons it said that Kent State "must mark the last time loaded rifles are issued as a matter of course to guardsmen confronting student demonstrators." The report charged that the deaths were "inexcusable," and that the guardsmen had fired "indiscriminately."

The above comparison begins with a conclusion that acts as a predictor for the two sets of opinions that are reported. Then the two blocks of opinion are quoted in turn. Though they are presented in sequence, each deals with items of information that can be compared, and the items are presented in the same order.

Some writers rely on exemplification—the use of examples and specific instances—as the means by which they develop their paragraphs. Here is one (used as an example!):

This myth, which extends to the whole judiciary, not just the Supreme Court, is further illustrated by the condemnation of any judge who indulges in any remotely political activity—except the deciding of cases. When Justice Douglas, a few years back, made a series of public speeches urging that the Constitution's Bill of Rights be zealously followed and zealously guarded, especially in explosive times like these—a sentiment scarcely out of keeping with the duties or office of a high judge sworn to uphold the Constitution—he was bitterly criticized by much of the press and most of the bar for stooping to political partisanship and so sullying his judicial robes and judicial integrity. Although not yet deprived of their right, as citizens, to cast their votes every November, Supreme Court Justices—off the bench as well as on it—are deemed by the myth to be, properly, apolitical persons, unaffected by what goes on in the nation outside their marble temple, aloof and remote from the workaday world.[21]

Mr. Rodell knows as well as anyone that we cannot generalize from one example. Yet his alternatives are not easy. One is to write something like this: "On 37 different occasions, Justices have been criticized . . ." and then footnote all 37 instances; another is to cite several examples; but the busy reader will probably not stand still for that. The third, and the one he has used, is to cite one example to make the point that he is sure we all are aware of.

Mr. Rodell's voice (at least in this paragraph) is a voice that pauses, stops, reconsiders, as it goes along—and constantly throws in exceptions, parenthetical asides, and qualifications.

[21] Fred Rodell, *Nine Men,* Random House, 1955, p. 29.

His is a voice much like the voice of anyone who knows how difficult it is to make a precise point.

The other type of proof open to a writer is exemplified in this paragraph:

There can be small and pleasant interludes in autumn's steady advance. Proof of this is a nooning hour spent by a countryman in a corner of what once was a pasture and will never be a woodlot. Behind a screen of young junipers, in an angle of old walls, there is a square of dry, tawny grass. It is a scrap of abandoned nature where nothing grows more valuable than reddening sumac, more useful to a winter woodpile than a dead elm, more fruitful of berries than oddly vigorous bittersweet vines possessing tumbled rocks. There is not a maple to redden . . . but goldenrod and asters have set up their colored borders undisturbed and every day will see more scarlet feathering the sumacs.[22]

This paragraph is developed through the use of particulars and details, proof of the writer's eye for observation and his ability to record or remember.

An analytical mind produces this kind of paragraph:

For me, as for many others, the reading of detective stories is an addiction like tobacco or alcohol. The symptoms of this are: Firstly, the intensity of the craving—if I have any work to do, I must be careful not to get hold of a detective story for, once I begin one, I cannot work or sleep till I have finished it. Secondly, its specificity—the story must conform to certain formulas. . . . And, thirdly, its immediacy. I forget the story as soon as I have finished it, and have no wish to read it again.[23]

Or this kind:

The insects of New Guinea are less known than the birds, but they seem almost equally remarkable for fine forms and brilliant colors. . . . The magnificent green and yellow Ornithopterae are abundant. . . . Among the smaller butterflies are several peculiar genera of Nymphalidae and Lycaenidae, remarkable for their large size singular markings, or brilliant coloration. The largest and most beautiful of the clear-winged moths (Cocytia d'urvillei) is found here, as well as the large and handsome green moth (Nyctalemon orontes). (Alfred Wallace)

[22] "Juniper Corners," *New York Herald Tribune*, September 16, 1951, p. 4.
[23] W. H. Auden, *The Dyer's Hand*, Random House, 1962, p. 146.

In other words, if the subject lends itself (and if the writer's mind is so inclined) to classification or analysis, those techniques may be used for paragraph development.

Paragraphs may be developed by a method that offers reasons in answer to the question "why." (The paragraph need not contain the question.) Sometimes such a paragraph explains one reason fully; sometimes it gives several reasons, each perhaps with a brief explanation. Sometimes this method is expanded into two or more paragraphs; the question is asked in the first (or a situation requiring reasons is set up), and the answers are given in the second:

Why should we go through the painful process of "unlearning" and relearning grammar simply because linguists have concocted some new theories? The first answer . . . is that the superseding of vague and sloppy thinking by clear and precise thinking is an exciting experience in and for itself. To acquire insight into the workings of our language, and to recognize the infinitely delicate system of relationship, balance, and interplay that constitutes its grammar, is to become closely acquainted with one of man's most miraculous creations, not unworthy to be set beside the equally beautiful organization of the physical universe. . . . [Furthermore,] it seems probable that a realistic, scientific grammar should vastly facilitate the teaching of English. . . . [Finally,] the new grammar can also be of use in improving the . . . speaker's proficiency in handling the structural devices of his . . . language.[24]

Paragraphs may be developed by a *cause and effect* method. When you use this method you begin with an initial step and then proceed in a logical sequence. Clear transitions between steps are essential:

The real nature of writing in its relation to language is so obvious on a moment's reflection that it might seem strange that so much misunderstanding could arise about it. Probably the confusion is due to two things: the nature of our English spelling system, and the age at which we start to learn the language. . . . Our traditional orthography for English is quite far removed from the reality of speech, and our letters do not stand in a wholly one-to-one relationship with the phonemes of our speech. [Therefore,] it takes considerable effort and many years (as we all know!) to master completely our English conventional spelling. . . . We learn to speak long before we are able

[24] W. Nelson Francis, "Revolution in Grammar," *Quarterly Journal of Speech,* October, 1954.

to do any kind of reflective or analytical intellectual work. . . . This entire situation has given results that are little short of disastrous for the understanding of the true nature of language.[25]

In this paragraph, "misunderstanding" in the first sentence becomes the "confusion" of the second sentence. The subject of spelling is introduced and carried on into the next sentence. Then the subject of the age at which we learn the language is picked up and explained. Finally, there is a summary which ties the whole together.

From all of this you may conclude that the paragraph exists as a strategic device for the writer. It also serves as a convenience for the reader. Typographically, it breaks up the large mass of matter that the narrative printed page would otherwise have— along that line, its use permits spacing at some points or the use of an illuminated or large block letter at another. In terms of the ideas being presented, the paragraph "signals" units of thought— although in many cases (as in the Einstein example in Chapter 11), a unit of thought may be spread out over several paragraphs. Winston Churchill who has been singled out as a great writer, both by critics and by himself, said that a paragraph should "embrace a distinct episode," but that rule, like most others aimed at producing a "classical English style," is no doubt broken as often as it is followed. Churchill also thought that "paragraphs must fit on to one another like the automatic couplings of railway carriages"—which, for the most part, is pretty good advice.

When a topic sentence is used in a paragraph, it may be used as the initial sentence, a middle sentence, or an end sentence. When it is used initially, the balance of the paragraph usually develops the predicate portion of the sentence. However, if the subject causes a question in our minds, the paragraph may be used to develop the subject. In that case the succeeding paragraph might answer our questions about the predicate.

One of my favorite paragraphs may seem to you to have no logical development to it at all:

Word has somehow got around that a split infinitive is always wrong. This is of a piece with the sentimental and outworn notion that it is always wrong to strike a lady. Everybody will recall at least one woman of his acquaintance whom, at one time or another, he has had to punch or slap. I have in mind a charming lady who is over-

[25] Robert A. Hall, Jr., *Leave Your Language Alone!* Second Revised Edition, Doubleday (Anchor Books), p. 41.

come by the unaccountable desire, at formal dinners with red and white wines, to climb up on the table and lie down. Her dinner companion used at first to pinch her under the cover of conversation, but she pinched right back, or, what is even less defensible, tickled. They finally learned that they could make her hold her seat only by fetching her a smart downward blow on the head. She would then sit quietly through the rest of the dinner, smiling dreamily and nodding at people, and looking altogether charming.[26]

Assignment for Discussion

Look for paragraphs that seem to you not to fit any of the patterns outlined in this chapter. Bring them in and challenge your classmates to find any pattern in them. Also, bring in paragraphs that exemplify patterns outlined in this chapter. Do you find that some writers stick to patterned paragraphs more than others? To prefer one pattern over others?

Assignment for Writing

Select subjects that can be developed by each of the methods discussed in the latter part of this chapter: particulars and details, comparison and contrast, exemplification, reasons, cause and effect. Write three paragraphs, using one of these methods for each paragraph. Identify the method used, at the beginning of the paragraph.

[26] Copyright © 1931, 1959 James Thurber. From "The Split Infinitive" in *The Owl in the Attic*, published by Harper & Row, New York. Originally published in *The New Yorker*.

11

Structure

In the same sense in which I earlier said that sentences in themselves are not important, so now I say that the paragraph is not important. It is possible to demonstrate styles of sentences; it is possible to demonstrate styles of paragraphs; but my own sense of fitness tells me that I consider neither as I construct a paper. I have my mind on a goal, and somehow the sentences and paragraphs evolve and fall into place as I move toward that goal.

Structure Through Subject

In his *Out of My Later Years*, Albert Einstein developed some of his ideas on the nature of education. At one point, in order to explain part of his subject, he put together four paragraphs. As you will see, no one of these four paragraphs will truly stand by itself; the four must operate as a unit:

If you have followed attentively my meditations up to this point, you will probably wonder about one thing. I have spoken fully about what in spirit, according to my opinion, youth should be instructed. But I have said nothing yet about the choice of subjects for instruction, nor about the method of teaching. Should language predominate or technical education in science?

To this I answer: In my opinion all of this is of secondary importance. If a young man has trained his muscles and physical endurance by gymnastics and walking, he will later be fitted for every physical work. This is also analogous to the training of the mind and the exercising of the mental and manual skill. Thus the wit was not wrong who defined education in this way: "Education is that which remains, if one has forgotten everything he learned in school." For this reason I am not at all anxious to take sides in the struggle between the followers of the classical philologic-historical education and the education more devoted to natural science.

On the other hand, I want to oppose the idea that the school has to teach directly that special knowledge and those accomplishments which one has to use directly later in life. The demands of life are much too manifold to let such a specialized training in school appear possible. Apart from that, it seems to me, moreover, objectionable to treat the individual like a dead tool. The school should always have as its aim that the young man leave it as a harmonious personality, not as a specialist. This in my opinion is true in a certain sense even for technical schools, whose students will devote themselves to a quite definite profession. The development of general ability for independent thinking and judgment should always be placed foremost, not the acquisition of special knowledge. If a person masters the fundamentals of his subject and has learned to think and work independently, he will surely find his way and besides will better be able to adapt himself to progress and changes than the person whose training principally consists in the acquiring of detailed knowledge.

Finally, I wish to emphasize once more what has been said here in a somewhat categorical form does not claim to mean more than the personal opinion of a man, which is founded upon *nothing but* his own personal experience, which he has gathered as a student and as a teacher.[1]

For all of his standing as a physicist, Einstein is no great shakes as a stylist and, in this sample at least, he is hardly concise. Nevertheless, we can learn something about the development of a theme from these paragraphs.

The theme is the question that is asked at the end of the first

[1] Albert Einstein, *Out of My Later Years,* 1950. Reprinted by permission of the Estate of Albert Einstein.

paragraph. Einstein has led up to this statement by three sentences that are essentially transitional and summary. They are also conversational in tone.

At the beginning of the second paragraph there is a transitional device that is rhetorical and actually redundant. The paragraph could have begun with the statement beginning: "All of this is. . . ."

Einstein uses transitional devices or signals in many of his sentences in the second paragraph: "This is also analogous . . . ," "Thus the wit . . . ," "For this reason. . . ." He concludes the paragraph with a sentence that is essentially a restatement of his theme question.

His third paragraph begins with a transitional phrase ("On the other hand") which not only ties this paragraph to the one before but also indicates that the trend of his coming remarks will be antithetical to those preceding. In this paragraph he continues to indicate the logical connections among his ideas by the use of more signals: "The demands of life . . . ," "Apart from that . . . ," "The school should . . . ," "This in my opinion . . . ," "The development of general ability . . . ," "If a person masters . . . ," "he will surely find. . . ." Each of these phrases picks up the stream of thought developed in the preceding sentence.

His last paragraph indicates that he has come to the close of his argument: "Finally. . . ." But he does not use the paragraph as a summary as much as he perhaps should; instead, he reiterates what he has said at least three times before: this is his opinion. But he knows, of course, that we will accept his opinion on the authority of his reputation "as a student and as a teacher."

Now I proceed to an analysis of the structure of four major essays in order to demonstrate how words, phrases, sentences, and paragraphs are used as building blocks to develop a theme, and how all of these may be fitted into a language structure that eventually makes a worthwhile point.

Randolph Bourne's "A Philosophy of Handicap" from *Youth and Life* (pages 309–316) is an example of what might be called the "classical model" of the essay. It is highly structured and well-organized and it reminds me, to use a figure of speech, of a brick wall in which every brick is laid professionally into place.

Bourne's thesis is that we are all handicapped and we must all learn to adjust to the terms of the world in which we live, despite our handicaps. This theme is expressed in two separated

sentences that serve as a fulcrum on which the essay is balanced:

> The difference between what the strongest of the strong and the
> most winning of the attractive can get out of life, and what I can, is
> after all so slight. . . . But one must have grown up, to get this atti-
> tude. And that is the best thing the handicapped man can do.

What comes before those fulcrum sentences is a series of comments about the handicapped person as the handicapped person
narcissistically sees himself. These comments are developed in
paragraphs that in turn are explications of these topic sentences:

> It would not be thought . . . that the man whom physical dis-
> abilities have made so helpless . . . can bear his lot more happily
> . . . than can the man whose handicaps are merely enough to mark
> him out . . .
> When the handicapped youth . . . is in full possession of his
> faculties . . . his road is apt to be hard . . .
> The handicapped man is always conscious that the world does not
> expect very much from him. . . .
> This sensitiveness has both its good and its bad sides. . . .
> The doors of the handicapped man are always locked, and the key
> is on the outside. . . .
> It thus takes the handicapped man a long time to get adjusted to
> his world. Childhood is perhaps the hardest time of all. . . .
> There is tragedy for those situated as I was. . . .
> When the world became one of dances and parties . . . I was to
> find myself still less adapted to it . . . the world of youth is a world
> of so many conventions, and the abnormal in any direction is so glar-
> ingly and hideously abnormal.
> . . . the bitterest struggles . . . come when he tackles the busi-
> ness world. . . . The environment of the big city is perhaps the
> worst possible. . . .

Then there comes a turn in the philosophy in which, within a
few sentences, the utter hopelessness of "I know of no particular
way of escape" changes into the optimism of,

> . . . college furnishes an ideal environment where the things at
> which a man handicapped like myself can succeed can really
> count . . .

and the growing sense of optimism is stated in topic sentences
such as these:

. . . his self-respect is so slow in growing up. . . .

If he could only . . . separate the factors that are due to his physical disability from those that are due to his weak will and character.   . .

But optimism must be tempered with caution:

If the handicapped youth is brought into harsh and direct touch with the real world, life proves a much more complex thing to him . . .

We are perhaps too prone to get our ideas and standards of worth from the successful . . . a philosophy gained through personal disability and failure [is] as just and true a method of appraising the life around us . . .

The difference between what the strongest of the strong and the most winning of the attractive can get out of life, and what I can, is after all so slight. . . . One's enemy is one's own weak will.

Now that the fulcrum has been reached, the balance is turned:

When one has grown up, he will find that people of his own age and experience are willing to make the large allowances . . .

But I leave it to you to locate the balance of the topic sentences in this essay.

Bourne's essay is interconnected through a number of transitional phrases and sentences:

It would not be thought . . . But the fact is . . . When the handicapped youth . . . Particularly . . . For he has all . . . This attitude . . . As a result . . . He becomes . . . On the other hand . . . This sensitiveness . . . For here . . . Except with those few . . .

Again I leave it to you to locate the balance of these and discuss with your classmates their effectiveness in providing a smooth flow of ideas through the essay.

Notice too how the language and tone are removed from the purely personal; although Bourne was severely handicapped, there is no whining or crying here. For example the young man referred to in the first paragraph is obviously Bourne himself, but by keeping the reference in the third person, the intended effect is achieved without any element of maudlinism being introduced.

Yet he does let us know that he is writing from experience; he is not trying to comfort the badly handicapped from a background that is alien to his subject. In this recounting of personal experience he sets himself as very much the average schoolboy trying to maintain the middle road.

In his last paragraph he shifts from the fairly impersonal third person he has been using most of the time and addresses himself directly to his reader. At this point he runs the risk of sermonizing, of alienating himself from his reader by a holier-than-thou attitude. But he neatly avoids this by eliminating all reference to himself, and by avoiding moralizing. As well he does not promise his reader the sun and the moon and the stars. On the other hand he puts it bluntly to his reader; happiness for the handicapped (that is, for all of us) is a matter of maturity.

In Bourne's essay we have seen how a personal situation can be used as a basis for a universal statement. In the next essay, E. B. White's "Once More to the Lake" from *One Man's Meat* (see pages 317–322), we see how an experience can become the basis of a similar generalization. Whereas the development in Bourne's essay is comparative (the pre-acceptance state versus the state of acceptance), the development in White's essay is chronological.

In his essay White accepts Giovanni Battista Vico's thesis that history repeats itself. Unlike the Greek philosopher who had argued that one can't wade in the same river twice (for both the river and the wader change), Vico had propounded a natural law of growth, decay, and regrowth:

> The evolution of civilization is paralleled to the child's acquisition of knowledge through broadening experience; man, like the child, passes through the ascending stages of the senses, the imagination, and reason in his progression towards knowledge.[2]

I have used this summary because it is a very good précis of White's essay. When White, at the end of his essay says,

> As he buckled the swollen belt suddenly my groin felt the chill of death.

he has achieved the state of knowledge that the events of his essay have been leading him toward.

The structure of White's essay follows a triple strand. One is epitomized in the title; the return of the man to the lake he had

---

[2] *The Reader's Encyclopedia,* Vol. II, p. 1057.

often enjoyed as a boy, but a return with his son. The second strand, which develops his thesis, begins with the sentences:

I began to wonder what it would be like. I wondered how time would have marred this unique, this holy spot.

The third—the progression through the senses, the imagination and the reason—is developed through passages such as this one:

The lake had never been what you would call a wild lake. There were cottages sprinkled around the shores. . . . I knew it, lying in bed the first morning, *smelling* the bedroom and *hearing* the boy. . . . I *felt* the same damp moss covering the worms in their bait can, and I *saw* the dragonfly alight. . . .

The sensory impressions lead to the play of the imagination:

There was a choice of pie for dessert, and one was blueberry and one was apple, and the waitresses were the same country girls, there having been no passage of time, only the illusion of it as in a dropped curtain. . . .

As these paragraphs demonstrate, White's essay, unlike Bourne's, makes excellent use of real-life imagery. Yet by playing off the sense of illusion against the reality of the vacation week, White keeps his three strands moving to the final statement.

The final statement opens up a new vista for us—the essay has been moving in what almost might be termed a fourth dimension. For now we see that in White's first visits to the lake he had been a romantic innocent. But this visit has been an initiation rite. Through the medium of his son's re-creation of his childhood experience, he has seen his philosophy demonstrated—history does repeat itself. But what reason tells him is that history does not allow man to repeat the experience. Ironically, history repeats itself only through the growth and decay of man. The lake goes on and on—but man must die.

White is much more of a stylist than either Einstein or Bourne. The epitome of his style may be seen in passages such as these:

The lake had never been what you would call a wild lake.

We caught two bass, hauling them in briskly as though they were mackerel, pulling them over the side of the boat in a businesslike manner without any landing net, and stunning them with a blow on the back of the head.

Assignment for Writing

Write an essay in which a personal experience becomes the basis for a general statement. Remember that without the thesis or theme, the experience is just another anecdote. Don't forget that when you are through, your audience will have one of two reactions—Hey, that reminds me of something that happened to me once, or, Yes, isn't it the truth. It is the second reaction that you are after.

When you have read the final essay, you may wonder why I have included it in a group with essays by Bourne and White. Ring Lardner's "How to Write Short Stories" from *How to Write Short Stories* (see pages 323–326) is so different in style, in its apparent lack of urbanity, even in its apparent pointlessness. For the present you will have to be satisfied with my explanation that Lardner is one of my favorite writers.

The characteristic that you will notice almost from the first is the quality of the language. ". . . may be shy of, learns you, most notorious, it don't, skin through, boys or gals, had win, phi beta skeleton," and so on, is the kind of diction we ordinarily associate with ungainly wads of bubble gum and girls who wear their hair-rollers in the department stores. But if we recall some earlier discussions in this book, we may begin to detect a bit of method in the madness; certainly the "phi beta skeleton" remark tells us that Lardner is after something, even if it is only the intellectual snob.

What he is seemingly after are those people who place ads in the slick magazines (they did it in 1924 and they still do it to-day), offering to teach people how to become successful writers. Well and good, but when he writes:

But a little group of our deeper thinkers has suggested that maybe boys and gals who wanted to take up writing as their life work would benefit if some person like I was to give them a few hints . . .

we begin to wonder if it isn't a case of the blind leading the blind. How can a man who writes in such an atrocious fashion teach anyone anything about writing? If we have our wits about us we will begin to suspect that it is not Lardner who is being put on by the "little group of deeper thinkers," but we who are being put on by the apparent guilelessness of the writer—who is not Lardner at all (any more than Jack Benny is the character he pretends to be), but a voice adopted by Lardner for the occasion.

The strategy adopted by Lardner is that made famous by the Marx Brothers in their zany films—the *non sequitur* (something that does not logically follow). For example, a person who mangles the language is chosen to teach "boys and gals." Jack Dempsey is not a writer but a prize fighter; the plot of a story involving two girls, an English Prince, and a Mexican is made from a series of unrelated and pointless incidents.

But Lardner uses other devices as well. His advice on the use of a "catchy" title and his note about the sheets of paper and the colored pencils is a parody of the advice given by the professionals who place the ads in the magazine. The term *"l'approchement"* is a satire on writers of the caliber of Henry James with their glosses of foreign words, necessary because the English language apparently isn't versatile enough for some novelists. Lardner's statement that Blasco Ibáñez "usually starts his stories with a Spanish word" is partially a topical joke, partially a trap for the unwary. Vicente Blasco Ibáñez was a Spanish writer whose two novels (*Four Horsemen of the Apocalypse* and *Blood and Sand* in their English translations) had been the vehicles for two immensely popular Rudolph Valentino films. If Lardner's reader is not aware that Blasco Ibáñez wrote in Spanish, he may be taken in by Lardner's joke.

The essay as a whole, down to the advice about "marketing of the complete work," is a parody of the advice often found in magazines published for people who will never be professional short-story writers and novelists. But is the essay merely that— merely another zany bit of humor—or is it something else?

I think it is something else. There is some good advice hidden in the comedy, and some of it is rather straightforward. When Lardner says that "you can't find no school . . . which can make a great author of a born druggist," he is speaking the truth. No serious-minded teacher of writing in the United States will claim that he can make a writer out of anyone—let alone the "born druggist." The best that a teacher can do (if he is a writer) is describe his own personal "technic"; and the "technics" of other successful writers as well. He can lead the horse to water, but if the animal takes a bath in the tank—

Lardner makes some of his points in a negative way. When he

tells you that a "catchy title" is important and then suggests "Basil Hargrave's Vermifuge" as an example, he is telling you that the title is not the story. While it might help trap the unwary reader, there had better be something else.

Some of his apparent nonsense is pretty good advice. How many bad writers have written the line, " 'Well,' said Mrs. Croot, for it was she," no one will ever know; but I for one have seen that "for it was she" in at least a dozen bad novels. And whereas Lardner knows what he is doing when he writes, "spending the heated term at a famous resort," the authors of "for it was she" happily remain in ignorance.

What is Lardner's real point, then? It is: don't be a sucker. Ignore those who hold forth promises of sudden wealth and fame to anyone. Read the fine print—ask the would-be teacher just how long it took that one bright star in his heaven to make that "$5000.00 and no hundreds dollars." Lardner is not joking. I know, for instance, of one case where one such teacher of writing accidentally stumbled on an amateur with a beautiful story already written, helped him market it (for a sizable fee, of course) —and for almost 25 years since has used this one example in his monthly magazine advertisement.

And what is my point in introducing this essay by Lardner? Well, first of all, I hope you laughed at it and as a result will read some more of Lardner. Second, I hope you see that good zany comedy can serve a serious purpose—something that I wish certain television comedians would learn. Third, that an essay can be apparently structureless (the structure in Lardner's essay is based on his models) and still have a structure. Fourth, if you want to write like Lardner, perhaps you'd better make sure that you are not a born druggist. Then, if you still persist, study what Lardner has done, word for word, line for line. Whether you believe it or not, this essay represents a very real talent.

Questions for Discussion

What is Lardner getting at when he says it would be his "tendency" to "take up the life of a mule in the Grand Canyon"?

Bourne says that "the world of youth is a world of so many conventions." Do you agree?

If, as Bourne says, the worlds of business and the "big city" are closed off to the handicapped, what solutions does he offer for the handicapped person in today's urbanized environment? What advice would you offer the handicapped?

In your opinion, what is the "ideal environment" that college offers the handicapped?

Do you agree with White that "history repeats itself." Or is your philosophy the Greek one that "you can't wade in the same river twice"? Or perhaps the French philosophy that "the more things change, the more things are the same"?

Have you ever had the feeling that you were one of your parents? What caused it? What was the experience like?

Why does White apostrophize summertime in the paragraph beginning "Summertime, oh summertime, pattern of life indelible"? What, if any, is the relationship between this paragraph and the final sentence?

Thomas Henry Huxley's essay is titled "On a Piece of Chalk." Can you think of a more appropriate title? Why do you suppose he used this one? You might do a little research into the problems of the scientists in persuading their nineteenth-century fellows to accept some of their findings as a means of understanding what Huxley was up to.

At what points in his paper do you become aware that his subject is something else than a piece of chalk? What is his true subject?

Huxley's essay is a good example of the strategy that begins with the known and acceptable and moves to the unknown and previously unacceptable. In rhetorical terms it is an argumentative or persuasive paper.

In his "The Method of Scientific Investigation" Huxley inserts this paragraph as a means of establishing a stage in his paper. He summarizes what he has said up to this point, and then prepares us for a shift to a new aspect of his topic:

So much, then, by way of proof that the method of establishing laws in science is exactly the same as that pursued in common life. Let us now turn to another matter . . . and that is, the method by which, from the relations of certain phenomena, we prove that some stand in the position of causes toward the others.

In a long paper such as the one before us, such paragraphs are quite useful—especially if the paper is to be read to a group. In a short paper such announcements and summaries are not so necessary. Has he used any such devices in "On a Piece of Chalk"?

Assignments for Writing

Try to find a passage of advice or instruction that seems to you to be fallacious or at best superficial. Write a parody of it. If you cannot find a passage to parody, write a humorous lesson for your classmates.

Use a common everyday item as a device by which you explain some difficult concept. For instance, what concept might you demonstrate with a ballpoint pen?

Or, explain how your notion of some fact about the universe was formed or changed. What, for instance, leads you to accept the notion that the earth is round? What is your theory about the creation of the universe? What everyday objects or incidents can you use as a basis for persuading others to your belief?

Structure Through Metaphor

Structure may also be achieved through metaphor; that is, you are faced with the matter of getting an idea across to someone, either to inform him or to persuade him, and you are aware either that the concept is a difficult one to explain or that the task of persuasion may not be an easy one. So you set up a metaphorical structure based on a set of metaphorical equivalents or analogies for your concept. You may, like Shakespeare in the example given back in the first chapter, be trying to explain what life and man are, and so you say that life is a drama and men and women are the actors in it. Or, on a larger scale, you may be trying to say that life is a voyage of discovery, and so you write a *Two Years Before the Mast* or a *Life on the Mississippi*.

Here is an *Esquire* writer who is trying to tell us about a United States Senator, and he comes upon the fact that the Senator and the President of the United States have gone to a football game together; from this latter fact, he structures his article:

A football stadium in Arkansas, where one may forget the war while another broods upon it, is not a bad place to suggest the difference between Nixon and Fulbright. Let us say that Nixon, the conscientious substitute who did not win his letter from Whittier College until 1968, is still living inside the American day-dream: God touches the dead-game halfback who scores the winning touchdown in the last ten seconds. . . . *Fulbright has been that halfback*. In 1922 [he] defeated S.M.U. virtually single-handed in the first Homecoming Game ever played by the Razorbacks.[3]

Here is Virginia Woolf trying to get across to you what words are:

Words . . . are the wildest, freest, most irresponsible, most unteachable of all things. Of course, you can catch them and sort them and place them in alphabetical order in dictionaries. But words do not live in dictionaries; they live in the mind. . . . Thus to lay down any laws for such irreclaimable vagabonds is worse than useless. A few trifling rules of grammar and spelling are all the constraint we can put on them. All we can say about them, as we peer at them over the edges of that deep, dark and only fitfully illuminated cavern in which they live—the mind—all we can say about them is that they seem to like people to think and feel before they use them, but to think and feel not about them, but about something different. They are highly sensitive, easily made self-conscious. They do not like to have their purity or their impurity discussed. . . . Nor do they like being lifted out on the point of a pen and examined separately. They hang together, in sentences, in paragraphs, sometimes for whole pages at a time. They hate being useful; they hate making money; they hate being lectured about in public. In short they hate anything that stamps them with one meaning or confines them to one attitude, for it is their nature to change.[4]

It is not easy to understand what words are or how they function, and Mrs. Woolf, as a sensitive writer, knew that. So she fixed upon the metaphor of words as living beings, because she thought that in that way she might be able to help you to understand how words work. You have likes and dislikes; you are emotional and changeable; you hate being categorized; you hate being dissected; you like being a vagabond—and so on. You are like the words you use, and the words you use are like you. Words, the invention of humans, are human.

A word of caution is in order. Because Virginia Woolf has used the metaphorical device of personification to *structure* her essay on words, you must not assume that *she* understood words through this metaphor. As a lifelong worker with words (and a very skillful one), Mrs. Woolf's understanding of words was certainly much more complex than one might assume from reading her paragraph. In her understanding of words, Mrs. Woolf

[3] "Mourning Becomes Senator Fulbright," *Esquire,* June, 1970, p. 116.

[4] Virginia Woolf, *The Death of a Moth,* Harcourt Brace Jovanovich, p. 131.

might be compared to Albert Einstein in his understanding of the universe. In trying to explain words to you, Mrs. Woolf was faced with a problem similar to that faced by Einstein as he tried to explain the universe. What I am saying in my circumlocutious way was described by C. S. Lewis in his *Rehabilitations and Other Essays;* we achieve understanding through the use of *one* metaphor or set of metaphors (what I would call a private or personal metaphor), and we pass our understanding on to others through the construction of *another* metaphor or set of metaphors (what I would call a public metaphor).

Topics for Discussion

In the essays we have looked at in this chapter what small and large metaphorical structures (if any) have been used to help you understand or to persuade you to accept a point of view? Is Huxley's piece of chalk a metaphor? Is Lardner's *persona* of a semiliterate author a metaphor? In White's essay is the lake a metaphor? What is the largest metaphorical structure you find?

Bring to class examples of metaphors you have found in other books or textbooks. Look for metaphors that helped you to understand, or that persuaded you to change an attitude; look for metaphors that, in your opinion, failed. Discuss the reasons for success and failure.

Topics for Writing

Develop metaphorical explanations for such concepts as: $(a + b)^2$ or $(x + y)^3$; what happens when sodium and chlorine come together; a business letter; a recipe; a clothing pattern or blueprint; student government; a college or university; student protest. Through what metaphors have you come to an understanding of subjects such as these? Will you explain your choice of concept through the metaphor by which you learned about it or through another metaphor which you devise? What reasoning underlies your choice?

12

Something
to Write About

A frequent complaint of the student is that he has "nothing to write about." This complaint often comes about because the student is sent from class with an assignment such as "My Vacation Last Summer," and after writing the first line— "I spent last summer working for the U-Smash-M-I-Fix-M body shop" or "I spent last summer as a 'dishout' in El Toro's Genuine Mexican Food and American Specialties"—*he* stops, remembering that while he was hammering out the dents in the Mustangs and Mavericks, the guys who owned them were down at El Toro's, having a swinging time with the chicks; or *she* stops, remembering that while she was being scolded for being a lousy dishout, the other chicks were over at El Encanto, sunning in their new bikinis.

My purpose in this chapter is to give you some notions for subjects you can write about. They are drawn from the experiences of persons who were your age when the experiences took place.

For instance, all of us, when we were younger, dreamed of growing up and being somebody. Perhaps we toyed with the notion of being a fireman, a policeman, an airplane pilot, a stewardess, a ballerina. Or perhaps we were fascinated by some young person in our neighborhood, someone who at the time seemed much older but who was actually only five or six years older—perhaps ten at the most. Here is Henry G. Felsen (who wrote *Hot Rod*) as he describes one such person:

As I set up my tripod and camera, the young Romans on the bridge ceased their aimless swarming and streamed toward me. They came like black flies crawling over sugar, following erratic individual courses and buzzing with noise. They saw that I was an American and, as such, was a fat stag for hunters. I might be heavy with cigarettes or candy, a customer for curios or in need of a guide.

In a moment they had me surrounded. Empty hands begged, full hands offered souvenirs at outrageous prices. A score of mouths competed shrilly to cajole, demand, plead and insult. They crowded about me, pushed and fought among themselves and threatened to overturn the camera. Knowing their light-fingered approach to pockets, I tried to protect myself from every angle, meanwhile bellowing "No!"

My shouts stimulated them to greater effort, and I was about to pack up my camera and leave when a penetrating voice called them off with one stinging word. Immediately their clamor ceased and they all lost interest in me. I saw their leader for the first time and I thanked him with a smile and a nod, but he ignored me. He stared past me, but I stared at him.

This leader, whose word was law among boys who defied authority for the sake of defiance, was no more than twelve or thirteen years old, and looked even younger. He leaned against the stone railing of the bridge with the cold stub of a cigarette hanging loosely from his lips. His face was small and thin and of that peculiar bluish color that swarthy people become when they are pale. His skin was very smooth and his large eyes seemed too large and intense for his face. He was dressed in cast-off adult clothing much too large for him. The legs of the trousers had been hacked off at ankle-length, but the sleeves of his jacket had been folded back. A torn, too-large fedora sat crookedly on his head and long, black uncut hair straggled out from beneath it. He wore no shirt, but had an old black scarf wrapped around his neck with one frayed end trailing free. He wore broken canvas shoes and no socks.

He was, at first glance, just another nondescript, ragged, aimless street boy, freed by war from every discipline including that of love. He lounged carelessly and lazily against stones warmed by the sun during the day and found whatever shelter he needed for the night in doorways, cellars or caves. He viewed human beings from the standpoint of what they might yield and how they might be harvested. He exulted over successful petty thieveries without suspecting that he was the victim of the most criminal robbery of all. He begged piteously when the situation demanded begging, stole whenever possible and lived by the weakness, debauchery, sentiment or carelessness of mankind.

But he was also a leader. He had something, invisible to ordinary eyes, that caused others to follow him and obey.

I thought of the leaders of American neighborhood gangs I had seen and belonged to. In our gang assaults on watermelon patches and our daring sessions when we smoked cigarettes behind barns or down by the tracks, leadership most often went to the boy who was best with his fists and intimidated his followers by brute force. A football letter on a husky chest gave us our local hero and our leader to follow.

In Italy, judging from the boy who leaned insolently against the bridge rail, brute force was not the requisite. I supposed leadership went to the lad with the sharpest wits or the most daring plans. It was hard to tell, looking at this boy, just what quality he did possess. But there had to be something. He led not in sport and play, but in battle. The issue was not glory, but life. He led a little band who lived in the eyes of children and looked at the world through the cynical eyes of old men. For every *centesimo* they got honestly, they acquired ten *lire* by appealing to the greed, credulity or lust of adults. They knew too much, and because they knew too soon, they were at once the most evil and innocent of children—in their surfeit of twisted knowledge they had become cunningly ignorant and wickedly naive. To be the leader of boys like these is not to be the leader of boys at play who have mothers to call them to supper, and suppers to which they can run.

It seemed to me then that whatever quality this boy had that made the others obey him, it must be something so evil or cruel that it frightened and so won them. And in their surrender to that at which he excelled, I saw a death of personal dignity and honor that made the future seem without hope.[1]

Felsen, in this essay, is writing from the viewpoint of an older American visiting a foreign land and trying to understand it.

[1] Henry G. Felsen, "Horatio." Reprinted from *Seventeen®*. Copyright © 1949 by Triangle Publications, Inc.

What viewpoint will you use in writing about a person? Will you write from the childish viewpoint that you had when you first dreamed about being somebody or first saw your subject? Or will you write from your present viewpoint, looking back at your childish innocence? Or some other viewpoint?

What strategies will you use in your essay? Felsen introduces us to his subject as the result of a casual meeting—and he shows us the young man only as a static form, almost a statue. Will you use this descriptive process—or will you show your subject in action? Why does Felson title his article "Horatio"?

In an earlier chapter I warned you against static prose and cautioned you that the adjective, rather than enlightening and giving life to a subject, tended to render it ambiguous and to deaden it. After reading Felsen's essay, do you agree with me? Or has Felsen used adjectives rather skillfully?

In the fourth paragraph Felsen is describing the leader. Does the passage seem monotonous to you? If so, why? How has Felsen tried to avoid monotony in the paragraph? How will you avoid monotony in similar paragraphs?

Felsen has also used comparison and contrast as a means of emphasizing his subject. Is his American boy familiar to you? If not, is the comparison any less effective?

All of us have known times when everything seemed to go well for us and times when nothing went well at all. Whether we realized it at the time or not, such experiences were a vital part of our education and, in fact, may have been more important in shaping our lives than any education we ever received in a classroom or from books. Here are reports of three experiences, one of which left its participant feeling as if he were a "dunderhead," one of which left its participant with a warm glow, and one— well, I'll let you decide on the third one for yourself:

    . . . one matchless summer's day I was bowling down the bend above island 66, brimful of self-conceit and carrying my nose high as a giraffe's when Mr. Bixby said—

    "I am going below a while. I suppose you know the next crossing?"

    This was almost an affront. It was about the plainest and simplest crossing in the whole river. One couldn't come to any harm, whether he ran it right or not; and as for depth, there never had been any bottom there. I knew all this, perfectly well.

    "Know how to *run* it? Why, I can run it with my eyes shut."

    "How much water is there in it?"

"Well, that is an odd question. I couldn't get bottom there with a church steeple."

"You think so, do you?"

The very tone of the question shook my confidence. That was what Mr. Bixby was expecting. He left, without saying anything more. I began to imagine all sorts of things. Mr. Bixby, unknown to me, of course, sent somebody down to the forecastle with some mysterious instruction to the leadsmen, another messenger was sent to whisper among the officers, and then Mr. Bixby went into hiding behind a smoke stack where he could observe results. Presently the captain stepped out on the hurricane deck; next the chief mate appeared; then a clerk. Every moment or two a straggler was added to my audience; and before I got to the head of the island I had fifteen or twenty people assembled down there under my nose. I began to wonder what the trouble was. As I started across, the captain glanced at me and said with a sham uneasiness in his voice—

"Where is Mr. Bixby?"

"Gone below, sir."

But that did the business for me. My imagination began to construct dangers out of nothing, and they multiplied faster than I could keep the run of them. All at once I imagined I saw shoal water ahead! The wave of coward agony that surged through me then came near dislocating every joint in me. All my confidence in that crossing vanished. I seized the bell rope; dropped it, ashamed; seized it and dropped it once more; clutched it tremblingly once again, and pulled it so feebly that I could hardly hear the stroke myself. Captain and mate sang out instantly, and both together—

"Starboard lead there! And quick about it!"

This was another shock. I began to climb the wheel like a squirrel; but I would hardly get the boat started to port before I would see new dangers on that side, and away I would spin to the other; only to find perils accumulating to starboard, and be crazy to get to port again. Then came the leadsman's sepulchral cry:

"D-e-e-p four!"

Deep four in a bottomless crossing! The terror of it took my breath away.

"M-a-r-k three! . . . M-a-r-k three . . . Quarter less three! . . . Half twain!"

This was frightful! I seized the bell ropes and stopped the engines.

"Quarter twain! Quarter twain! *Mark* twain!"

I was helpless. I did not know what in the world to do. I was quaking from head to foot, and I could have hung my hat on my eyes, they stuck out so far.

"Quarter *less* twain! Nine and a *half!*"

We were *drawing* nine! My hands were in a nervous flutter. I could not ring a bell intelligibly with them. I flew to the speaking tube and shouted to the engineer—

"Oh, Ben, if you love me, *back* her! Quick, Ben! Oh, back the immortal *soul* out of her!"

I heard the door close gently. I looked around, and there stood Mr. Bixby, smiling a bland, sweet smile. Then the audience on the hurricane deck sent up a thundergust of humiliating laughter. I saw it all, now, and I felt meaner than the meanest man in history. I laid in the lead, set the boat in her marks, came ahead on the engines, and said:

"It was a fine trick to play on an orphan, *wasn't* it? I suppose I'll never hear the last of how I was ass enough to heave the lead at the head of 66."

"Well, no you won't, maybe. In fact I hope you won't; for I want you to learn something by that experience. Didn't you *know* there was no bottom in that crossing?"

"Yes, sir, I did."

"Very well, then. You shouldn't have allowed me or anybody else to shake your confidence in that knowledge. Try to remember that. And another thing: when you get into a dangerous place, don't turn coward. . . ." It was a good enough lesson, but pretty hardly learned. (*Life on the Mississippi*)

What experience have you had that proved disastrous at the moment, yet resulted in your learning a valuable lesson?

In Twain's essay, he lets you in on the fact that a practical joke was being played on him. Would his essay have been a better one or a worse one if he had not revealed the practical joke until it was over? For instance, would the revelation of the joke have interfered with the discussion of what he learned?

(1) I also connected with our arrival here another circumstance, which more nearly concerns myself; viz., my first act of what the sailors will allow to be seamanship—sending down a royal-yard. I had seen it done once or twice at sea; and an old sailor, whose favour I had taken some pains to gain, had taught me carefully everything which was necessary to be done, and in its proper order, and advised me to take the first opportunity when we were in port, and try it. I told the second mate, with whom I had been pretty *thick* when he was before the mast, that I could do it, and got him to ask the mate to send me up the first time the royal yards were struck. Accordingly, I was called upon, and went aloft, repeating the operations over in my mind, taking care to get each thing in its order, for the slightest mistake spoils the whole. Fortunately, I got through without any word from the officer, and heard the "well done" of the mate, when the yard reached the deck, with as much satisfaction as I ever felt at Cambridge on seeing a *"bene"* at the foot of a Latin exercise. . . .

(2) Here we were again in this romantic spot—a perpendicular hill, twice the height of the ship's mast-head, with a single circuitous path to the top, and long sand-beach at its base, with the swell of the whole Pacific breaking high upon it, and our hides ranged in piles on the over-hanging summit. The captain sent me, who was the only one of the crew that had ever been there, to the top to count the hides and to pitch them down. There I stood again, as six months before, throwing off the hides, and watching them pitching and scaling to the bottom, while the men, dwarfed by the distance, were walking to and fro on the beach, carrying the hides, as they picked them up, to the distant boats, upon the tops of their heads. Two or three boat-loads were sent off, until at last all were thrown down, and the boats nearly loaded again, when we were delayed by a dozen or twenty hides which had lodged in the recesses of the bank, and which we could not reach by any missiles, as the general line of the side was exactly perpendicular, and these places were caved in, and could not be seen or reached from the top. As hides are worth in Boston twelve and a half cents a pound, and the captain's commission was one per cent, he determined not to give them up, and sent on board for a pair of top-gallant studding-sail halyards and requested some one of the crew to go to the top and come down by the halyards. The older sailors said the boys, who were light and active, ought to go; while the boys thought that strength and experience were necessary. Seeing the dilemma, and feeling myself to be near the medium of these requisites, I offered my services, and went up, with one man to tend the rope, and prepared for the descent.

We found a stake fastened strongly to the ground, and apparently capable of holding my weight, to which we made one end of the halyard well fast, and taking the coil, threw it over the brink. The end, we saw, just reached to a landing place, from which the descent to the beach was easy. Having nothing on but shirt, trousers, and hat, the common sea rig of warm weather, I had no stripping to do, and began my descent by taking hold of the rope with both hands, and slipping down, sometimes with hands and feet round the rope, and sometimes breasting off with one hand and foot against the precipice, and holding on to the rope with the other. In this way I descended until I came to a place which shelved in, and in which the hides were lodged. Keeping hold of the rope with one hand, I scrambled in, and by aid of my feet and the other hand succeeded in dislodging all the hides, and continued on my way. Just below this place the precipice projected again, and, going over the projection I could see nothing below me but the sea and the rocks upon which it broke, and a few gulls flying in mid-air. I got down in safety, pretty well covered with dirt, and for my pains was told, "What a d——d fool you were to risk your life for half a dozen hides!" (*Two Years Before the Mast*)

Both of these incidents required a similar amount of risk on the part of the narrator, but nevertheless he volunteered for each duty. Have you ever engaged in a task that was either physically or psychologically hazardous, and in which you succeeded? Were you praised or scolded afterward?

Which is easier to report—an incident in which we succeeded or an incident in which we failed? Is the brevity of Dana's first report due to any sense of modesty on his part?

Twain's strategy in reporting his near-disaster is the one of setting off scene against action, summary against dramatic dialogue. Dana, on the other hand, prefers summary for both. Which do you find more interesting? Which technique seems easier to you to use? Dana was reporting his actions three or four years after they happened—Twain many years later. Yet Twain's memory for dialogue is pretty good, it seems. Or has he merely contrived the dialogue?

Assignment for Writing

Report an activity in which you either succeeded or failed and for which you were either praised or scolded.

Each of the above selections reports an instance of a man's education. As we become more educated, we move away (or should) from the fantasies of childhood. Life becomes less romantic, more realistic. The moment when we become aware of our past romanticizing and seem to take on a new awareness of ourselves and our place in the world has been termed an "initiation rite." The following selection does not report the rite itself but demonstrates how a man's attitude might change as a result of education:

The face of the water, in time, became a wonderful book—a book that was a dead language to the uneducated passenger, but which told its mind to me without reserve, delivering its most cherished secrets as clearly as if it uttered them with a voice. And it was not a book to be read once and thrown aside, for it had a new story to tell every day.

. . . Now when I had mastered the language of this water and had come to know every trifling feature that bordered the great river as familiarly as I knew the letters of the alphabet, I had made a valuable acquisition. But I had lost something too. I had lost something which could never be restored to me while I lived. All the grace, the beauty, the poetry had gone out of the majestic river! I still keep in mind a certain wonderful sunset which I witnessed when steamboating was new to me. A broad expanse of the river was turned to blood; in the middle distance the red hue brightened into gold, through which a solitary log came floating, black and conspicuous; in one place a long slanting mark lay sparkling upon the water; in another the surface was broken by boiling, tumbling rings, that were as many-tinted as an opal; where the ruddy flush was faintest, was a smooth spot that was covered with graceful circles and radiating lines, ever so delicately traced; the shore on our left was densely wooded and the somber shadow that fell from this forest was broken in one place by a long, ruffled trail that shone like silver, and high above the forest wall a clean-stemmed dead tree waved a single leafy bough that glowed like a flame in the unobstructed splendor that was flowing from the sun. There were graceful curves, reflected images, woody heights, soft distances; and over the whole scene, far and near, the dissolving lights drifted steadily, enriching it, every passing moment with new marvels of coloring.

I stood like one bewitched. I drank it in, in a speechless rapture. The world was new to me, and I had never seen anything like this at home. But as I have said, a day came when I began to cease from noting the glories and the charms which the moon and the sun and the twilight wrought upon the river's face; another day when I ceased altogether to note them. Then, if that sunset scene had been repeated, I should have looked upon it without rapture, and should have commented upon it, inwardly, after this fashion: This sun means that we are going to have wind tomorrow; that floating log means that the river is rising, small thanks to it; that slanting mark on the river refers to a bluff reef which is going to kill somebody's steamboat one of these nights, if it keeps on stretching out like that; those tumbling "boils" show a dissolving bar and a changing channel there; the lines and circles in the slick water over yonder are a warning that the troublesome place is shoaling up dangerously; that silver streak in the shadow of the forest is the "break" from a new snag, and he has located himself in the very best place he could have found to fish for steamboats; that tall dead tree, with a single living branch, is not going to last long . . . the romance and the beauty were all gone from the river. (*Life on the Mississippi*)

What experiences have you undergone that parallel this one? Each one of them can be the basis for an essay.

Sometimes a brief experience taken in the context of one's faith, one's philosophy about existence, can be meaningful:

To live alone as I have lived, a man should have the confidence of God, the tranquil faith of a monastic saint, the stern impregnability of Gibraltar. Lacking these, there are times when anything, everything, all or nothing, the most trivial incidents, the most casual words, can in an instant strip me of my armor, palsy my hand, constrict my heart with frozen horror, and fill my bowels with the gray substance of shuddering impotence.

Sometimes it is nothing but a shadow passing on the sun; sometimes nothing but the torrid milky light of August, or the naked sprawling ugliness and squalid decencies of streets in Brooklyn fading in the weary vistas of that milky light and evoking the intolerable misery of countless drab and nameless lives. Sometimes it is just the barren horror of raw concrete, or the heat blazing on a million beetles of machinery darting through the torrid streets, or the cindered weariness of parking spaces, or the slamming smash and racket of the El, or the driven manswarm of the earth, thrusting on forever in exacerbated fury, going nowhere in a hurry.[2]

As Virginia Woolf says, such emotions may be triggered by recalling

some event that has left a distinct impression on you—how at the corner of the street, perhaps, you passed two people talking. A tree shook; an electric light danced, the tone of the talk was comic, but also tragic; a whole vision, an entire conception, seemed contained in that moment.[3]

Do you believe that seemingly unimportant events such as these condition our behavior, perhaps more significantly than formal education can? Or is your philosophy of another kind?

When I was a boy I would walk along the streets of the downtown district of my hometown and play a game—a very private one. As I approached a corner, I would stop and say to myself: As I turn this corner, I am going to bring existence to a world that does not now exist. Until I turn the corner, there is nothing there. The moment I turn the corner, all of the buildings will take form and people will come to life. But as long as I stand here neither the buildings nor the people exist. Imagine my astonishment when I grew up and went to college to discover that I had been, in play, expounding a philosophy that many people, at one

[2] From pp. 187–188 in *The Hills Beyond* by Thomas Wolfe (Harper & Row).

[3] Virginia Woolf, "How Should One Read a Book?" *The Second Common Reader*, Harcourt Brace Jovanovich.

time or another at least, had taken seriously. When you were young, did you play games like this one?

The experience of death is another one we come to know. Here is a report of death in the life of a girl in the Amana Colonies of Iowa—a set of villages with a unique way of life:

My first awareness of death came when Grandpa Schneider died. Henry and I were still very young and had not grasped the significance of his last illness. One day mother dressed us as if for church, and took us to the home of Grandma and Grandpa Schneider. We liked to go there for we knew that these old people loved us and wanted to have us with them. Theirs was a place of pleasant times and happy hours. Grandpa would make tiny wooden toys for us and Grandma always had a surprise, usually a sweet.

But on this day, before we went in, mother stooped down and took us each by the arm and said, "Now children, be very quiet today." We wondered about this, for mother seldom made such a point of our conduct.

Inside, people stood around and no one talked. It was strange to find so many people at Grandma's. Uncle Albert was there, but he did not look as jolly as I had remembered him. He barely nodded recognition to Henry and me. The door to the ever-closed parlor stood open and the room was quite dark. I had seldom been in that parlor, so it was as strange as if it belonged to another house. Grandma came forward and took my hand. She did not smile nor make a little joke as was usual for her. She said, "Come with me."

I followed her into the parlor and there, the ends resting on two chairs, was a long, polished, brown wooden box, the largest I had ever seen. Grandma brought me up close and said that I should look.

"Do you know who it is?" she asked. She seemed to be crying.

I could barely see over the edge of the box, by standing on my toes. "Yes," I answered, "that is my Grandpa Schneider." [4]

Mrs. Yambura's account of her grandfather's death maintains the viewpoint of the little girl, even though the book was written when Mrs. Yambura was an adult. Thus there is no emotion—merely a matter-of-fact accounting of the few events that impressed her on that day.

What are your memories of death? Perhaps, if you have been a soldier, they involve violence and sudden unexpected death. In such a case do you agree with the philosophy of Richard Henry

[4] Yambura, Barbara S. and Eunice Bodine, *A Change and a Parting* 1st edition, © 1960, Iowa State University Press, Ames, Iowa, pp. 213–214.

Dana, reported elsewhere in this book, when he compares death at sea with death in battle?

Perhaps your memories of death coincide with a last visit with a parent as in this quotation from *One Foot in Heaven:*

The next week his condition suddenly became serious. I, being nearest of the children, hurried home.

But I found father laughing, though he could scarcely move. "If you came for the obsequies," he challenged as I entered the room, "I am happy to disappoint you."

He seemed to gain strength during my brief stay. Guiltily I told him that I had left my work without reporting to Chicago and that when my superiors discovered my absence I might be in difficulty.

"Then you mustn't stay," he said at once. "Your life has a long uphill run ahead, and your work is important. Mine is coasting down-grade and what's left of it isn't worth any risks."

But he was happy to talk on and on, principally about my future. He wanted to be sure that my home training was so strong that without him I could go on alone.

"You are an egotistical youngster," he said at one point, "but don't worry too much about that. Someone will come along at the proper time and pin your ears back. You just go on about your work with everything that's in you and trust in God, and you'll be all right. But don't run up and down stairs, or put your heart to needless excitement."

He kept looking at me as though he were never going to see me again and wanted something to remember.

"A little egotism is a good thing. I have often been called egotistical myself. It used to worry me. But one day in the mountains I figured it out. I respect myself. That is a good thing. A man must respect himself first if he is to command respect from others."

We talked on and on. . . . The telephone rang. I answered. The call was from Chicago, informing me that I had been transferred to New York and must leave immediately. Quickly I told father and looked up bus schedules. I just had time to catch the last bus that day.

As I turned to leave, father held out both his hands and took mine. His grasp was firm.

"Son," he said, "I am very happy over your promotion. I like to be proud of my sons. You are going far away. When you return, I probably will not be here."

He caught his breath.

"But don't worry about me. We are both moving up to new jobs. You know that you are going to New York; and just as surely, I know where I am going. You know what to expect when you get there; so, too, do I."

His clear eyes held mine for a long moment. I could not reply. We both knew we would not see each other again.

"God bless you, son," he said, "good-by." [5]

So you see it is possible to capitalize on personal experience for writing subjects, even if that personal experience doesn't include hanging around the El Encanto Park Pool last summer or taking a long-awaited trip to Timbuktu. The examples given here demonstrate that; they also demonstrate techniques for the handling of personal experience in writing. As such, they are well worth your close study.

But perhaps you feel at this point that you want something with some meat in it, an issue you can sink your teeth into. Well, here are two issues; they're meaty enough and very real:

The issue was defined by Walter Lippmann, a distinguished Harvard graduate, 33 years ago, on the occasion of the 300th anniversary of the founding of the university.

"If the universities are to do their work," he said on that occasion, "they must be independent, and they must be disinterested . . . they are places to which men can turn for judgments which are unbiased by partisanship and special interest. Obviously, the moment the universities fall under political control, or under the control of private interests, or the moment they themselves take a hand in politics and the leadership of government, their value as independent and disinterested sources of judgment is impaired. . . ."

This is part of the argument that is going on at Harvard today. Another part is the argument of the militant and even many moderate students: that a university is the keeper of our ideals and morals, and should not be "disinterested" but activist in bringing the nation's ideals and actions together.[6]

Dear Abby: When young people date one of a different race (and I mean "color") they tend to develop stronger relationships because they are defensive about the raised eyebrows and stares that follow them in public.

A child will say to his parents, "If I marry one of another race, it's my life and my business!"

This is not quite true, because the parents will have to bear the stares and raised eyebrows with him.

And if their "great love" miraculously survives the rejection they

[5] From *One Foot in Heaven* by Hartzell Spence. Copyright 1940 by Hartzell Spence. Used with permission of McGraw-Hill Book Company.

[6] James Reston, *The New York Times*, December 3, 1969. © 1969 by The New York Times Company. Reprinted by permission.

are sure to meet on both sides, their children will have to pay the price of never fully belonging to one race or the other.

Don't we have the right to speak for our unborn grandchildren who cannot as yet speak for themselves?

I am sure that if the truth were told, most Oriental and Negro parents are as much opposed to these mixed marriages as we Caucasian parents. And where do the "white" kids get the supreme arrogance to think that other races have less pride and are better off diluted by Caucasian blood?

What is wrong with evaluating an individual for his own worth, but not accepting interracial marriage as the answer?

There are two issues for you to write about. But if neither of these "grabs" you for any reason, they ought to suggest others. The editorial columns of the daily newspapers, of the news magazines, and the letters to the editors and columnists of these media ought to intrigue you. Finally, many of the stories appearing in the mass media are themselves the fruit of controversy worthy of your concern.

And, if you don't wish to be "involved" in social and political issues, perhaps you might like to prepare an essay in which you attempt to persuade others to accept your point of view.

Topics for Discussion and Writing

1. Rewrite the incident of dislodging the hides from the cliff, supplying it with appropriate dialogue. Is the expanded product livelier and better or not? Aside from imagining what the dialogue would be, what kinds of problems did you have?
2. Discuss the philosophies of life held by you and your classmates. Then discuss some specific experiences some of you have had in which these philosophies played a part.
3. Discuss or write about an instance when you attempted to accomplish some goal, job, or task. Perhaps you were on your own; perhaps you were a member of an athletic team, a debate team, a musical group, or a theatrical production. What were your goals and how were they achieved? To what extent did your own capabilities control your success or failure or the group's? To what extent did outside forces (man, climate, and the like) control the success or failure of the project?
4. Analyzing your life as a dynamic process, what are the significant stages so far? What are the junctions? Assuming

that birth might be the first junction, beginning school the second, how do you make a distinction between stage and junction in such cases?

5. What considerations are necessary if we are to give point to an essay regarding our own experience? Did you think that any of the excerpts quoted in this chapter were pointless? If so, why? In any such instance, what would be necessary in the way of an addition to give the excerpt point? If you felt that any of the excerpts made a point, what was the point, and how was it made?

6. Prepare an outline of one of the essays in the Appendix, following the suggestions in the discussion of Bourne's essay in Chapter 11, and any other suggestions that may come to you from your reading of this book. (Remember that outlining is largely a matter of reading carefully, then determining the levels of abstraction of sentences and paragraphs in relation to each other and to the whole essay.) What problems do you have as you attempt this task? Do you find any evidence that White, Huxley, or Lardner used an outline?

7. Write a brief essay about either the most valuable bit of advice you found in this book, or the least valuable. Use an argumentative or persuasive approach. Then try your essay on your fellow classmates. Are they persuaded to your point of view? If not, why not?

Appendix

On a

Piece

of Chalk

THOMAS HENRY HUXLEY

(1825–1895)

*Thomas Henry Huxley, although he had little formal
education until he enrolled in a course of medical studies
at seventeen, became a biologist, educator, philosopher,
lecturer, and author. With his friend, Charles Darwin, he
became one of those nineteenth-century men of science
who helped bring science to the position of eminence in our
culture that it occupies today. One of his strategies for
popularizing scientific study was to lecture before workingmen's groups. This essay was first delivered "to the workingmen of Norwich." Workingmen responded strongly to him;
the story is told that*

*he felt a strong interest in workingmen, and was much beloved
by them. On one occasion, having taken a cab home, on his
arrival there, when he held out his fare to the cabman, the
latter replied: "Oh no, Professor; I have had too much pleasure
and profit from hearing you lecture to take any money from
your pocket; proud to have driven you, Sir!"*

*As you read this essay try to visualize what there was
about it that made it attractive to workingmen. Is there
any evidence that Huxley is "talking down" to his audience? What are the "stages" in his talk, and what are the
transitions from stage to stage? Against whom does he
seem to be debating, and what are the types of proofs he
offers? Which of the patterns of organization mentioned in
Chapter 7 does he use? Are his strategies successful for
you?*

*Some of the scientific evidence Huxley presents in this
essay was later acknowledged by him to be in error; I must
"eat the leek," he said. Does that knowledge lessen the
power of his argument? Why or why not?*

If a well were sunk at our feet in the midst of the city of Norwich, the diggers would very soon find themselves at work in that white substance almost too soft to be called rock, with which we are all familiar as "chalk."

Not only here, but over the whole county of Norfolk, the well-sinker might carry his shaft down many hundred feet without coming to the end of the chalk; and, on the sea-coast, where the waves have pared away the face of the land which breasts them, the scarped faces of the high cliffs are often wholly formed of the same material. Northward, the chalk may be followed as far as Yorkshire; on the south coast it appears abruptly in the picturesque western bays of Dorset, and breaks into the Needles of the Isle of Wight; while on the shores of Kent it supplies that long line of white cliffs to which England owes her name of Albion.

Were the thin soil which covers it all washed away, a curved band of white chalk, here broader, and there narrower, might be followed diagonally across England from Lulworth in Dorset, to Flamborough Head in Yorkshire—a distance of over 280 miles as the crow flies. From this band to the North Sea, on the east, and the Channel, on the south, the chalk is largely hidden by other deposits; but, except in the Weald of Kent and Sussex, it enters into the very foundation of all the south-eastern counties.

Attaining, as it does in some places, a thickness of more than a thousand feet, the English chalk must be admitted to be a mass of considerable magnitude. Nevertheless, it covers but an insignificant portion of the whole area occupied by the chalk formation of the globe, much of which has the same general characters as ours, and is found in detached patches, some less, and others more extensive, than the English. Chalk occurs in north-west Ireland; it stretches over a large part of France,—the chalk which underlies Paris being, in fact, a continuation of that of the London basin; it runs through Denmark and Central Europe, and extends southward to North Africa; while eastward, it appears in the Crimea and in Syria, and may be traced as far as the shores of the Sea of Aral, in Central Asia. If all the points at which true chalk occurs were circumscribed, they would lie within an irregular oval about 3,000 miles in long diameter—the area of which would be as great as that of Europe, and would many times exceed that of the largest existing inland sea—the Mediterranean.

Thus the chalk is no unimportant element in the masonry of the earth's crust, and it impresses a peculiar stamp, varying with the conditions to which it is exposed, on the scenery of the districts in which it occurs. The undulating downs and rounded coombs, covered with sweet-grassed turf, of our inland chalk country, have a peacefully domestic and mutton-suggesting prettiness, but can hardly be called either grand or beautiful. But on our southern coasts, the wall-sided cliffs, many hundred feet high, with vast needles and pin-nacles standing out in the sea, sharp and solitary enough to serve as perches for the wary cormorant, confer a wonderful beauty and grandeur upon the chalk headlands. And, in the East, chalk has its share in the formation of some of the most venerable of mountain ranges, such as the Lebanon.

What is this wide-spread component of the surface of the earth? and whence did it come?

You may think this no very hopeful inquiry. You may not un-naturally suppose that the attempt to solve such problems as these can lead to no result, save that of entangling the inquirer in vague speculations, incapable of refutation and of verification. If such were really the case, I should have selected some other subject than a "piece of chalk" for my discourse. But, in truth, after much delibera-tion, I have been unable to think of any topic which would so well enable me to lead you to see how solid is the foundation upon which some of the most startling conclusions of physical science rest.

A great chapter of the history of the world is written in the chalk. Few passages in the history of man can be supported by such an overwhelming mass of direct and indirect evidence as that which testifies to the truth of the fragment of the history of the globe, which I hope to enable you to read, with your own eyes, to-night. Let me add, that few chapters of human history have a more profound significance for ourselves. I weigh my words well when I assert, that the man who should know the true history of the bit of chalk which every carpenter carries about in his breeches-pocket, though ignorant of all other history, is likely, if he will think his knowledge out to its ultimate results, to have a truer, and therefore a better, conception of this wonderful universe, and of man's relation to it, than the most learned student who is deep-read in the records of humanity and ignorant of those of Nature.

The language of the chalk is not hard to learn, not nearly so hard as Latin, if you only want to get at the broad features of the story it has to tell; and I propose that we now set to work to spell that story out together.

We all know that if we "burn" chalk the result is quicklime. Chalk, in fact, is a compound of carbonic acid gas, and lime, and when you make it very hot the carbonic acid flies away and the lime is left. By this method of procedure we see the lime, but we do not see the carbonic acid. If, on the other hand, you were to powder a little chalk and drop it into a good deal of strong vinegar, there would be a great bubbling and fizzing, and, finally, a clear liquid, in which no sign of chalk would appear. Here you see the carbonic acid in the bubbles; the lime, dissolved in the vinegar, vanishes from sight. There are a great many other ways of showing that chalk is essentially nothing but carbonic acid and quicklime. Chemists enunciate the result of all the experiments which prove this, by stating that chalk is almost wholly composed of "carbonate of lime."

It is desirable for us to start from the knowledge of this fact, though it may not seem to help us very far towards what we seek. For carbonate of lime is a widely-spread substance, and is met with under very various conditions. All sorts of limestones are composed of more or less pure carbonate of lime. The crust which is often deposited by waters which have drained through limestone rocks, in the form of what are called stalagmites and stalactites, is carbonate of lime. Or, to take a more familiar example, the fur on the inside of a tea-kettle is carbonate of lime; and, for anything chemistry tells us to the contrary, the chalk might be a kind of gigantic fur upon the bottom of the earth-kettle, which is kept pretty hot below.

Let us try another method of making the chalk tell us its own history. To the unassisted eye chalk looks simply like a very loose and open kind of stone. But it is possible to grind a slice of chalk down so thin that you can see through it—until it is thin enough, in fact, to be examined with any magnifying power that may be thought desirable. A thin slice of the fur of a kettle might be made in the same way. If it were examined microscopically, it would show itself to be a more or less distinctly laminated mineral substance, and nothing more.

But the slice of chalk presents a totally different appearance when placed under the microscope. The general mass of it is made up of very minute granules; but, imbedded in this matrix, are innumerable bodies, some smaller and some larger, but, on a rough average, not more than a hundredth of an inch in diameter, having a well-defined shape and structure. A cubic inch of some specimens of chalk may contain hundreds of thousands of these bodies, compacted together with incalculable millions of the granules.

The examination of a transparent slice gives a good notion of the manner in which the components of the chalk are arranged, and of their relative proportions. But, by rubbing up some chalk with a brush in water and then pouring off the milky fluid, so as to obtain sediments of different degrees of fineness, the granules and the minute rounded bodies may be pretty well separated from one another, and submitted to microscopic examination, either as opaque or as transparent objects. By combining the views obtained in these various methods, each of the rounded bodies may be proved to be a beautifully-constructed calcareous fabric, made up of a number of chambers, communicating freely with one another. The chambered bodies are of various forms. One of the commonest is something like a badly-grown raspberry, being formed of a number of nearly globular chambers of different sizes congregated together. It is called *Globigerina,* and some specimens of chalk consist of little else than *Globi-*

gerinæ and granules. Let us fix our attention upon the *Globigerina*. It is the spoor of the game we are tracking. If we can learn what it is and what are the conditions of its existence, we shall see our way to the origin and past history of the chalk.

A suggestion which may naturally enough present itself is, that these curious bodies are the result of some process of aggregation which has taken place in the carbonate of lime; that, just as in winter, the rime on our windows simulates the most delicate and elegantly arborescent foliage—proving that the mere mineral water may, under certain conditions, assume the outward form of organic bodies—so this mineral substance, carbonate of lime, hidden away in the bowels of the earth, has taken the shape of these chambered bodies. I am not raising a merely fanciful and unreal objection. Very learned men, in former days, have even entertained the notion that all the formed things found in rocks are of this nature; and if no such conception is at present held to be admissible, it is because long and varied experience has now shown that mineral matter never does assume the form and structure we find in fossils. If any one were to try to persuade you that an oyster-shell (which is also chiefly composed of carbonate of lime) had crystallized out of sea-water, I suppose you would laugh at the absurdity. Your laughter would be justified by the fact that all experience tends to show that oyster-shells are formed by the agency of oysters, and in no other way. And if there were no better reasons, we should be justified, on like grounds, in believing that *Globigerina* is not the product of anything but vital activity.

Happily, however, better evidence in proof of the organic nature of the *Globigerinæ* than that of analogy is forthcoming. It so happens that calcareous skeletons, exactly similar to the *Globigerinæ* of the chalk, are being formed, at the present moment, by minute living creatures, which flourish in multitudes, literally more numerous than the sands of the sea-shore, over a large extent of that part of the earth's surface which is covered by the ocean.

The history of the discovery of these living *Globigerinæ*, and of the part which they play in rock building, is singular enough. It is a discovery which, like others of no less scientific importance, has arisen, incidentally, out of work devoted to very different and exceedingly practical interests. When men first took to the sea, they speedily learned to look out for shoals and rocks; and the more the burthen of their ships increased, the more imperatively necessary it became for sailors to ascertain with precision the depth of the waters they traversed. Out of this necessity grew the use of the lead and sounding line; and, ultimately, marine-surveying, which is the recording of the form of coasts and of the depth of the sea, as ascertained by the sounding-lead, upon charts.

At the same time, it became desirable to ascertain and to indicate the nature of the sea-bottom, since this circumstance greatly affects its goodness as holding ground for anchors. Some ingenious tar, whose name deserves a better fate than the oblivion into which it has fallen, attained this object by "arming" the bottom of the lead with a lump of grease, to which more or less of the sand or mud, or broken shells, as the case might be, adhered, and was brought to the surface. But, however well adapted such an apparatus might be for rough nautical purposes, scientific accuracy could not be expected from the armed lead, and to remedy its defects (especially when applied to sounding in great depths) Lieut. Brooke, of the American Navy, some years ago invented a most ingenious machine, by which a considerable portion of the superficial layer of the sea-bottom can be scooped out and brought up from any depth to which the lead descends. In 1853, Lieut. Brooke obtained mud from the bottom of the North Atlantic, between Newfoundland and the Azores, at a depth of more than 10,000 feet, or two miles, by the help of this sounding apparatus. The specimens were sent for examination to Ehrenberg of Berlin, and to Bailey of West Point, and those able microscopists found that this deep-sea mud was almost entirely composed of the skeletons of living organisms—the greater proportion of these being just like the *Globigerinæ* already known to occur in the chalk.

Thus far, the work had been carried on simply in the interests of science, but Lieut. Brooke's method of sounding acquired a high commercial value, when the enterprise of laying down the telegraph-cable between this country and the United States was undertaken. For it became a matter of immense importance to know, not only the depth of the sea over the whole line along which the cable was to be laid, but the exact nature of the bottom, so as to guard against chances of cutting or fraying the strands of that costly rope. The Admiralty consequently ordered Captain Dayman, an old friend and shipmate of mine, to ascertain the depth over the whole line of the cable, and to bring back specimens of the bottom. In former days, such a command as this might have sounded very much like one of the impossible things which the young Prince in the Fairy Tales is ordered to do before he can obtain the hand of the Princess. However, in the months of June and July, 1857, my friend performed the task assigned to him with great expedition and precision, without, so far as I know, having met with any reward of that kind. The specimens of Atlantic mud which he procured were sent to me to be examined and reported upon.

The result of all these operations is, that we know the contours and the nature of the surface-soil covered by the North Atlantic for a distance of 1,700 miles from east to west, as well as we know that of any part of the dry land. It is a prodigious plain—one of the widest and most even plains in the world. If the sea were drained off, you might drive a waggon all the way from Valentia, on the west coast of Ireland, to Trinity Bay, in Newfoundland. And, except upon one sharp incline about 200 miles from Valentia, I am not quite sure that it would even be necessary to put the skid on, so gentle are the ascents and descents upon that long route. From Valentia the road would lie down-hill for about 200 miles to the point at which the bottom is now covered by 1,700 fathoms of sea-water. Then would come the central plain, more than a thousand miles wide, the inequalities of the surface of which would be hardly perceptible, though the depth of water upon it now varies from 10,000 to 15,000 feet; and there are places in which Mont Blanc might be sunk without showing its peak above water. Beyond this, the ascent on the American side commences, and gradually leads, for about 300 miles, to the Newfoundland shore.

Almost the whole of the bottom of this central plain (which extends for many hundred miles in a north and south direction) is covered by a fine mud, which, when brought to the surface, dries into a greyish white friable substance. You can write with this on a blackboard, if you are so inclined; and, to the eye, it is quite like very soft, grayish chalk. Examined chemically, it proves to be composed almost wholly of carbonate of lime; and if you make a section of it, in the same way as that of the piece of chalk was made, and view it with the microscope, it presents innumerable *Globigerinæ* embedded in a granular matrix. Thus this deep-sea mud is substantially chalk. I say substantially, because there are a good many minor differences; but as these have no bearing on the question immediately before us,—which is the nature of the *Globigerinæ* of the chalk,—it is unnecessary to speak of them.

Globigerinæ of every size, from the smallest to the largest, are associated together in the Atlantic mud, and the chambers of many are filled by a soft animal matter. This soft substance is, in fact, the remains of the creature to which the *Globigerina* shell, or rather skeleton, owes its existence—and which is an animal of the simplest imaginable description. It is, in fact, a mere particle of living jelly, without defined parts of any kind—without a mouth, nerves, muscles, or distinct organs, and only manifesting its vitality to ordinary observation by thrusting out and retracting from all parts of its surface, long filamentous processes, which serve for arms and legs. Yet this amorphous particle, devoid of everything which, in the higher animals, we call organs, is capable of feeding, growing, and multiplying; of separating from the ocean the small proportion of carbonate of lime which is dissolved in sea-water; and of building up that substance into a skeleton for itself, according to a pattern which can be imitated by no other known agency.

The notion that animals can live and flourish in the sea, at the vast depths from which apparently living *Globigerinæ* have been brought up, does not agree very well with our usual conceptions respecting the conditions of animal life; and it is not so absolutely impossible as it might at first sight appear to be, that the *Globigerinæ* of the Atlantic sea-bottom do not live and die where they are found.

As I have mentioned, the soundings from the great Atlantic plain are almost entirely made up of *Globigerinæ*, with the granules which have been mentioned, and some few other calcareous shells; but a small percentage of the chalky mud—perhaps at most some five per cent of it—is of a different nature, and consists of shells and skeletons composed of silex, or pure flint. These silicious bodies belong partly to the lowly vegetable organisms which are called *Diatomaccæ*, and partly to the minute, and extremely simple, animals, termed *Radiolaria*. It is quite certain that these creatures do not live at the bottom of the ocean, but at its surface—where they may be obtained in prodigious numbers by the use of a properly constructed net. Hence it follows that these silicious organisms, though they are not heavier than the lightest dust, must have fallen, in some cases, through fifteen thousand feet of water, before they reached their final resting-place on the ocean floor. And considering how large a surface these bodies expose in proportion to their weight, it is probable that they occupy a great length of time in making their burial journey from the surface of the Atlantic to the bottom.

But if the *Radiolaria* and Diatoms are thus rained upon the bottom of the sea, from the superficial layer of its waters in which they pass their lives, it is obviously possible that the *Globigerinæ* may be similarly derived; and if they were so, it would be much more easy to understand how they obtain their supply of food than it is at present. Nevertheless, the positive and negative evidence all points the other way. The skeletons of the full-grown, deep-sea *Globigerinæ* are so remarkably solid and heavy in proportion to their surface as to seem little fitted for floating; and, as a matter of fact, they are not to be found along with the Diatoms and *Radiolaria* in the uppermost stratum of the open ocean. It has been observed, again, that the abundance of *Globigerinæ*, in proportion to other organisms, of like kind, increases with the depth of the sea; and that deep-water *Globigerinæ* are larger than those which live in shallower parts of the sea; and such facts negative the supposition that these organisms have been swept by currents from the shallows into the deeps of the Atlantic. It therefore seems to be hardly doubtful that these wonderful creatures live and die at the depths in which they are found.

However, the important points for us are, that the living *Globigerinæ* are exclusively marine animals, the skeletons of which abound at the bottom of deep seas; and that there is not a shadow of reason for believing that the habits of the *Globigerinæ* of the chalk differed from those of the existing species. But if this be true, there is no escaping the conclusion that the chalk itself is the dried mud of an ancient deep sea.

In working over the soundings collected by Captain Dayman, I was surprised to find that many of what I have called the "granules" of that mud were not, as one might have been tempted to think at first, the mere powder and waste of *Globigerinæ*, but that they had a definite form and size. I termed these bodies "*coccoliths*," and doubted their organic nature. Dr. Wallich verified my observation, and added the interesting discovery that, not unfrequently, bodies similar to these "coccoliths" were aggregated together into spheroids, which he termed "*coccospheres*." So far as we knew, these bodies, the nature of which is extremely puzzling and problematical, were peculiar to the Atlantic soundings. But, a few years ago, Mr. Sorby, in making a careful examination of the chalk by means of thin sections and otherwise, observed, as Ehrenberg had done before him, that much of its granular basis possesses a definite form. Comparing these formed particles with those in the Atlantic soundings, he found the two to be identical; and thus proved that the chalk, like the surroundings, contains these mysterious coccoliths and coccospheres. Here was a further and most interesting confirmation, from internal evidence, of the essential identity of the chalk with modern deep-sea mud. *Globigerinæ*, coccoliths, and coccospheres are found as the chief constituents of both, and testify to the general similarity of the conditions under which both have been formed.

The evidence furnished by the hewing, facing, and superposition of the stones of the Pyramids, that these structures were built by men, has no greater weight than the evidence that the chalk was built by *Globigerinæ*; and the belief that those ancient pyramid-builders were terrestrial and air-breathing creatures like ourselves, is not better based than the conviction that the chalk-makers lived in the sea. But as our belief in the building of the Pyramids by men is not only grounded on the internal evidence afforded by these structures, but gathers strength from multitudinous collateral proofs, and is clinched by the total absence of any reason for a contrary belief; so the evidence drawn from the *Globigerinæ* that the chalk is an ancient sea-bottom, is fortified by innumerable independent lines of evidence; and our belief in the truth of the conclusion to which all positive testimony tends, receives the like negative justification from the fact that no other hypothesis has a shadow of foundation.

It may be worth while briefly to consider a few of these collateral proofs that the chalk was deposited at the bottom of the sea. The great mass of the chalk is composed, as we have seen, of the skeletons of *Globigerinæ*, and other simple organisms, imbedded in granular matter. Here and there, however, this hardened mud of the ancient sea reveals the remains of higher animals which have lived and died, and left their hard parts in the mud, just as the oysters die and leave their shells behind them, in the mud of the present seas.

There are, at the present day, certain groups of animals which are never found in fresh waters, being unable to live anywhere but in the sea. Such are the corals; those corallines which are called *Polyzoa;* those creatures which fabricate the lamp-shells, and are called *Brachiopoda;* the pearly *Nautilus,* and all animals allied to it; and all the forms of sea-urchins and star-fishes. Not only are all these creatures confined to salt water at the present day; but, so far as our records of the past go, the conditions of their existence have been the same: hence, their occurrence in any deposit is as strong evidence as can be obtained, that that deposit was formed in the sea. Now the remains of animals of all the kinds which have been enumerated, occur in the chalk, in greater or less abundance; while not one of those forms of shell-fish which are characteristic of fresh water has yet been observed in it.

When we consider that the remains of more than three thousand distinct species of aquatic animals have been discovered among the fossils of the chalk, that the great majority of them are of such forms as are now met with only in the sea, and that there is no reason to believe that any one of them inhabited fresh water—the collateral evidence that the chalk represents an ancient sea-bottom acquires as great force as the proof derived from the nature of the chalk itself. I think you will now allow that I did not overstate my case when I asserted that we have as strong grounds for believing that all the vast area of dry land, at present occupied by the chalk, was once at the bottom of the sea, as we have for any matter of history whatever; while there is no justification for any other belief.

No less certain it is that the time during which the countries we now call south-east England, France, Germany, Poland, Russia, Egypt, Arabia, Syria, were more or less completely covered by a deep sea, was of considerable duration. We have already seen that the chalk is, in places, more than a thousand feet thick. I think you will agree with me, that it must have taken some time for the skeletons of animalcules of a hundredth of an inch in diameter to heap up such a mass as that. I have said that throughout the thickness of the chalk the remains of other animals are scattered. These remains are often in the most exquisite state of preservation. The valves of the shell-fishes are commonly adherent; the long spines of some of the sea-urchins, which would be detached by the smallest jar, often remain in their places. In a word, it is certain that these animals have lived and died when the place which they now occupy was the surface of as much of the chalk as had then been deposited; and that each has been covered up by the layer of *Globigerina* mud, upon which the creatures imbedded a little higher up have, in like manner, lived and died. But some of these remains prove the existence of reptiles of vast size in the chalk sea. These lived their time, and had their ancestors and descendants, which assuredly implies time, reptiles being of slow growth.

There is more curious evidence, again, that the process of covering up, or, in other words, the deposit of *Globigerina* skeletons, did not go on very fast. It is demonstrable that an animal of the cretaceous sea might die, that its skeleton might lie uncovered upon the sea-bottom long enough to lose all its outward coverings and appendages by putrefaction; and that, after this had happened, another animal might attach itself to the dead and naked skeleton, might grow to maturity, and might itself die before the calcareous mud had buried the whole.

Cases of this kind are admirably described by Sir Charles Lyell. He speaks of the frequency with which geologists find in the chalk a fossilized sea-urchin, to which is attached the lower valve of a *Crania*. This is a kind of shell-fish, with a shell composed of two pieces, of which, as in the oyster, one is fixed and the other free.

"The upper valve is almost invariably wanting, though occasionally found in a perfect state of preservation in the white chalk at some distance. In this case, we see clearly that the sea-urchin first lived from youth to age, then died and lost its spines, which were carried away. Then the young *Crania* adhered to the bared shell, grew and perished in its turn; after which, the upper valve was separated from the lower, before the Echinus became enveloped in chalky mud."

A specimen in the Museum of Practical Geology, in London, still further prolongs the period which must have elapsed between the death of the sea-urchin, and its burial by the *Globigerinæ*. For the outward face of the valve of a *Crania*, which is attached to a sea-urchin, (*Micraster*), is itself overrun by an incrusting coralline, which spreads thence over more or less of the surface of the sea-urchin. It follows that, after the upper valve of the *Crania* fell off, the surface of the attached valve must have remained exposed long enough to allow of the growth of the whole coralline, since corallines do not live embedded in mud.

The progress of knowledge may, one day, enable us to deduce from such facts as these the maximum rate at which the chalk can have accumulated, and thus to arrive at the minimum duration of the chalk period. Suppose that the valve of the *Crania* upon which a coralline has fixed itself in the way just described, is so attached to the sea-urchin that no part of it is more than an inch above the face upon which the sea-urchin rests. Then, as the coralline could not have fixed itself, if the *Crania* had been covered up with chalk mud, and could not have lived had itself been so covered, it follows, that an inch of chalk mud could not have accumulated within the time between the death and decay of the soft parts of the sea-urchin and the growth of the coralline to the full size which it has attained. If the decay of the soft parts of the sea-urchin; the attachment, growth to maturity, and decay of the *Crania;* and the subsequent attachment and growth of the coralline, took a year (which is a low estimate enough), the accumulation of the inch of chalk must have taken more than a year: and the deposit of a thousand feet of chalk must, consequently, have taken more than twelve thousand years.

The foundation of all this calculation is, of course, a knowledge of the length of time the *Crania* and the coralline needed to attain their full size; and, on this head, precise knowledge is at present wanting. But there are circumstances which tend to show, that nothing like an inch of chalk has accumulated during the life of a *Crania;* and, on any probable estimate of the length of that life, the chalk period must have had a much longer duration than that thus roughly assigned to it.

Thus, not only is it certain that the chalk is the mud of an ancient sea-bottom; but it is no less certain, that the chalk sea existed during an extremely long period, though we may not be prepared to give a precise estimate of the length of that period in years. The relative duration is clear, though the absolute duration may not be definable. The attempt to affix any precise date to the period at which the chalk sea began, or ended, its existence, is baffled by difficulties of the same kind. But the relative age of the cretaceous epoch may be determined with as great ease and certainty as the long duration of that epoch.

You will have heard of the interesting discoveries recently made, in various parts of Western Europe, of flint implements, obviously worked into shape by human hands, under circumstances which show conclusively that man is a very ancient denizen of these regions. It has been proved that the whole populations of Europe, whose existence has been revealed to us in this way, consisted of savages, such as the Esquimaux are now; that, in the country which is now France, they hunted the reindeer, and were familiar with the ways of the mammoth and the bison. The physical geography of France was in those days different from what it is now—the river Somme, for instance, having cut its bed a hundred feet deeper between that time and this; and, it is probable, that the climate was more like that of Canada or Siberia, than that of Western Europe.

The existence of these people is forgotten even in the traditions of the oldest historical nations. The name and fame of them had utterly vanished until a few years back; and the amount of physical change which has been effected since their day renders it more than probable that, venerable as are some of the historical nations, the workers of the chipped flints of Hoxne or of Amiens are to them, as they are to us, in point of antiquity. But, if we assign to these hoar relics of long-vanished generations of men the greatest age that can possibly be claimed for them, they are not older than the drift, or boulder clay, which, in comparison with the chalk, is but a very juvenile deposit. You need go no further than your own sea-board for evidence of this fact. At one of the most charming spots on the coast of Norfolk,

Cromer, you will see the boulder clay forming a vast mass, which lies upon the chalk, and must consequently have come into existence after it. Huge boulders of chalk are, in fact, included in the clay, and have evidently been brought to the position they now occupy by the same agency as that which has planted blocks of syenite from Norway side by side with them.

The chalk, then, is certainly older than the boulder clay. If you ask how much, I will again take you no further than the same spot upon your own coasts for evidence. I have spoken of the boulder clay and drift as resting upon the chalk. That is not strictly true. Interposed between the chalk and the drift is a comparatively insignificant layer, containing vegetable matter. But that layer tells a wonderful history. It is full of stumps of trees standing as they grew. Fir-trees are there with their cones, and hazel-bushes with their nuts; there stand the stools of oak and yew trees, beeches and alders. Hence this stratum is appropriately called the "forest-bed."

It is obvious that the chalk must have been upheaved and converted into dry land, before the timber trees could grow upon it. As the bolls of some of these trees are from two to three feet in diameter, it is no less clear that the dry land thus formed remained in the same condition for long ages. And not only do the remains of stately oaks and well-grown firs testify to the duration of this condition of things, but additional evidence to the same effect is afforded by the abundant remains of elephants, rhinoceroses, hippopotamuses, and other great wild beasts, which it has yielded to the zealous search of such men as the Rev. Mr. Gunn. When you look at such a collection as he has formed, and bethink you that these elephantine bones did veritably carry their owners about, and these great grinders crunch, in the dark woods of which the forest-bed is now the only trace, it is impossible not to feel that they are as good evidence of the lapse of time as the annual rings of the tree stumps.

Thus there is a writing upon the wall of cliffs at Cromer, and whoso runs may read it. It tells us, with an authority which cannot be impeached, that the ancient sea-bed of the chalk sea was raised up, and remained dry land, until it was covered with forest, stocked with the great game the spoils of which have rejoiced your geologists. How long it remained in that condition cannot be said; but "the whirligig of time brought its revenges" in those days as in these. That dry land, with the bones and teeth of generations of long-lived elephants, hidden away among the gnarled roots and dry leaves of its ancient trees, sank gradually to the bottom of the icy sea, which covered it with huge masses of drift and boulder clay. Sea-beasts, such as the walrus, now restricted to the extreme north, paddled about where birds had twittered among the topmost twigs of the fir-trees. How long this state of things endured we know not, but at length it came to an end. The upheaved glacial mud hardened into the soil of modern Norfolk. Forests grew once more, the wolf and the beaver replaced the reindeer and the elephant; and at length what we call the history of England dawned.

Thus you have, within the limits of your own county, proof that the chalk can justly claim a very much greater antiquity than even the oldest physical traces of mankind. But we may go further and demonstrate, by evidence of the same authority as that which testifies to the existence of the father of men, that the chalk is vastly older than Adam himself. The Book of Genesis informs us that Adam, immediately upon his creation, and before the appearance of Eve, was placed in the Garden of Eden. The problem of the geographical position of Eden has greatly vexed the spirits of the learned in such matters, but there is one point respecting which, so far as I know, no commentator has ever raised a doubt. This is, that of the four rivers which are said to run out of it, Euphrates and Hiddekel are identical with the rivers now known by the names of Euphrates and Tigris. But the whole country in which these mighty rivers take their origin, and through which they run, is composed of rocks which are either of the same age as the chalk, or of later date. So that the chalk must not only have been formed, but, after its formation, the time required for the deposit of these later rocks, and for their upheaval into dry land, must have elapsed, before the smallest brook which feeds the swift stream of "the great river, the river of Babylon," began to flow.

Thus, evidence which cannot be rebutted, and which need not be strengthened, though if time permitted I might indefinitely increase its quantity, compels you to believe that the earth, from the time of the chalk to the present day, has been the theatre of a series of changes as vast in their amount, as they were slow in their progress. The area on which we stand has been first sea and then land, for at least four alternations; and has remained in each of these conditions for a period of great length.

Nor have these wonderful metamorphoses of sea into land, and of land into sea, been confined to one corner of England. During the chalk period, or "cretaceous epoch," not one of the present great physical features of the globe was in existence. Our great mountain ranges, Pyrenees, Alps, Himalayas, Andes, have all been upheaved since the chalk was deposited, and the cretaceous sea flowed over the sites of Sinai and Ararat. All this is certain, because rocks of cretaceous, or still later, date have shared in the elevatory movements which gave rise to these mountain chains; and may be found perched up, in some cases, many thousand feet high upon their flanks. And evidence of equal cogency demonstrates that, though, in Norfolk, the forest-bed rests directly upon the chalk, yet it does so, not because the period at which the forest grew immediately followed that at which the chalk was formed, but because an immense lapse of time, represented elsewhere by thousands of feet of rock, is not indicated at Cromer.

I must ask you to believe that there is no less conclusive proof that a still more prolonged succession of similar changes occurred, before the chalk was deposited. Nor have we any reason to think that the first term in the series of these changes is known. The oldest sea-beds preserved to us are sands, and mud, and pebbles, the wear and tear of rocks which were formed in still older oceans.

But, great as is the magnitude of these physical changes of the world, they have been accompanied by a no less striking series of modifications in its living inhabitaints. All the great classes of animals, beasts of the field, fowls of the air, creeping things, and things which dwell in the waters, flourished upon the globe long ages before the chalk was deposited. Very few, however, if any, of these ancient forms of animal life were identical with those which now live. Certainly not one of the higher animals was of the same species as any of those now in existence. The beasts of the field, in the days before the chalk, were not our beasts of the field, nor the fowls of the air such as those which the eye of men has seen flying, unless his antiquity dates infinitely further back than we at present surmise. If we could be carried back into those times, we should be as one suddenly set down in Australia before it was colonized. We should see mammals, birds, reptiles, fishes, insects, snails, and the like, clearly recognizable as such, and yet not one of them would be just the same as those with which we are familiar, and many would be extremely different.

From that time to the present, the population of the world has undergone slow and gradual, but incessant, changes. There has been no grand catastrophe—no destroyer has swept away the forms of life of one period, and replaced them by a totally new creation: but one species has vanished and another has taken its place; creatures of one type of structure have diminished, those of another have increased, as time has passed on. And thus, while the differences between the living creatures of the time before the chalk and those of the present day appear startling, if placed side by side, we are led from one to the other by the most gradual progress, if we follow the course of Nature through the whole series of those relics of her operations which she has left behind. It is by the population of the chalk sea that the ancient and the modern inhabitants of the world are most completely connected. The groups which are dying out flourish, side by side, with groups which are now the dominant forms of life. Thus the chalk contains remains of those strange flying and swimming reptiles, the pterodactyl, the ichthyosaurus, and the plesiosaurus, which are found in no later deposits, but abounded in preceding

ages. The chambered shells called ammonites and belemnites, which
are so characteristic of the period preceding the cretaceous, in like
manner die with it.

But, amongst these fading remainders of a previous state of things,
are some very modern forms of life, looking like Yankee pedlars
among a tribe of Red Indians. Crocodiles of modern type appear; bony
fishes, many of them very similar to existing species, almost supplant
the forms of fish which predominate in more ancient seas; and many
kinds of living shell-fish first become known to us in the chalk. The
vegetation acquires a modern aspect. A few living animals are not
even distinguishable as species, from those which existed at that remote epoch. The *Globigerina* of the present day, for example, is not
different specifically from that of the chalk; and the same may be said
of many other *Foraminifera*. I think it probable that critical and un-
prejudiced examination will show that more than one species of
much higher animals have had a similar longevity; but the only
example which I can at present give confidently is the snake's-head
lampshell (*Terebratulina caput serpentis*), which lives in our English
seas and abounded (as *Terebratulina striata* of authors) in the chalk.

The longest line of human ancestry must hide its diminished head
before the pedigree of this insignificant shell-fish. We Englishmen
are proud to have an ancestor who was present at the Battle of
Hastings. The ancestors of *Terebratulina caput serpentis* may have
been present at a battle of *Ichthyosauria* in that part of the sea which,
when the chalk was forming, flowed over the site of Hastings. While
all around has changed, this *Terebratulina* has peacefully propagated
its species from generation to generation, and stands to this day, as
a living testimony to the continuity of the present with the past history of the globe.

Up to this moment I have stated, so far as I know, nothing but
well-authenticated facts, and the immediate conclusions which they
force upon the mind. But the mind is so constituted that it does not
willingly rest in facts and immediate causes, but seeks always after
a knowledge of the remoter links in the chain of causation.

Taking the many changes of any given spot of the earth's surface,
from sea to land and from land to sea, as an established fact, we
cannot refrain from asking ourselves how these changes have occurred. And when we have explained them—as they must be explained—by the alternate slow movements of elevation and depres-
sion which have affected the crust of the earth, we go still further
back, and ask, Why these movements?

I am not certain that any one can give you a satisfactory answer
to that question. Assuredly I cannot. All that can be said, for certain,
is that such movements are part of the ordinary course of nature,
inasmuch as they are going on at the present time. Direct proof may

be given, that some parts of the land of the northern hemisphere are at this moment insensibly rising and others insensibly sinking; and there is indirect, but perfectly satisfactory, proof, that an enormous area now covered by the Pacific has been deepened thousands of feet, since the present inhabitants of that sea came into existence. Thus there is not a shadow of a reason for believing that the physical changes of the globe, in past times, have been effected by other than natural causes. Is there any more reason for believing that the concomitant modifications in the forms of the living inhabitants of the globe have been brought about in other ways?

Before attempting to answer this question, let us try to form a distinct mental picture of what has happened in some special case. The crocodiles are animals which, as a group, have a very vast antiquity. They abounded ages before the chalk was deposited; they throng the rivers in warm climates, at the present day. There is a difference in the form of the joints of the back-bone, and in some minor particulars, between the crocodiles of the present epoch and those which lived before the chalk; but, in the cretaceous epoch, as I have alread mentioned, the crocodiles had assumed the modern type of structure. Notwithstanding this, the crocodiles of the chalk are not identically the same as those which lived in the times called "older tertiary," which succeeded the cretaceous epoch; and the crocodiles of the older tertiaries are not identical with those of the newer tertiaries, nor are these identical with existing forms. I leave open the question whether particular species may have lived on from epoch to epoch. But each epoch has had its peculiar crocodiles; though all, since the chalk, have belonged to the modern type, and differ simply in their proportions, and in such structural particulars as are discernible only to trained eyes.

How is the existence of this long succession of different species of crocodiles to be accounted for? Only two suppositions seem to be open to us—Either each species of crocodile has been specially created, or it has arisen out of some pre-existing form by the operation of natural causes. Choose your hypothesis; I have chosen mine. I can find no warranty for believing in the distinct creation of a score of successive species of crocodiles in the course of countless ages of time. Science gives no countenance to such a wild fancy; nor can even the perverse ingenuity of a commentator pretend to discover this sense, in the simple words in which the writer of Genesis records the proceedings of the fifth and six days of the Creation.

On the other hand, I see no good reason for doubting the necessary alternative, that all these varied species have been evolved from pre-existing crocodilian forms, by the operation of causes as completely a part of the common order of nature as those which have effected the changes of the inorganic world. Few will venture to affirm that the reasoning which applies to crocodiles loses its force among other animals, or among plants. If one series of species has come into existence by the operation of natural causes, it seems folly to deny that all may have arisen in the same way.

A small beginning has led us to a great ending. If I were to put the bit of chalk with which we started into the hot but obscure flame of burning hydrogen, it would presently shine like the sun. It seems to me that this physical metamorphosis is no false image of what has been the result of our subjecting it to a jet of fervent, though no-wise brilliant, thought to-night. It has become luminous, and its clear rays, penetrating the abyss of the remote past, have brought within our ken some stages of the evolution of the earth. And in the shifting "without haste, but without rest" of the land and sea, as in the endless variation of the forms assumed by living beings, we have observed nothing but the natural product of the forces originally possessed by the substance of the universe.

A Philosophy

of

Handicap

RANDOLPH BOURNE

(1886–1918)

*This essay was published in a collection of essays in the
year of their author's graduation from Columbia University (1913). The maturity shown in such a youthful writer
is all the more remarkable when it is known Randolph
Bourne was small, hunchbacked, and in poor health—in
other words, the handicapped person of his essay. Nevertheless, the book is an idealistic prophecy of a youth movement in American culture which many students of the
1970's would be able to appreciate. Bourne was also a paci-
fist, a militant intellectual radical, whose sympathies and
enthusiasms were shared by the equally young Floyd Dell,
to whose magazine,* The Masses, *Bourne contributed. Russel Nye has called this essay "one of the most moving and
ho..est documents ever written of the impact of a physical
handicap on a brilliant, sensitive, and ambitious man."*

It would not be thought, ordinarily, that the man whom physical
disabilities have made so helpless that he is unable to move around
among his fellows, can bear his lot more happily, even though he
suffer pain, and face life with a more cheerful and contented spirit,
than can the man whose handicaps are merely enough to mark him
out from the rest of his fellows without preventing him from entering
with them into most of their common affairs and experiences. But
the fact is that the former's very helplessness makes him content to
rest and not to strive. I know a young man so helplessly disabled that
he has to be carried about, who is happy in reading a little, playing
chess, taking a course or two in college, and all with the sunniest good
will in the world, and a happiness that seems strange and unaccountable to my restlessness. He does not cry for the moon.

When the handicapped youth, however, is in full possession of his
faculties, and can move about freely, he is perforce drawn into all
the currents of life. Particularly if he has his own way in the world
to make, his road is apt to be hard and rugged, and he will penetrate

From *Youth and Life* by Randolph Bourne, Houghton Mifflin Company, 1913.

309

to an unusual depth in his interpretation both of the world's attitude toward such misfortunes, and of the attitude toward the world which such misfortunes tend to cultivate in men like him. For he has all the battles of a stronger man to fight, and he is at a double disadvantage in fighting them. He has constantly with him the sense of being obliged to make extra efforts to overcome the bad impression of his physical defects, and he is haunted with a constant feeling of weakness and low vitality which makes effort more difficult and renders him easily faint-hearted and discouraged by failure. He is never confident of himself, because he has grown up in an atmosphere where nobody has been very confident of him; and yet his environment and circumstances call out all sorts of ambitions and energies in him which, from the nature of his case, are bound to be immediately thwarted. This attitude is likely to keep him at a generally low level of accomplishment unless he have an unusually strong will, and a strong will is perhaps the last thing to develop under such circumstances.

The handicapped man is always conscious that the world does not expect very much from him. And it takes him a long time to see in this a challenge instead of a firm pressing down to a low level of accomplishment. As a result, he does not expect very much from himself; he is timid in approaching people, and distrustful of his ability to persuade and convince. He becomes extraordinarily sensitive to other people's first impressions of him; those who are to be his friends he knows instantly, and further acquaintance adds little to the intimacy and warm friendship that he at once feels for them. On the other hand, those who do not respond to him immediately cannot by any effort either on his part or theirs overcome that first alienation.

This sensitiveness has both its good and its bad sides. It makes friendship the most precious thing in the world to him, and he finds that he arrives at a much richer and wider intimacy with his friends than do ordinary men with their light, surface friendships, based on good fellowship or the convenience of the moment. But on the other hand this sensitiveness absolutely unfits him for business and the practice of a profession, where one must be "all things to all men," and the professional manner is indispensable to success. For here, where he has to meet a constant stream of men of all sorts and conditions, his sensitiveness to these first impressions will make his case hopeless. Except with those few who by some secret sympathy will seem to respond, his physical deficiencies will stand like a huge barrier between his personality and other men's. The magical good fortune of attractive personal appearance makes its way almost without effort in the world, breaking down all sorts of walls of disapproval and lack of interest. Even the homely person can attract by personal charm.

The doors of the handicapped man are always locked, and the key is on the outside. He may have treasures of charm inside, but they will never be revealed unless the person outside cooperates with him in unlocking the door. A friend becomes, to a much greater degree than with the ordinary man, the indispensable means of discovering one's own personality. One only exists, so to speak, with friends. It is easy to see how hopelessly such a sensitiveness incapacitates a man for business, professional or social life, where the hasty and super-ficial impression is everything, and disaster is the fate of the man who has not all the treasures of his personality in the front window, where they can be readily inspected and appraised.

It thus takes the handicapped man a long time to get adjusted to his world. Childhood is perhaps the hardest time of all. As a child he is a strange creature in a strange land. It was my own fate to be just strong enough to play about with the other boys, and attempt all their games and "stunts," without being strong enough actually to succeed in any of them. It never used to occur to me that my failures and lack of skill were due to circumstances beyond my control, but I would always impute them, in consequence of my rigid Calvinistc upbringing, I suppose, to some moral weakness of my own. I suffered tortures in trying to learn to skate, to climb trees, to play ball, to con-form in general to the ways of the world. I never resigned myself to the inevitable, but overexerted myself constantly in a grim determina-tion to succeed. I was good at my lessons, and through timidity rather than priggishness, I hope, a very well-behaved boy at school; I was devoted, too, to music, and learned to play the piano pretty well. But I despised my reputation for excellence in these things, and instead of adapting myself philosophically to the situation, I strove and have been striving ever since to do the things I could not.

As I look back now it seems perfectly natural that I should have followed the standards of the crowd, and loathed my high marks in lessons and deportment, and the concerts to which I was sent by my aunt, and the exhibitions of my musical skill that I had to give before admiring ladies. Whether or not such an experience is typical of handicapped children, there is tragedy there for those situated as I was. For had I been a little weaker physically, I should have been thrown back on reading omnivorously and cultivating my music, with some possible results; while if I had been a little stronger, I could have participated in the play on an equal footing with the rest. As it was, I simply tantalized myself, and grew up with a deepening sense of failure, and a lack of pride in that at which I really excelled.

When the world became one of dances and parties and social eve-nings and boy-and-girl attachments,—the world of youth,—I was to find myself still less adapted to it. And this was the harder to bear because I was naturally sociable, and all these things appealed tre-mendously to me. This world of admiration and gayety and smiles and favors and quick interest and companionship, however, is only for the well-begotten and the debonair. It was not through any cruelty or dislike, I think, that I was refused admittance; indeed they were always very kind about inviting me. But it was more as if a ragged urchin had been asked to come and look through a window at the light and warmth of a glittering party; I was truly in the world, but not of the world. Indeed there were times when one would almost prefer conscious cruelty to this silent, unconscious, gentle oblivion. And this is the tragedy, I suppose, of all the ill-favored and unattractive to a greater or less degree; the world of youth is a world of so many conventions, and the abnormal in any direction is so glaringly and hideously abnormal.

Although it took me a long time to understand this, and I continued to attribute my failure mostly to my own character, trying hard to compensate for my physical deficiencies by my skill and cleverness, I suffered comparatively few pangs, and got much better adjusted to this world than the other. For I was older, and I had acquired a lively interest in all the social politics; I would get so interested in watching how people behaved, and in sizing them up, that only at rare intervals would I remember that I was really having no hand in the game. This interest just in the ways people are human, has become more and more a positive advantage in my life, and has kept sweet many a situation that might easily have cost me a pang. Not that a person with disabilities should be a sort of detective, evil-mindedly using his social opportunities for spying out and analyzing his friends' foibles, but that, if he does acquire an interest in people quite apart from their relation to him, he may go into society with an easy conscience and a certainty that he will be entertained and possibly entertaining, even though he cuts a poor enough social figure. He must simply not expect too much.

Perhaps the bitterest struggles of the handicapped man come when he tackles the business world. If he has to go out for himself to look for work, without fortune, training, or influence, as I personally did, his way will indeed be rugged. His disability will work against him for any position where he must be much in the eyes of men, and his general insignificance has a subtle influence in convincing those to whom he applies that he is unfitted for any kind of work. As I have suggested, his keen sensitiveness to other people's impressions of him makes him more than usually timid and unable to counteract that fatal first impression by any display of personal force and will. He cannot get his personality over across that barrier. The cards seem stacked against him from the start. With training and influence something might be done, but alone and unaided his case is almost hopeless. The attitude toward him ranges from, "You can't expect us to create a place for you," to "How could it enter your head that we should find any use for you?" He is discounted at the start: it is not business to make allowances for anybody; and while people are not cruel or unkind, it is the hopeless finality of the thing that fills one's heart with despair.

The environment of the big city is perhaps the worst possible that a man in such a situation could have. For the thousands of seeming opportunities lead one restlessly on and on, and keep one's mind perpetually unsettled and depressed. There is a poignant mental torture that comes with such an experience,—the urgent need, the repeated failure, or rather the repeated failure even to obtain a chance to fail, the realization that those at home can ill afford to have you idle, the growing dread of encountering people,—all this is something that those who have never been through it can never realize. Personally I know of no particular way of escape. One can expect to do little by one's own unaided efforts. I solved my difficulties by evading them, by throwing overboard some of my responsibility, and taking the desperate step of entering college on a scholarship. Desultory work is not nearly so humiliating when one is using one's time to some advantage, and college furnishes an ideal environment where the things at which a man handicapped like myself can succeed really count. One's self-respect can begin to grow like a weed.

For at the bottom of all the difficulties of a man like me is really the fact that his self-respect is so slow in growing up. Accustomed from his childhood to being discounted, his self-respect is naturally not very strong, and it would require pretty constant success in a congenial line of work really to confirm it. If he could only more easily separate the factors that are due to his physical disability from those that are due to his weak will and character, he might more quickly attain self-respect, for he would realize what he is responsible for, and what he is not. But at the beginning he rarely makes allowances for himself; he is his own severest judge. He longs for a "strong will," and yet the experience of having his efforts promptly nipped off at the beginning is the last thing on earth to produce that will.

If the handicapped youth is brought into harsh and direct touch with the real world, life proves a much more complex thing to him than to the ordinary man. Many of his inherited platitudes vanish at the first touch. Life appears to him as a grim struggle, where ability does not necessarily mean opportunity and success, nor piety sympathy, and where helplessness cannot count on assistance and kindly interest. Human affairs seem to be running on a wholly irrational plan, and success to be founded on chance as much as on anything. But if he can stand the first shock of disillusionment, he may find himself enormously interested in discovering how they actually do run, and he will want to burrow into the motives of men, and find the reasons for the crass inequalities and injustices of the world he sees around him. He has practically to construct anew a world of his own, and explain a great many things to himself that the ordinary person never dreams of finding unintelligible at all. He will be filled with a profound sympathy for all who are despised and ignored in the world. When he has been through the neglect and struggles of a handicapped and ill-favored man himself, he will begin to understand the feelings of all the horde of the unpresentable and unemployable, the incompetent and the ugly, the queer and crotchety people who make up so large a proportion of human folk.

We are perhaps too prone to get our ideas and standards of worth from the successful, without reflecting that the interpretations of life which patriotic legend, copy-book philosophy, and the sayings of the wealthy give us, are pitifully inadequate for those who fall behind in the race. Surely there are enough people to whom the task of making a decent living and maintaining themselves and their families in their social class, or of winning and keeping the respect of their fellows, is a hard and bitter task, to make a philosophy gained through personal disability and failure as just and true a method of appraising the life around us as the cheap optimism of the ordinary professional man. And certainly a kindlier, for it has no shade of contempt or disparagement about it. . . .

The difference between what the strongest of the strong and the most winning of the attractive can get out of life, and what I can, is after all so slight. Our experiences and enjoyments, both his and mine, are so infinitesimal compared with the great mass of possibilities; and there must be a division of labor. If he takes the world of physical satisfactions and of material success, I can at least occupy the far richer kingdom of mental effort and artistic appreciation. And on the side of what we are to put into life, although I admit that achievement on my part will be harder relatively to encompass than on his, at least I may have the field of artistic creation and intellectual achievement for my own. Indeed, as one gets older, the fact of one's disabilities fades dimmer and dimmer away from consciousness. One's enemy is now one's own weak will, and the struggle is to attain the artistic ideal one has set.

But one must have grown up, to get this attitude. And that is the best thing the handicapped man can do. Growing up will have given him one of the greatest satisfactions of his life, and certainly the most durable one. It will mean at least that he is out of the woods. Childhood has nothing to offer him; youth little more. They are things to be gotten through with as soon as possible. For he will not understand, and he will not be understood. He finds himself simply a bundle of chaotic impulses and emotions and ambitions, very few of which, from the nature of the case, can possibly be realized or satisfied. He is bound to be at cross-grains with the world, and he has to look sharp that he does not grow up with a bad temper and a hateful disposition, and become cynical and bitter against those who turn him away. By growing up, his horizon will broaden; he will get a better perspective, and will not take the world so seriously as he used to, nor will failure frighten him so much. He can look back and see how inevitable it all was, and understand how precarious and problematic even the best regulated of human affairs may be. And if he feels that there were times when he should have been able to count upon the help and kindly counsel of relatives and acquaintances who remained dumb and uninterested, he will not put their behavior down as proof of the depravity of human nature, but as due to an unfortunate blindness which it will be his work to avoid in himself by looking out for others when he has the power.

When he has grown up, he will find that people of his own age and experience are willing to make those large allowances for what is out of the ordinary, which were impossible for his younger friends, and that grown-up people touch each other on planes other than the purely superficial. With a broadening of his own interests, he will find himself overlapping with other people's personalities at new points, and will discover with rare delight that he is beginning to be understood and appreciated,—at least to a greater degree than when he had to keep his real interests hid as something unusual. For he will begin to see in his friends, his music and books, and his interest in people and social betterment, his true life; many of his restless ambitions will fade gradually away, and he will come to recognize all the more clearly some true ambition of his life that is within the range of his capabilities. He will have built up his world, and have sifted out the things that are not going to concern him, and the participation in which will only serve to vex and harass him. He may well come to count his disabilities even as a blessing, for it has made impossible to him at last many things in the pursuit of which he would only fritter away his time and dissipate his interest. He must not think of "resigning himself to his fate"; above all, he must insist on his own personality. For once really grown up, he will find that he has acquired self-respect and personality. Grownup-ness, I think, is not a mere question of age, but of being able to look back and understand and find satisfaction in one's experience, no matter how bitter it may have been.

So to all the handicapped and unappreciated, I would say,—Grow up as fast as you can. Cultivate the widest interests you can, and cherish all your friends. Cultivate some artistic talent, for you will find it the most durable of satisfactions, and perhaps one of the surest means of livelihood as well. Achievement is, of course, on the knees of the gods; but you will at least have the thrill of trial, and, after all, not to try is to fail. Taking your disabilities for granted, and assuming constantly that they are being taken for granted, make your social intercourse as broad and as constant as possible. Do not take the world too seriously, nor let too many social conventions oppress you. Keep sweet your sense of humor, and above all do not let any morbid feelings of inferiority creep into your soul. You will find yourself sensitive enough to the sympathy of others, and if you do not find people who like you and are willing to meet you more than halfway, it will be because you have let your disability narrow your vision and shrink up your soul. It will be really your own fault, and not that of your circumstances. In a word, keep looking outward; look out eagerly for those things that interest you, for people who will interest you and be friends with you, for new interests and opportunities to express yourself. You will find that your disability will come to have little meaning for you, that it will begin to fade quite completely out of your sight; you will wake up some fine morning and find yourself, after all the struggles that seemed so bitter to you, really and truly adjusted to the world.

Once More to the Lake

E. B. WHITE

(1899–   )

*Like Lardner, White was also a newspaperman, but with
the advent of* The New Yorker, *he was lured from an advertising job to the staff of that illustrious magazine. A year
later (1927) James Thurber came along; with White and
Harold Ross there was formed one of the great editor-
writer teams of this century. White is a master of style and
a perfectionist as one may see by reading the essays collected in* One Man's Meat (*based on his* Harper's *column,
1941*), The Second Tree from the Corner (*1953*), *and*
The Points of My Compass (*1962*).

One summer, along about 1904, my father rented a camp on a lake
in Maine and took us all there for the month of August. We all got
ringworm from some kittens and had to rub Pond's Extract on our
arms and legs night and morning, and my father rolled over in a
canoe with all his clothes on; but outside of that the vacation was a
success and from then on none of us ever thought there was any place
in the world like that lake in Maine. We returned summer after summer—always on August first for one month. I have since become a
salt-water man, but sometimes in summer there are days when the
restlessness of the tides and the fearful cold of the sea water and the
incessant wind which blows across the afternoon and into the evening make me wish for the placidity of a lake in the woods. A few
weeks ago this feeling got so strong I bought myself a couple of bass
hooks and a spinner and returned to the lake where we used to go, for
a week's fishing and to revisit old haunts.

I took along my son, who had never had any fresh water up his
nose and who had seen lily pads only from train windows. On the
journey over to the lake I began to wonder what it would be like. I
wondered how time would have marred this unique, this holy spot—
the coves and streams, the hills that the sun set behind, the camps
and the paths behind the camps. I was sure that the tarred road
would have found it out and I wondered in what other ways it would

be desolated. It is strange how much you can remember about places like that once you allow your mind to return into the grooves which lead back. You remember one thing, and that suddenly reminds you of another thing. I guess I remembered clearest of all the early morning, when the lake was cool and motionless, remembered how the bedroom smelled of the lumber it was made of and of the wet woods whose scent entered through the screen. The partitions in the camp were thin and did not extend clear to the top of the rooms, and as I was always the first up I would dress softly so as not to wake the others and sneak out into the sweet outdoors and start out in the canoe, keeping close along the shore in the long shadows of the pines. I remembered being very careful never to rub my paddle against the thwart for fear of disturbing the stillness of the cathedral.

The lake had never been what you would call a wild lake. There were cottages sprinkled around the shores, and it was in farming country although the shores of the lake were quite heavily wooded. Some of the cottages were owned by nearby farmers, and you would live at the shore and eat your meals at the farmhouse. That's what our family did. But although it wasn't wild, it was a fairly large and undisturbed lake and there were places in it which, to a child at least, seemed infinitely remote and primeval.

I was right about the tar: it led to within half a mile of the shore. But when I got back there, with my boy, and we settled into a camp near a farmhouse and into the kind of summertime I had known, I could tell that it was going to be pretty much the same as it had been before—I knew it, lying in bed the first morning, smelling the bedroom, and hearing the boy sneak quietly out and go off along the shore in a boat. I began to sustain the illusion that he was I, and therefore, by simple transposition, that I was my father. This sensation persisted, kept cropping up all the time we were there. It was not an entirely new feeling, but in this setting it grew much stronger. I seemed to be living a dual existence. I would be in the middle of some simple act, I would be picking up a bait box or laying down a table fork, or I would be saying something, and suddenly it would be not I but my father who was saying the words or making the gesture. It gave me a creepy sensation.

We went fishing the first morning. I felt the same damp moss covering the worms in the bait can, and saw the dragonfly alight on the tip of my rod as it hovered a few inches from the surface of the water. It was the arrival of this fly that convinced me beyond any doubt that everything was as it always had been, that the years were a mirage and there had been no years. The small waves were the same, chucking the rowboat under the chin as we fished at anchor, and the boat was the same boat, the same color green and the ribs broken in the same places, and under the floor-boards the same fresh-water leavings and debris—the dead hell-grammite, the wisps of moss, the rusty discarded fishhook, the dried blood from yesterday's catch. We stared silently at the tips of our rods, at the dragonflies that came and went. I lowered the tip of mine into the water, tentatively, pensively dislodging the fly, which darted two feet away, poised, darted two feet back, and came to rest again a little farther up the rod. There had been no years between the ducking of this dragonfly and the other one—the one that was part of memory. I looked at the boy, who was silently watching his fly, and it was my hands that held his rod, my eyes watching. I felt dizzy and didn't know which rod I was at the end of.

We caught two bass, hauling them in briskly as though they were mackerel, pulling them over the side of the boat in a businesslike manner without any landing net, and stunning them with a blow on the back of the head. When we got back for a swim before lunch, the lake was exactly where we had left it, the same number of inches from the dock, and there was only the merest suggestion of a breeze. This seemed an utterly enchanted sea, this lake you could leave to its own devices for a few hours and come back to, and find that it had not stirred, this constant and trustworthy body of water. In the shallows, the dark, watersoaked sticks and twigs, smooth and old, were undulating in clusters on the bottom against the clean ribbed sand, and the track of the mussel was plain. A school of minnows swam by, each minnow with its small individual shadow, doubling the attendance, so clear and sharp in the sunlight. Some of the other campers were in swimming, along the shore, one of them with a cake of soap, and the water felt thin and clear and unsubstantial. Over the years there had been this person with the cake of soap, this cultist, and here he was. There had been no years.

Up to the farmhouse to dinner through the teeming, dusty field, the road under our sneakers was only a two-track road. The middle track was missing, the one with the marks of the hooves and the splotches of dried, flaky manure. There had always been three tracks to choose from in choosing which track to walk in; now the choice was narrowed down to two. For a moment I missed terribly the middle alternative. But the way led past the tennis court, and something about the way it lay there in the sun reassured me; the tape has loosened along the backline, the alleys were green with plantains and other weeds, and the net (installed in June and removed in September) sagged in the dry noon, and the whole place steamed with midday heat and hunger and emptiness. There was a choice of pie for dessert, and one was blueberry and one was apple, and the waitresses were the same country girls, there having been no passage of time, only the illusion of it as in a dropped curtain—the waitresses were still fifteen; their hair had been washed, that was the only difference— they had been to the movies and seen the pretty girls with the clean hair.

Summertime, oh summertime, pattern of life indelible, the fade-proof lake, the woods unshatterable, the pasture with the sweetfern and the juniper forever and ever, summer without end; this was the background, and the life along the shore was the design, the cottages with their innocent and tranquil design, their tiny docks with the flag-pole and the American flag floating against the white clouds in the blue sky, the little paths over the roots of the trees leading from camp to camp and the paths leading back to the outhouses and the can of lime for sprinkling, and at the souvenir counters at the store the miniature birchbark canoes and the post cards that showed things looking a little better than they looked. This was the American family at play, escaping the city heat, wondering whether the newcomers in the camp at the head of the cover were "common" or "nice," wonder-ing whether the people who drove up for Sunday dinner at the farm-house were turned away because they were Jews or because there wasn't enough chicken.

It seemed to me, as I kept remembering all this, that those times and those summers had been infinitely precious and worth saving. There had been jollity and peace and goodness. The arriving (at the beginning of August) had been so big a business in itself, at the rail-way station the farm wagon drawn up, the first smell of the pine-laden air, the first glimpse of the smiling farmer, and the great im-portance of the trunks and your father's enormous authority in such matters, and the feel of the wagon under you for the long ten-mile haul, and at the top of the last long hill catching the first view of the lake after eleven months of not seeing this cherished body of water. The shouts and cries of the other campers when they saw you, and the trunks to be unpacked, to give up their rich burden. (Arriving was less exciting nowadays, when you sneaked up in your car and parked it under a tree near the camp and took out the bags and in five min-utes it was all over, no fuss, no loud wonderful fuss about trunks.)

Peace and goodness and jollity. The only thing that was wrong now, really, was the sound of the place, an unfamiliar nervous sound of the outboard motors. This was the note that jarred, the one thing that would sometimes break the illusion and set the years moving. In those other summertimes all motors were inboard; and when they were at a little distance, the noise they made was a sedative, an in-gredient of summer sleep. They were one-cylinder and two-cylinder engines, and some were make-and-break and some were jump-spark, but they all made a sleepy sound across the lake. The one-lungers throbbed and fluttered, and the twin-cylinder ones purred and purred, and that was a quiet sound too. But now the campers all had out-boards. In the daytime, in the hot mornings, these motors made a petulant, irritable sound; at night, in the still evening when the after-glow lit the water, they whined about one's ears like mosquitoes. My boy loved our rented outboard, and his great desire was to achieve singlehanded mastery over it, and authority, and he soon learned the trick of choking it a little (but not too much), and the adjustment of the needle valve. Watching him I would remember the things you could do with the old one-cylinder engine with the heavy flywheel, how you could have it eating out of your hand if you got really close to it spiritually. Motor boats in those days didn't have clutches, and you would make a landing by shutting off the motor at the proper time and coasting in with a dead rudder. But there was a way of reversing them, if you learned the trick, by cutting the switch and putting it on again exactly on the final dying revolution of the flywheel, so that it would kick back against compression and begin reversing. Approaching a dock in a strong following breeze it was difficult to slow up sufficiently by the ordinary coasting method, and if a boy felt he had complete mastery over his motor, he was tempted to keep it running beyond its time and then reverse it a few feet from the dock. It took a cool nerve, because if you threw the switch a twentieth of a second too soon you would catch the flywheel when it still had speed enough to go up past center, and the boat would leap ahead, charging bull-fashion at the dock.

We had a good week at the camp. The bass were biting well and the sun shone endlessly, day after day. We would be tired at night and lie down in the accumulated heat of the little bedrooms after the long hot day and the breeze would stir almost imperceptibly outside and the smell of the swamp drift in through the rusty screens. Sleep would come easily and in the morning the red squirrel would be on the roof, tapping out his gay routine. I kept remembering everything, lying in the bed in the mornings—the small steamboat that had a long rounded stern like the lip of a Ubangi, and how quietly she ran on the moonlight sails, when the older boys played their mandolins and the girls sang and we ate doughnuts dipped in sugar, and how sweet the music was on the water in the shining night, and what it had felt like to think about girls then. After breakfast we would go up to the store and the things were in the same place—the minnows in a bottle, the plugs and spinners disarranged and pawed over by the youngsters from the boys' camp, the fig newtons and the Beeman's gum. Outside, the road was tarred and cars stood in front of the store. Inside, all was just as it had always been, except there was more Coca-Cola and not so much Moxie and root beer and birch beer and sarsaparilla. We would walk out with a bottle of pop apiece and sometimes the pop would backfire up our noses and hurt. We explored the streams, quietly, where the turtles slid off the sunny logs and dug their way into the soft bottom; and we lay on the town wharf and fed worms to the tame bass. Everywhere we went I had trouble making out which was I, the one walking at my side, the one walking in my pants.

One afternoon while we were there at that lake a thunderstorm came up. It was like the revival of an old melodrama that I had seen

long ago with childish awe. The second-act climax of the drama of
the electrical disturbance over a lake in America had not changed in
any important respect. This was the big scene, still the big scene. The
whole thing was so familiar, the first feeling of oppression and heat
and a general air around camp of not wanting to go very far away. In
midafternoon (it was all the same) a curious darkening of the sky,
and a lull in everything that had made life tick; and then the way the
boats suddenly swung the other way at their moorings with the coming of a breeze out of the new quarter, and the premonitory rumble.
Then the kettle drum, then the snare, then the bass drum and cymbals, then crackling light against the dark, and the gods grinning and
licking their chops in the hills. Afterward the calm, the rain steadily
rustling in the calm lake, the return of light and hope and spirits, and
the campers running out in joy and relief to go swimming in the rain,
their bright cries perpetuating the deathless joke about how they were
getting simply drenched, and the children screaming with delight at
the new sensation of bathing in the rain, and the joke about getting
drenched linking the generations in a strong indestructible chain. And
the comedian who waded in carrying an umbrella.

When the others went swimming my son said he was going in too.
He pulled his dripping trunks from the line where they had hung all
through the shower, and wrung them out. Languidly, and with no
thought of going in, I watched him, his hard little body, skinny and
bare, saw him wince slightly as he pulled up around his vitals the
small, soggy, icy garment. As he buckled the swollen belt suddenly
my groin felt the chill of death.

How to Write
Short Stories

RING (RINGGOLD) LARDNER
(1885–1933)

*Ring Lardner was a lifelong newspaperman and sports-
writer. His 1920 collection of essays about the World Series
of that year (entitled "A World's Serious") is one of the
classics of that genre. He early acquired a reputation as
a humorist who wrote about baseball in slang, particularly
because of* You Know Me, Al *(1916) and "Alibi Ike." The
essay reproduced here first appeared as a preface to a volume of short stories of the same title. With the publication
of this volume Lardner also acquired fame as a writer of
short stories. His "Haircut" and "Champion" are among the
best American short tales.*

A glimpse at the advertising columns of our leading magazines
shows that whatever else this country may be shy of, there is certainly
no lack of correspondence schools that learns you the art of short-
story writing. The most notorious of these schools makes the boast
that one of their pupils cleaned up $5000.00 and no hundreds dollars
writing short stories according to the system learnt in their course,
though it don't say if that amount was cleaned up in one year or fifty.

However, for some reason another when you skin through the pages
of high class periodicals, you don't very often find them cluttered up
with stories that was written by boys or gals who had win their phi
beta skeleton keys at this or that story-writing college. In fact, the
most of the successful authors of the short fiction of to-day never
went to no kind of a college, or if they did, they studied piano tuning
or the barber trade. They could of got just as far in what I call the
literary game if they had of stayed home those four years and helped
mother carry out the empty bottles.

The answer is that you can't find no school in operation up to date,
whether it be a general institution of learning or a school that special-
izes in story writing, which can make a great author out of a born
druggist.

Reprinted by permission of Charles Scribner's Sons from *How to Write Short
Stories,* pages v–x, by Ring Lardner. Copyright 1924 Charles Scribner's Sons; re-
newal copyright 1952 Ellis A. Lardner.

But a little group of our deeper drinkers has suggested that maybe boys and gals who wants to take up writing as their life work would be benefited if some person like I was to give them a few hints in regards to the technic of the short story, how to go about planning it and writing it, when and where to plant the love interest and climax, and finally how to market the finished product without leaving no bad taste in the mouth.

Well, then, it seems to me like the best method to use in giving out these hints is to try and describe my own personal procedure from the time I get inspired till the time the manuscript is loaded on to the trucks.

The first thing I generally always do is try and get hold of a catchy title, like for instance, "Basil Hargrave's Vermifuge," Or "Fun at the Incinerating Plant." Then I set down to a desk or flat table of any kind and lay out 3 or 4 sheets of paper with as many different colored pencils and look at them cock-eyed a few moments before making a selection.

How to begin—or, as we professionals would say, "how to commence"—is the next question. It must be admitted that the method of approach (*"l'approchement"*) differs even among first class fictionists. For example, Blasco Ibáñez usually starts his stories with a Spanish word, Jack Dempsey with an "I" and Charley Peterson with a couple of simple declarative sentences about his leading character, such as "Hazel Gooftree had just gone mah jong. She felt faint."

Personally it has been my observation that the reading public prefers short dialogue to any other kind of writing and I always aim to open my tale with two or three lines of conversation between characters—or, as I call them, my puppets—who are to play important rôles. I have often found that something one of these characters says, words I have perhaps unconsciously put into his or her mouth, directs my plot into channels deeper than I had planned and changes, for the better, the entire sense of my story.

To illustrate this, let us pretend that I have laid out a plot as follows: Two girls, Dorothy Abbott and Edith Quaver, are spending the heated term at a famous resort. The Prince of Wales visits the resort, but leaves on the next train. A day or two later, a Mexican reaches the place and looks for accommodations, but is unable to find a room without a bath. The two girls meet him at the public filling station and ask him for a contribution to their autograph album. To their amazement, he utters a terrible oath, spits in their general direction and hurries out of town. It is not until years later that the two girls learn he is a notorious forger and realize how lucky they were after all.

Let us pretend that the above is the original plot. Then let us begin the writing with haphazard dialogue and see whither it leads:

"Where was you?" asked Edith Quaver.

"To the taxidermist's," replied Dorothy Abbott.

The two girls were spending the heated term at a famous watering trough. They had just been bathing and were now engaged in sorting dental floss.

"I am getting sick in tired of this place," went on Miss Quaver.

"It is mutual," said Miss Abbott, shying a cucumber at a passing paper-hanger.

There was a rap at their door and the maid's voice announced that company was awaiting them downstairs. The two girls went down and entered the music room. Garnett Whaledriver was at the piano and the girls tiptoed to the lounge.

The big Nordic, oblivious of their presence, allowed his fingers to form weird, fantastic minors before they strayed unconsciously into the first tones of Chopin's 121st Fugue for the Bass Drum.

From this beginning, a skilled writer could go most anywhere, but it would be my tendency to drop these three characters and take up the life of a mule in the Grand Canyon. The mule watches the trains come in from the east, he watches the trains come in from the west, and keeps wondering who is going to ride him. But he never finds out.

The love interest and climax would come when a man and a lady, both strangers, got to talking together on the train going back east.

"Well," said Mrs. Croot, for it was she, "what did you think of the Canyon?"

"Some cave," replied her escort.

"What a funny way to put it!" replied Mrs. Croot. "And now play me something."

Without a word, Warren took his place on the piano bench and at first allowed his fingers to form weird, fantastic chords on the black keys. Suddenly and with no seeming intention, he was in the midst of the second movement of Chopin's Twelfth Sonata for Flute and Cuspidor. Mrs. Croot felt faint.

That will give young writers an idea of how an apparently trivial thing such as a line of dialogue will upset an entire plot and lead an author far from the path he had pointed for himself. It will also serve as a model for beginners to follow in regards to style and technic. I will not insult my readers by going on with the story to its obvious conclusion. That simple task they can do for themselves, and it will be good practice.

So much for the planning and writing. Now for the marketing of the completed work. A good many young writers make the mistake of enclosing a stamped, self-addressed envelope, big enough for the manuscript to come back in. This is too much of a temptation to the editor.

Personally I have found it a good scheme to not even sign my name to the story, and when I have got it sealed up in its envelope and stamped and addressed, I take it to some town where I don't live and mail it from there. The editor has no idea who wrote the story, so how can he send it back? He is in a quandary.

In conclusion let me warn my pupils never to write their stories—or, as we professionals call them, "yarns"—on used paper. And never to write them on a post-card. And never to send them by telegraph (Morse code).

Index

ABC of Reading, The (Pound), 225
Abracadabra, 72
Absalom and Achitophel (Dryden),
  89
Absolute judgment, 198, 213
  use of specifications in, 213
Abstract, 36–45
  as aid to reading, 26–27
  of articles, 37
  of books, 36, 37–38
  example of, 37–38
  how to write, 38–39
  as introduction, 37
  one form of, 36–37
  organization of, 38
  as source of power, 38
Abstracter
  Reader's Digest as, 39
  secretary as, 41
Abstraction, levels of, 103–104,
    105–107, 109, 143, 227–228, 231,
    238–239, 242, 244, 246–248
  example of, 143
  in a sentence, 106–107
Abstract noun, 91
Abstract term (word), 143
Acceptable to unacceptable, pattern or
    structure, 269
Action through verbs, 126–130
Active voice, 137–139
Additions to noun, 226–227
Additions to verb, 226–227
Adjectives, 276
  faulty use of, 132
  in specifications, 202
Adventures of Huckleberry Finn
    (Twain), 10–11, 244
Adventures of Tom Sawyer, The
    (Twain), 170
Adverbs, use of in specifications, 202
"Advice to a Young Critic" (Nathan),
    149

Aeneid, The (Dryden's translation),
    21
Agamemnon, 244
Agenda, 40
Ali Baba and the Forty Thieves, 72
"Alibi Ike" (Lardner), 323
Allegory, 82
Alliteration, 87, 233
Ambiguity, 91, 143
American College Dictionary, The, 69
*American Heritage Dictionary of the
    English Language*, 69
American Language, The (Mencken),
    123
The American Mercury [Reader], 88,
    148, 149, 150, 151, 174, 229
American Scientist, 174
Analogous (contiguous) magic, 72
Analogy, 199
  as definition, 170
  examples of, 3, 252
  as means of explanation, 192
Analysis, as basis for operational
    definition, 174
  in developing patterns for writing,
    88, 254–255
  dynamic, 113–114
  and fact, 116
  and point of view, 209
  static, 110–113
  structural, 180
  in writing directions, 215
And, variety of meanings and
    functions of, 96–97
". . . And Sudden Death" (Furnas),
    156
Anecdote, in writing patterns, 146
*Annals of English Literature
    1475–1925*, 31
Annotated bibliography, 36–37, 38
Anthony Trant (Downing), 98
Anthropomorphism, 78, 252

Antithesis, 235–236
Antonym, definition by, 172
Aphorism, 89–90, 156
Apostrophe, 88
  as opener, 153
Apparatus, description of, 183
Appositive modifier, 226
  used in definition, 169–170
Argot, 92
Argumentative form of discourse. *See*
  Persuasion
Aristotle, 176
Arizona Republic, The, 23, 93, 118,
  120, 170, 241
"Arketall" (Nicolson), 227–228
Armed Services Technical Information
  System (ASTIA), 30
Army, U. S., approach to evaluation of
  audience, 17
Arrow of Love (Manfred), 27, 31
Art of Fiction, The (James), 19–20
Assertion, 114, 115
Assonance, 87
Assorted Prose (Updike), 73–74, 153
ASTIA, 30
Atlantic, 165
Auden, W. H., 254
Audience
  assumptions about, 137, 240
  decision about, 15
  for definitions, 167
  for directions, 215
  estimating, 15–18, 142, 144, 157
  and language, 192
  motivation of, 17–18, 19
  and style, 222
Author, 4, 10, 111
  patterns determined by role of,
  148–151
Authority, our reliance on, 147
Authors League of America, Inc., 37,
  151
Autobiography of Lincoln Steffens,
  223

Bacon, Francis, 187–188
Bakken, Aimee, 239–240
Baldwin, Hanson W., 244–245
Bartlett's Familiar Quotations, 84–85
Baugh, Albert C., 69
Beard, Charles A., 150
Beckham, Barry, 153
Beerbohm, Max, 250
Beginnings (introductions, openings),
  151–155, 193–194
Benét, William Rose, 38

Benny, Jack, 267
Better Homes and Gardens, 28
Bible, 56, 72, 88
Bibliographies, 31
  annotated, 36–37, 38
  form of notation, 48–49
Billings, Josh, 90
Bishop, Barry C., 153
Blasco Ibáñez, Vicente, 267, 318
Bloomfield, Leonard, 68, 111
Bodine, Eunice, 194, 283
Body of composition, 155
Book of Prefaces, A (Mencken), 71
Books, 27–28
  abstract of (example), 37–38
  indexes, 24
  reading, 23–24
  tables of contents, 24
Bourne, Randolph, 97, 144, 146,
  261–264, 265, 266, 287, 309–316
Bowen, Elizabeth, 19, 20
Braithwaite, R. B., 240–242
Brevity, 142–143
Bridge, The (Talese), 190–191
Brief, 36
British Museum, 30
Brogan, Dennis, 152
Brooks, Charles S., 252
Brougham, Henry Peter, Lord, 143
Brown, John Mason, 1
Brussel, Isidore R., 37
Bryan, William Jennings, 88–89, 115,
  229
Burke, Edmund, 143

Caesar and Cleopatra (Shaw), 30–31
*Cambridge Bibliography of English
  Literature*, 31
Canby, Henry Seidel, 75
Cant, 92
Carey, Henry, 87
Carroll, Lewis, 250
Catalog, 86
Catholic Press Directory, 29
Cause and effect patterns, 146
  in paragraph development, 255
Cecil, David, 195
Chain-of-command, 157, 159
"Champion" (Lardner), 323
Change and a Parting, A (Yambura
  and Bodine), 194, 283
Charts, 207
Chase, Stuart, 69
Chevrolet's *Friends*, 147
Chicago *Tribune*, 58
Chimney-Pot Papers (Brooks), 252

Chinese technique for definition, 224
Christensen, Francis, 226, 245
Christmas Garland, A (Beerbohm),
    250
Chronological patterns, 145
    in paragraph development, 264
Chrononhotonthologos (Carey), 87
Churchill, Winston, 256
Circumlocution, 91
    example of, 272
    as form of definition, 169
Clarke, Kenneth B., 93
Classical writing patterns, 144
Classification, 101–108
    deductive, 109
    and facts, 116
    and generalizations, 103
    as indexing, 103, 104
    inductive, 109
    and logical definition, 172–173
    by means of outline, 108–109
    as means of paragraph
        development, 255
    in polling, 35
    as process, 104
    and sentence, 227–229
    by synonyms, 102
    by words, 102
Clemens, Samuel Langhorne. *See*
    Twain, Mark
Cliché, 90
Closings (endings), 155–157
"Clowning of Danny Kaye, The"
    (Dworkin), 171
Coca-Cola Company, The, 72
Coleridge, Samuel Taylor, 108, 178
College English, 151
Collier's, 155
Commission on English, CEEB, 11
Committees, 163
Common terms (couplets), 58, 200
Comparative terms, in judgments,
    202
Comparison
    in "A Philosophy of Handicap,"
        264
    for emotional purposes, 201
    limited literary, 201
    as means of definition (example),
        173
    as means of semantic growth, 78
    report of, 204–208
    in reviews and criticisms, 43
Comparison and contrast, 198–201
    example of, 276

Comparison and contrast—*(Continued)*
    of known and unknown, 188
    in paragraph development, 251–252
Compositions
    body of, 155
    closings, 155–157
    introductions, 151–155
    patterns of, 144–148
    writing of, 144
Conceptual definitions, 174
*Concise Bibliography for Students of
    English, A,* 31
*Concise Dictionary of American
    History,* 31
Conciseness, 142–144
Concrete illustration, 148
Concrete terms (words), 143, 225
Condensed Novels (Harte), 250
Conley, Harold T., 92
Connotations, connotative qualities of
    words, 76–77, 95
Consonance, 87
Constitutive and contextual
    definitions, 174
Contagious magic, 72
Contrast, 198–201. *See also*
    Comparison *and* Comparison
    and Contrast
Conventional aspects of language, 55
Cooper, James Fenimore, 82–85
Copyright, 46
Corinthians, I, 88
Couplets, words with common terms,
    58, 98, 200
Court reporter, 40
Cousins, Norman, 251
Crane, Stephen, 232
Crist, Judith, 152
Criteria, 198
Criticism, 43
"Crusade for Air Power"
    (DeSeversky), 151

Dana, Richard Henry, Jr. See *Two
    Years Years Before the Mast*
Darwin, Charles, 22, 291
Data and language, 110–111
David Cooperfield (abstract), 37–38,
    51
Davis, Elmer, 148–149, 174
Dead Sea Scrolls, 85
"Death of All Children, The"
    (Sternglas), 155
Death of a Moth, The (Woolf), 271
"Death of King John, The" (*Collier's*),
    155

Deductive classification, 109
Deductive outline, 109
Deerslayer, The (Cooper), 82–85
Definition, 167–177
  by analogy, 170
  by antonym, 172
  by appositive, 169–170
  in article, 149–150
  by circumlocution, 169
  by comparison, 173–174
  by etymology, 171
  European vs. Chinese, 225
  evaluation of audience for, 167
  extended, 175–176, 193
  logical, 104, 170, 172–173, 193, 238
  negative, 170–171, 176
  operational, 174–175, 193, 238
  as parenthetical part of subject, 190
  partial, 169–171, 173
  by pointing, 170
  of problem, 162, 163
  by specific instance, 170
  by synonym, 171–172, 238
Definitive edition, 31
Degree, 202
Dell, Floyd, 309
Dempsey, Jack, 267, 324
Denotations, denotative language,
  94–97, 101
Description, 177–178
  of apparatus, 183
  contrasted with definition, 177
  contrasted with directions, 214–215
  of department, 184–185
  detail in, 192
  as judgment, 210
  of layout, 184
  of motion, 186–191
  of one-piece object, 185
  patterns of, 180–182
  of simple mechanism, 182
  tone in, 192
Descriptive approach to language, 68
Descriptive dictionaries, 123
DeSeversky, Alexander, 151
Detail in description, 192, 228
Detail in developing paragraphs, 254
Details, use of, 228
Deutsch, Babette, 151
Devil, meaning of, 25
"Devil" terms, 76, 97. *See also*
  Ultimate terms
DeVoe, Alan, 149
DeVries, Julian, 241
Dewey, John, 162, 163
Dewey Decimal System, 27

Dialogue, as introductory strategy,
  153
Dialect, 90
Diaries, 40
Dickens, Charles, 37–38, 98
Dickinson, Emily, 15
Dictionaries, 31, 68, 123–124, 168,
  171–172
  characteristics of, 68
  descriptive, 123
  list of, 64
  methods for word selection, 124
  prescriptive, 123
  and reading, 25
  of synonyms (thesaurus), 102
  use of, 231–232
  *Webster's New International
    Dictionary of the English
    Language, Unabridged,* Second
    Edition, 67, 87, 123
  *Webster's Third New International
    Dictionary, Unabridged,* 123
Dictionary of American Slang, 73
*Dictionary of English-American
  Usage,* 69
Digest. *See* Abstract
Directions (instructions), 198, 214
  analysis necessary for, 215
  audience for, 215
  contrasted with description,
    214–215
  example of, 148–149
  imperative mood used in, 214
  preparation for writing, 216
  purpose of, 214
  voice of, 135, 140, 214
  writing, 216–218
Directory of American Scholars, 31
*Directory of Newspapers and
  Periodicals,* 28
Directories, 28, 31
"Disclaimer," as strategic device, 146
  Example of, 221
Dodd, William E., 148
Donne, John, 9
Double entendre (double entente),
  86
Downing, J. Hyatt, 98
Down to Earth (DeVoe), 149
Dryden, John, 21, 89
Dworkin, Martin, 171
Dyer's Hand, The (Auden), 254
Dynamic analysis, 113–114

Eastman Kodak Company, 235
Editorial "we," 13–14, 153

Einstein, Albert, 115, 142, 147, 259–261, 265, 272
Elegant variation, 91–92, 112
Elimination pattern, 146–147
Emerson, Ralph Waldo, 15
Eminent Victorians (Strachey), 194–195
Emotional characteristics of words, 95
Encyclopaedia Britannica, 31, 49, 242
Encyclopedias, 31
Endings (closings), 155–157, 194–195
English Prose Style (Read), 166
Erskine, John, 226, 242, 243
Esquire, 22, 23, 28, 50, 61, 151, 152, 153, 154, 155, 165, 179, 237, 242, 270–271
  analysis of *Newsweek*, 237
Essays on Language and Usage (Dean and Wilson), 122
Establishing fact, 116–118
Ethics of Rhetoric, The (Weaver), 76
Etymological definition, 17
  examples: bibliography, 31; synonym, 102; teleology, 171
Euphemism, 64–65, 72
European definition contrasted with Chinese, 225
Evaluations, 43
  examples of, 43–44, 150–151, 245–246
  in reviews and criticisms, 43
Evans, Bergen and Cornelia, 69
Excellence (Gardner), 248
"Exclusive and unauthorized . . ." (*Esquire*), 154
Exemplification in paragraph, 240, 253
Experience, 8, 278, 285
Experiment as source of information, 22
Explanation, 180–182
  by analogy, 192
  scientific, 240
  by simile, 78, 192
Explicit information, 23
Extended definition, 175–177, 193
  Aristotle's *Poetics* as example, 176
External fact, 117

Fabulous Toby and Me, The (Shaffner and Johnson), 193
Fact, 116–118
  analysis and, 116
  classification and, 116

Fact—(*Continued*)
  external, 117
  hypothetical (analogous), 117–118
  internal, 117
  literary or poetic, 118
  ways of establishing, 116–118
Fales, E.D., Jr., 152
Fallacy, sentimental, 232
Faraday, Michael, 183
Felsen, Henry G., 274–276
Fiction and life, 5–8
Figurative language, 77–81
  in description, 185
Fitzgerald, F. Scott, 4, 80–81, 127, 170–171, 228
Fitzimmons, Thomas, 44
Flashback, 146
Flexner, Stuart Bergl, 73
Folger Shakespeare Library, 31
Following the Equator (Twain), 20
Footnoting, 47–50
Ford Times, 29
Formal Logic (Schiller), 174
Formal report, 163–165
Forms of reports, 164
Fortune, 22
Francis, W. Nelson, 255
Frazier, Sir James, 73
Friend, The (Coleridge), 178
Friends (Chevrolet), 147
Fulbright, J. W., 270–271
Fulcrum sentence, 262–263
Functions of sentence, 224–225
Furnas, J. C., 156

"Gaining Respect on Woodward Avenue" (Jedlicka), 151
Gardner, John W., 248
Garland, Hamlin, 98, 118, 138
Gebbie Press House Magazine Directory, 28
Generalities, levels of in sentences, 107. *See also* Abstraction
Genesis, 73
Ghost writers, 210
Gibson, Walker, 11
Gilbert, William S., 87
Gingrich, Arnold, 50, 51
"God" terms 76, 97
Golden Bough, The (Frazier), 73
Goldwyn, Samuel, 98
Good Housekeeping, 152
"Good Night, Lady" (Kennedy), 157
Gorrell, Robert M., 151
Grady, Daniel M., 8
Grammar, 58, 118–121

Grammatical patterns, 2
Grange, Harold "Red," 32
Granger's Index to Poetry, 31
Grant, Martin, 28
Great Gatsby, The (Fitzgerald), 4, 81, 229
Green Bay Packers, 32
Grimm's Law, 67
Growth and Structure of the English Language (Jespersen), 68
Guide to Reference Material, 31
Guide to Reference Works, 31
Gutenberg Galaxy, The (McLuhan), 69

Hadrian the Seventh (Rolfe), 87
"Haircut" (Lardner), 323
Hall, Robert A., Jr., 255–256
"Halo" effect, 76
Hamlet, 5, 6, 9
Harper's, 165
Harper's Dictionary of Classical Antiquities, 36
Harte, Bret, 250
Hayakawa, S. I., 69
"Heart—Wondrous and Courageous Organ" (Robinson), 154
Hecht, Ben, 148, 150
Henry IV, Part I, 178
Henry, Joseph, 199
Henry, O., 221
Hewes, Henry, 250
Hills Beyond, The (Wolfe), 150, 282
Historian, 148
Homonymic quality of language, 85
"Hook" (introductory device), 153
Hopkins, Gerard Manley, 15
"Horatio" (Felsen), 275–276
Hot Rod (Felsen), 274
Houghton Library, 30
Howells, William Dean, 98
"How It Looks from the Colonies" (Brogan), 152
"How Should One Read a Book?" (Woolf), 229, 230, 282
"How to Write Short Stories" (Lardner), 83, 144, 323–326
"How We Climbed Mount Everest" (Bishop), 153
Hughes, Langston, 177
Hull, Helen, 37
Humor
  contrasted with wit, 252
  as opener, 152
Huntington Library, 30
Huxley, Aldous, 69, 151

Huxley, Thomas Henry, 106–107, 138, 146, 269, 272, 287, 291–308
Hyperbole, 84
Hypothesis, 114, 115–116
Hypothetical (analogous) fact, 117–118

Identity of the writer, 2, 4–8, 10–11, 12
Iliad, The (Homer), 59, 86
"Imagination—and a Few Mothers" (Fitzgerald), 171
Immaturity (Shaw), 7
Imperative mood (command voice), 12, 214
Implicit information, 23–24
"Impossible Rescue, The" (Fales), 152
Index, 24
Indexing, 50–51
  and classification, 103, 104
Indo-European family of languages, 56
Inductive classification, 109
Inductive outline, 109
Inductive paragraph, 223
Infinitive, split (Thurber), 256–257
Information, 22–52
  from experimentation, 22
  explicit, 23
  forms of, 23
  implicit, 23–24
  locating sources of, 22–23, 27
  from observation, 22, 32–33
  from polling, 23, 34–35
  from reading, 23–27
  from research and retrieval, 23
  from sampling, 22, 34–35
Informative paragraph, 238
"Initiation rite," 280
In media res, 146, 194, 244
Inquiry into the Policy of European Powers (Lord Brougham), 143
Instructions. *See* Directions
Internal fact, 117
Interviewing, 22, 34–35, 147
Introductory Readings on Language (Anderson and Stageberg), 123
Introductory strategies, 151–155, 193–194
Invective (name-calling), 73–74, 84
Inverted pyramid pattern of reporting, 147
Iowa place names, 98
Irony, 82–83, 244, 245, 265
  as a closing device, 157, 195

Jacobs, Hayes B., 166
Jacobs, Joe, 98
James, Henry, 19–20, 98, 156, 267
Jargon, 90–91, 143
Jedlicka, Daniel A., 151
Jespersen, Otto, 68
Jesus, 55
"Joe Namath as World Metaphor"
    (*Esquire*), 153
Johnson, Kenneth, 122
Johnson, Vance, 193
Jolson, Al, 98
Journal, 15
Joyce, James, 19
Judgments, 202–203
    absolute, 198, 213
    in comparative form, 210
    in descriptive form, 210
    hypothetical (deductive), 208
    patterns of, 210–212
    relative, 198, 202–204
    in specifications, 210
    in syllogisms (inductive), 208
"Juniper Corners" (*Herald Tribune*),
    254

"kaPOOMcha: The Mimeograph
    Revolution" (Kunen), 154
Kaul, Donald, 233
Kaye, Danny, 171
Keats, John, 22, 102, 127, 148
Kennedy, John B., 157
King Kong, 179
Kingsley, Charles, 4
Known to unknown, structural
    pattern, 188, 199, 269
Koch, Robert, 185
Kodak Flexichrome Process, 189–190
Kottler, Barnet, 69, 122
"Kubla Khan" (Coleridge), 108
Kunen, James Simon, 154

Ladies' Home Journal, The, 170–171
LaGuardia, Fiorella, 98
Laird, Charlton, 68, 135
Language
    and audience, 192
    basis for social distinctions, 18, 93
    borrowings, 58
    characteristics of oral, 58–59
    connotative, 76–77, 95
    as convention, 55
    denotative, 94–97, 101
    descriptive approach to, 68
    as an extension of man, 53
    forms of, 54–55

Language—(*Continued*)
    history of, 58
    homonymic qualities of, 85
    inadequacy of, 178–179
    Indo-European family of, 56
    kinds of, 55
    Latinate qualities of, 62
    levels of usage, 2, 68, 72–73,
        120–122
    metaphorical, 66
    oral vs. written traditions, 58–61
    organization of, 221–257
    origins of, 55
    prescriptive approach to, 68, 222
    of proposals, 161
    readings on, 68–69
    secret, 73
    semantic growth of, 66–67
    slang, 93
    as social marker, 64–65
    sources of, 61–64
    standards, 93–94, 98
    static, 132–134
    structure, 261
    symbolic aspects of, 54–55
    usage, 18, 68, 93–94
    used on data, 110–111
    "Wardour Street English," 62
Language (Bloomfield), 68
Language in Thought and Action
    (Hayakawa), 69
Language, Thought and Reality
    (Whorf), 69, 111
Lardner, Ring, Jr., 80, 83, 85, 144,
    266–268, 272, 287, 317, 323–326
Latinisms, 62–63
Layout, 184
Leave Your Language Alone! (Hall),
    256
Legal prose, 25
Lehman, Rosamond, 6
Leitmotif, 81
Letters of F. Scott Fitzgerald, The
    (ed. Turnbull), 127
Levels of generality in sentences,
    105–107. *See also* Abstraction
Levels of language usage, 2, 68,
    72–73, 120–122
Levin, Martin, 250
Lewis, C. S., 272
Libraries, 23, 27–28, 30–32
Library card catalog, 31, 36–37
Library of Congress, 27, 30
Life, 22, 25–26, 28, 45, 64, 86, 165,
    179

Life on the Mississippi (Twain), 6,
    128, 129, 130, 131, 134, 135, 138,
    193, 201, 244, 270, 276–278,
    280–281
Light, Martin, 69, 122
Limited literary comparisons, 201
Lippmann, Walter, 285
"Listen to the Black Graduate. . ."
    (Beckham), 153
Literary or poetic fact, 118
"Little Annie Fannie," 250
Lockyer, Sir Norman, 240, 241
Logical definition, 104, 172–173
    example of, 66. *See also* Metaphor
Logical patterns, 180
Lord, Walter, 243–244
Los Angeles Times, The, 86
Lowes, John Livingston, 108

Mad, 250
Madame Bovary (Flaubert), 169
Magazines, 24, 28–29
Magazines in the Twentieth Century
    (Peterson), 47, 48, 187
Magic, 72–73
Malapropism, 232
Manfred, Frederick, 27, 31
Marsh, Robert C., 154
Marx Brothers, 267
Masses, The, 309
Masterplots, 27, 37
Mathison, Richard, 248
Max (Cecil), 195
Maxwell, James Clerk, 199
McCall's, 28
McLuhan, Marshall, 60–61, 69
Meaning, nuances of, 102, 170,
    171–172
Mechanical Bride, The (McLuhan),
    69
Mechanism, description of simple,
    182
Melville, Herman, 24, 175
Memory. *See* Mnemonic devices
Mencken, H. L., 71, 88, 89, 115, 123,
    229
Metaphor, 66
    private and public, 272
    and structure, 270–272
Method, scientific, 200
"Method of Scientific Investigation,
    The" (Huxley), 269
Michener, James, 169
Milton, John, 199–200
Mimicry, 85
Minnelli, Liza, 246

Minto, John, 31
Minutes of meetings, 40–43
Mnemonic (memory) devices, 59
Moby Dick (Melville), 24, 175, 244
MLA (Modern Language Association)
    Style Sheet, 47
"Modern Minuteman" (Mathison),
    248
Modifiers, 106–107, 226–227
    appositive position of, 227
    bound, fixed, or free, 107, 226–227,
    230
    prepositional, 227
    verbal, 132
Moral, 156
Morris, William, 62
"Mortician, The" (Davis), 148–149,
    174
Motif. *See* Leitmotif
Motion, 186–191
Motivation of audience, 17–18, 19,
    141–142
Moynihan, Daniel Patrick, 25–26
Museums, 30

Namath, Joe, 153, 179, 180
Name-calling (invective), 73–74, 84
Naming, 73, 98–99
Narration, 193–195
Narrator, 4–5, 10–11, 148
Nathan, George Jean, 149
National Geographic, 51, 153
Negative definition, 170–171, 176
Newberry Library, 30
"New Boys for the FCC" (Shayon),
    154
Newspapers, 24–25, 28
Newsweek, 165, 236, 237, 241
New Yorker, The, 45, 256–257, 321
New York Herald Tribune, 254
New York Times, The, 28, 285
Nicolson, Harold, 227–229
Night to Remember, A (Lord),
    243–244
Nine Men (Rodell), 253
Nixon, Richard M., 24–26, 270
Non sequitur, 267
Nouns
    abstract, 91
    additions to, 226–227
    formed from verbs, 132–134
"Note on the Writer's Craft, A"
    (Erskine), 226
Nuances of meaning, 102, 199
Nye, Russel, 309

Observation
  in collecting information, 22, 32–33
  example of report of, 22
Odyssey, The (Homer), 59, 244
Old English, 56–57
Olympia Brewing Company, 86
"On a Piece of Chalk" (Huxley),
  106–107, 269, 291–308
On Conciliation With America
  (Burke), 143
"Once More to the Lake" (White), 81
  229, 264–265, 317–322
One Man's Meat (White), 264, 317
One-piece object, description of, 185
On the Art of Writing
  (Quiller-Couch), 91, 143
"Open Boat, The" (Crane), 232
Openers (beginnings and
  introductions), 151–155,
  193–194
Operational definition, 174–175, 238
Opinion, 24–25, 114–115
Oppenheimer, Robert S., 118
Oral vs. written traditions of
  language, 58–61
Organic writing patterns, 144
Organization of language, 221–257
Origins of language, 55
Orthography (spelling), 57, 60
Outlines, 108–110
  deductive, 109
  example of, 108–109
  inductive, 109
  sentence form, 109
  as a system of classification, 109
  tables of contents as, 24
  use of verbs in, 131–132
  used by professional writers, 109,
    287
Outlines of Shakespeare's Plays, 36
Out of My Later Years (Einstein),
  115, 259–261
Owl in the Attic, The (Thurber),
  256–257
"Ozawa in Transit" (Marsh), 154

Pace, 6
Panther and the Lash, The (Hughes),
  177
Paradox, 83, 88, 156, 244, 245
Paragraphs, 230–257, 259
  analytical, 254–255
  as building blocks in larger
    structures, 259, 261–270
  by cause and effect, 255
  by classification, 255

Paragraphs—(*Continued*)
  by comparison and contrast,
    251–252
  as convenience for reader, 256
  by exemplification, 253
  functions of, 256
  inductive, 223
  informative, 238
  parallelism in, 236
  by particulars and details, 254
  patterns of, 255, 264
  by reasons why, 255
  as signals of units of thought, 256
  stages in, 269
  as strategic device, 256
  as summary and announcement of
    new stage, 269
  syllogistic, 224
Parallelism, 131, 236. *See also*
  Abstraction, Generalities, *and*
  Repetition
Paraphrase, 25–26, 46
Parenthetical expression, 237
Parody, 229, 232, 245, 248–249, 250,
  267, 270
  of *King Kong,* 179
Paronomasia (punning), 85
Partial definition, 169–170
Particulars and details in developing
  paragraphs, 254
Passive voice, 42, 91, 137–139
Pasteur, Louis, 136, 139
Patience (Gilbert), 87
Patterns, 146, 180–182
  acceptable to unacceptable, 269
  through analysis, 254–255
  anecdotal, 146, 147
  basic, 187–189
  cause and effect, 146, 255
  chronological, 145, 264
  classical, 144
  of description, 180–182
  determined by role of author,
    148–151
  for directions, 216–218
  elimination, 146–147
  for getting and holding attention,
    144–148
  grammatical, 2
  inverted pyramid, 147
  interview, 22, 147
  of judgment, 198–199, 210–212
  known to unknown, 269
  logical, 180
  of motion, 187–193
  organic, 144

Patterns—(*Continued*)
  of persuasive writing, 144–148, 291
  sequential, 250
  spatial, 145, 180
  temporal, 180
  verbal, 5, 9, 134–136
Patterson, Helen M., 166
People in Quandaries (Johnson), 69
Periodical Directory, Ulrich's, 29
Periodical Literature, Poole Index to, 29
Periodical Literature, Reader's Guide to, 29
Periodic syllogistic sentence, 237
Persona, 11, 272
Personification, 78, 82, 271
"Perspective" (Plumb), 152
Persuasion, 233–234, 235, 269
Peterson, Theodore, 47, 48, 187
"Philosophy of Handicap, A"
    (Bourne), 144, 146, 261–264,
    309–316
Phoenix Nest, The, 248, 249, 250
Plagiarism, 46
Playboy, 165, 250
Plumb, J. H., 152
Poetic or literary fact, 118
Poetics (Aristotle), 176
Point (purpose), 2, 222
Point of view, 13–14, 153–154, 224.
    See also Viewpoint
  and analysis, 209
  opposite, 24
Points of My Compass, The (White),
    317
Polling, 23, 34–36
Poole Index to Periodical Literature,
    29
Pope, Alexander, 66, 71
Porter, J. R., 28
Porter, Jane, 99
Pound, Ezra, 225
Précis, 36, 51, 264
Prescriptive approach to language,
    68, 222
Prescriptive dictionaries, 123
Presentational (referential) words,
    74, 95–97
Price, Richard, 7
Princess, The (Tennyson), 87
Printing press, 56, 57, 60–61
Problem, definition of, 162, 163
Problem-solving, 162, 163
Process, Coleridgean concept of, 178
Progressive, The, 171

Projections, author's or narrator's,
    4–8, 10–11, 114, 115
Pronoun, personal, 13–14
Proposals, 159–161, 212
  example of use of, 159
  language of, 161
  specifications for, 160–161
  style of, 161
Prose
  legal, 25
  purple, 232, 233
  scientific, 238–239
Puddin'head Wilson's New Calendar
    (Twain), 20
Puns (paronomasia), 59, 85
Purpose, 2, 72
"Purr" words 97. *See also* Ultimate
    terms

Quarterly Journal of Speech, 255
Quick, Herbert, 99
Quiller-Couch, Sir Arthur, 91–92, 143
Quoting, quotations (standards for),
    42, 46–47

Rapoport, Anatol, 174
Read, Herbert, 166
Reader, 141–142
Reader's Digest, 39, 152, 154, 156,
    165, 201, 248
  as abstracter, 39
Reader's Encyclopedia, The, 37–38,
    264
*Reader's Guide to Periodical
    Literature,* 29
Reading, 23–26
  abstracts as aid to, 26
Reasons, in developing paragraphs,
    255
Reference Books (Minto), 31
Referent, 55
Referential (presentational) words,
    74, 95–97
Rehabilitations and Other Essays
    (Lewis), 272
Relational words, 96–97
Relationships, 178
Relative judgments, 198
"Remember Us" (Hecht), 148, 150
Repetitive writing, 91, 236
Reports, 157–159
  of comparison, 204–208
  formal, 163–165
  forms of, 164
Research (information retrieval), 23,
    40

Reston, James, 285
Reviews, 24, 43
  contrasted with criticism, 43
  example of, 245–246
  organization of, 44
  standards for, 43–45
"Revolution in Grammar" (Francis),
    255
Rhetorical questions, 88–89
  examples of, 152, 223, 240, 251
Rhetorical strategies, 2
Rice, Grantland, 32
"R. M. S. *Titanic*" (Baldwin),
    244–245
Robinson, Henry Morton, 154
Robinson, Mabel Louise, 37
Rockne, Knute, 32
Rodell, Fred, 253
Role, 11
Rolfe, Frederick, 87
Romantic view of writer, 22
Romeo and Juliet (Shakespeare), 74,
    85, 152
Ross, Harold, 317
Ruskin, John, 177, 232

Sampling, 22–23, 34–35
Samson Agonistes (Milton), 199–200
Satire, 89, 248–249
Saturday Review (*Saturday Review of
    Literature*), 26, 28, 39, 44, 45,
    51, 79, 91, 152, 224, 248, 249,
    250, 251
Schiller, F. C. S., 174
Scientific explanation, 240
Scientific Explanation (Braithwaite),
    241
Scientific method, 200
Scottish Chiefs (Porter), 99
Second Common Reader, The
    (Woolf), 89–90
Second Tree from the Corner, The
    (White), 75, 317
Secret language, 73
Seeing (understanding), 177–178,
    179
Semantic growth, 67, 78, 199
Sentences, 224–230
  basic form in English, 234
  as building blocks in paragraphs,
    261–270
  complete, in outline, 131–132
  F. Scott Fitzgerald on, 127
  fulcrum, 262–263
  functions of, 224
  levels of generality in, 105–107

Sentences—(*Continued*)
  syllogistic, 237
  topic, in development of
    paragraphs and larger structures,
    256, 262–263
  "undecidable," 88
Sentimental fallacy, 232
Sevareid, Eric, 208
Seventeen, 275
"Sex and Violence in Movies and
    TV. . ." (Crist), 152
Shaffner, Neil E., 193
Shakespeare, William, 5, 6, 8, 9, 15,
    22, 31, 36, 74, 85, 152, 178, 222,
    270
Shaw, George Bernard, 7, 30–31
Shayon, Robert Louis, 154
"She Didn't Mean to Do It"
    (Woollcott), 156
Sheed, Wilfred, 152
Sheridan, Richard Brinsley, 232
Simile, similitude, similarity, 78,
    199, 252
  as a means of comparison, 192
Slang, 90, 93, 149
"Slur" words, 97. *See also* Ultimate
    terms
Small group operations (committees),
    163
Smith, Bradford, 249
"Snarl" words, 97. *See also* Ultimate
    terms
Social distinctions based on language
    usage, 18, 64–65, 97–98
Socrates, 55
Solving problems, 162–163
Sors, sortes, 123
Sources of information
  acknowledging, 46
  locating, 22, 23, 27
"Sour Grapes Statement, The"
    (*Esquire*), 153
Southey, James W., 166
Spatial patterns, 145, 180
Specifications (standards), 202, 203
    207
  in absolute judgments, 212–213
  example of, 25
  intellectual basis for, 212–213
  as judgments, 210
  legal bases of, 211
Specific instance, definition by, 170
Spelling, 57, 60
Spence, Hartzell, 194, 284–285
Split infinitive, 257
Spock, Benjamin, 64, 147

Sports Illustrated, 32, 39
Stages in analysis, 188
Standards. *See* Specifications
Standards of language, 98
State Historical Society of Iowa, 51
Statement, 114
Static analysis, 110–113
Static language, 132–134, 276
Statistics, use of, 24–25
Steffens, Lincoln, 223
Sterile Cuckoo, The, 244–245
Sternglas, Ernest J., 155
Stevenson, Robert Louis, 4
Stong, Phil, 99
Strachey, Lytton, 194–195
Strategy
    in paragraph, 256, 267
    rhetorical, 2, 154, 276, 291
"Straw man," 146
Structural analysis, 180
Structure, 144, 259–272
    through metaphor, 270–272
    through subject, 259–270
"Structure in Thought" (Gorrell),
    151
Style, 2, 50, 222, 223, 239–240, 249,
    265
Subject, 21, 106–107, 223
Suckow, Ruth, 78
Summary, 36, 51, 148, 155, 280
    as beginning, 194
    paragraph as, 261
Summers, Richard, 170
Superlative terms, in judgments, 202
Superstition, 72
Sutherland, Mason, 51
Syllogisms, 164, 236
    as judgment, 208, 210
    in paragraphs, 224
    style, 222–223, 224
    in sentences, 237
Symbol, language as, 54–55
Symbols, 54, 79–80
    private, 80
    public, 80
Synonyms, 199
    as classifiers, 102
    as form of definition, 171–172
    dictionary of (thesaurus), 102
Synopsis, 36
Syntactical devices, 2

Table of contents, 24
Tables, 207
Taboo words, 72–73
Talese, Gay, 190–191

Technical Report Writing (Southey),
    166
Temporal patterns, 180
Tennyson, Alfred, Lord, 87
Tetragrammaton, 73
"Theatre" (Sheed), 152
Thematic usage, 81
Theme, development of, 260–262, 265
Thesaurus, 102
Thesis. *See* Theme
Thinking About Language (Laird),
    68
Thompson, Sir Benjamin, 185–186
Thoreau, Henry David, 5–6, 8
Thurber, James, 85, 256–257, 317
Time, 28, 45, 76–77, 165, 201,
    237–238, 241, 242, 245–247
    style analyzed, 237–238
Titles as abstracts, 36
"Tom Paine" (Dodd), 148
Tone, 11, 238, 263
    in description, 192
Topic sentence, 38, 223, 256, 262–263
*Toward a New Rhetoric—Six Essays
    for Teachers* (Christensen), 226
Tragedy in real life, 5, 9
Transitional devices, 260, 261, 263,
    291
Transitional words, 97
Treasure Island (Stevenson), 4
Truman, Harry S, 142
Twain, Mark, 6, 10–11, 20, 51, 82–85,
    128, 129, 130, 131, 134, 135, 138,
    170, 193, 230–232, 276–278, 280–
    281
Two Years Before the Mast (Dana),
    5–6, 7–8, 23, 30, 48, 188, 204,
    205, 207, 209, 244, 270, 278–280,
    283–284
Tyranny of Words, The (Chase), 69

Ulrich's Periodical Directory, 29
Ultimate terms, 76
"Undecidable" sentence, 88
Understanding and "seeing,"
    177–178, 179
Understatement, 84
*Union List of Serials in the U. S. and
    Canada,* 28, 29
University of Notre Dame, 32
Unknown from known, 199
Updike, John, 73–74, 96, 153
Up From Slavery (Washington), 193
"Up the Coulee" (Garland), 118
Usage, 120–123
    levels of, 2, 68, 72–73, 120–122

Usage—(*Continued*)
  with reference to audience, 18
  and social distinction, 93–94

Valentino, Rudolph, 267
Value judgments, 177
Vend, 29
Verbs, 127–137
  additions to, 226–227
  become nouns, 132–134
  as carriers of action, 128–129
  describing action, 134–136
  in other forms, 130
  in outlines, 131–132
  uses of, 131
  in writing, 127
Verner's Law, 67
Vico, Giovanni Battista, 264
Viewpoint in writing, 276, 283
Vocabulary, 2
Vogue, 233
Voice, 1–19, 88, 91, 223, 231, 238,
    240, 243, 248, 253–254, 267
  active, 135, 137–139, 140
  passive, 42, 91, 137–139, 140
Von Helmholtz, Herman, 201

Walden (Thoreau), 5–6
Walford, Arthur J., 31
Wallace, Alfred, 254
"Wardour Street English," 62
Ward Ritchie Press, 48
Warga, Wayne, 86
Washington, Booker T., 193
Washington Post Service, 65
Weaver, Richard, 76
Webster's New Collegiate Dictionary,
    69, 171
*Webster's New International
    Dictionary of the English
    Language, Unabridged*, Second
    Edition, 67, 86, 87, 123
*Webster's New World Dictionary of
    the American Language*, 67, 69
*Webster's Third New International
    Dictionary, Unabridged*, 123
"What Is a Statesman?" (Beard),
    150
What-when-where-who-why-and-how
    of sentences, 234
White, E. B., 75, 81, 229, 264–265,
    266, 269, 272, 287, 317–322
Whitman, Walt, 150
Whorf, Benjamin Lee, 69, 77, 111
Who's Who in America, 31, 34

Williamson, Samuel T., 79, 91
Winchell, Constance M., 31
"Winter is icumen in" (Smith), 249
Wit, 252
Wolfe, Thomas, 77, 150, 282
Woolf, Virginia, 89–90, 229, 230, 271,
    282
Woollcott, A., 156
Word-mongers, 75
Words, 271
  belief in power of, 72–73, 75
  borrowings, 62–63
  as building blocks, 261–270
  as classifiers, 101–102
  coinages, 63
  concrete, 143
  connotative, 76–77, 95
  couplets based on common terms,
    58, 98
  denotative, 94–97, 101
  emotional characteristics of, 95,
    124
  kinds of, 61–62
  levels of acceptance of, 93
  logical characteristics of, 95, 124
  not the thing, 55, 65
  pair concept, 62
  presentational (referential), 74,
    95–97
  "purr," 97. *See also* Ultimate terms
  referential (presentational), 74,
    95–97
  relational, 95–97
  sensory characteristics of, 95, 124
  shifts in functions, 61–62
  "slur" and "snarl," 97. *See also*
    Ultimate terms
  as social unequals, 64
  sources, 62–64
  taboo, 72–73
  take on additional meaning
    (semantic growth), 66–67
  transitional, 97
  "treacherous weapons," 25
Words and Their Meaning (Huxley),
    69
Wordsworth, William, 6
World of Words, The (Kottler and
    Light), 69, 122
Writer, 1–2
  advice to, 323–326
  projections of, 4–8, 10–11, 114, 115
  and how he works, 222–224, 225,
    240
  identity of, 4–8
  learning from good, 242

Writer—(*Continued*)
  philosophy of, 21
  point—the chief business of, 222
  power of, 209, 210
  problems of, 142
  romantic view of, 22
Writer's Book, The, 37, 151
Writer's Market, 166
Writing, 1–2
  bad, 222
  to inform, 234, 238
  and language, 255–256
  and outlines, 109
  patterns. *See* Writing patterns
  to persuade, 233–234, 235, 269
  problem of concurrent strands in,
    3–4
  propriety in, 18
  purpose, 2
Writing and Selling Feature Articles
  (Patterson), 166

Writing and Selling Non-Fiction
  (Jacobs), 166
"Writing for the Younger Generation"
  (Robinson), 37
Writing patterns, 144–151
  classical, 144
  determined by role of author,
    148–151
  form of, 18
  logical, 180
  of narrative beginnings, 151–154,
    193–194
  organic, 144
  spatial, 180–181
  temporal, 180–181
  verbal, 9

Yambura, Barbara S., 194, 283
You Know Me, Al (Lardner), 323
Youth and Life (Bourne), 309–316